# Five Stones In a Bovril Bottle

## Growing up in Ireland in the 1950s

# Monica Argue Bahm

Edited by Sandra Mackey

PUBLISHED BY

Fairtown Publishing

# Five Stones in a Bovril Bottle

## Growing up in Ireland in the 1950s

By Monica Argue Bahm

Version 7 with corrections 2021

PUBLISHED BY Fairtown Publishing

Printed in the United States of America

ISBN-13: 978-1492292593
ISBN-10: 1492292591

*Robert Lewis Stevenson's works became common domain in December 1944*

*Thank you to Thom Moore for giving his permission to use "My Cavan Girl" in this story and for providing me with the proper, original lyrics. This Cavan Girl is most grateful.*

*Cover picture of house in Fairtown painted by Monica Bahm*

# Acknowledgements

I thank God for the gift of growing up in Ireland for the first fourteen years of my life, and I thank Him for the desire to share my memories here. Thank you to my wonderful family for giving me a reason to share these reminiscences. Thank you to Dell for giving me the courage to complete this work. To Uncle John Clarke for giving me the incentive to finish it.

Thank you to my friend, my editor, Sandra Mackey, whose professional assistance has enhanced my work.

A special thank you to my amazing husband, Joe for all his help, work and patience in bringing this to fruition.

# Dedication

I dedicate my story to:

My husband, Joe

Our daughters;

Catherine and Brigid, her husband Travis

Our Grandchildren;

Kiera and Coleman

# Introduction

Many years ago I started making notes about my memories of growing up in Ireland in the late nineteen forties and fifties. I wanted to one day share them with our children so that they would know and understand what and who formed the person that they know. My life in Ireland was so different than anything they ever experienced and I wanted them to know the story of my journey. These stories are my memories of my childhood. Time and age may have affected their accuracy at times; but they are how this child, this woman, perceived her life and those around her. It is my hope and prayer that this story will give the reader the opportunity to experience the happiness of my childhood in a time that was uncomplicated, simple and filled with God's grace.

# Table of Contents

# Chapter 1

# My Memories of Ireland

It is early morning. I go to the kitchen sink and there they are, waiting for me, reminding me of a time and place so long ago. They bring me back to my childhood, a time I cherish. They remind me of where I came from and what makes me who I am. Sometimes their presence here by the sink makes me happy, makes me smile. Other times they fill me with sadness; they are all I have of what once was. Who could know that five stones in a Bovril bottle could mean so much?

I'm Irish! What exactly does that mean to me? How does it make me who I am? And what are those experiences which have shaped me so much? I was fourteen years old when I left Ireland for the first time. For fourteen years I lived there and this is my story.

On a cold February day I was born in a small, three-roomed, thatched cottage at the end of a steep hilly lane about three miles from Cavan town. Now that house no longer exists, but it was once the beautiful home of the Argue family. That house and farm had been in my Dad's family for generations. My father and his grandfather and his grandfather before him were born there.

*My mother and me, a baby picture*

*My Mother, Uncle John, Tessie Mooney*
*Monica and Tiny*

*Grandfather Clarke, My Mother and Me*

*My grandparents, James and Margaret Argue*

*James and Margaret Argue
with my father and two of his sisters*

*My grandparents James and Margaret Argue and four of*
*their five children*
*Margaret, Helen, John and Mollie*

*Grandfather Argue with Visitors*

The house was a cozy, thick-walled, mud cabin with three rooms. The kitchen served as the core of the house, indeed of the whole farm. The entry to the house was

14

through a half-door, then the big green door. On warm, sunny days the big door was open and only the half-door kept out inquisitive chickens, pigs and whatever happened to wander onto the street. We called it the street but in reality it was a cobblestone yard.

Occasionally a brave chicken perched itself on top of the door only to be swatted away by my mother, and every once in a while a hungry cow slipped her head in to see if dinner was on the fire. She, too, was shushed away with waving arms and guided to where she should be. It was also the barnyard where chickens, a big white duck, turkeys and sometimes the sow meandered around getting in each others' way. Many times a great cackling emanated from the foul as they fought over a piece of stale bread or a grain of oats thrown out by my mother. There were several breeds of chickens, but the ones I remember most were the Rhode Island reds, great big auburn roosters and hens. Usually my mother threw out scraps and food for them on the cobbles, and with wings flapping and loud chatter they were like bees around a hive trying to be first to get it. Otherwise they had to fend for themselves in the surrounding fields, pecking the ground as they went, searching for seeds and worms.

The outhouses with their corrugated iron roofs which replaced thatched roofs, were at right angles to the house, with just a small gap kept closed by a gate between them. The end nearest to the house was the henhouse, with lots of perches and some benches covered with hay where chickens could form a nest and lay their eggs, though quite often they choose to build their nests beneath the hedges between fields, proudly surprising us weeks later when they arrived on the street with their new families. At night when the chickens and duck had tucked their heads under their wings in sleep my parents made sure the door was securely closed to ward off the foxes that, given the opportunity, enjoyed a hearty chicken for supper.

The other end of the building was the byre with room for four cows at one end and the horse had a stall in the other end. In between the two was the pig sty, this was usually occupied by a huge sow.

*Out Buildings*

Outside in front of the byre was the dunghill, surrounded by egg tree bushes. These bushes had spindly branches packed so thick a bird could hardly pass through

16

them. In summer between the small green leaves they were covered with tiny round, inedible white fruit that I enjoyed picking and popping open. The dunghill seemed hardly noticeable as we came up onto the street, in spite of the fact that it was full of cow manure and pig droppings. Except in spring when the dung was hauled out to the potato field to fertilize the potato crop, I don't ever remember it smelling bad. It was a part of family life and very necessary to our existence. Farm life in Ireland was not always glamorous, but it was always practical!

# Chapter 2

# The Kitchen

Memories of the house are still crystal clear in my mind as I anticipate seeing it once more. Behind the door, well out of the way, coats were hung on good sturdy hooks. As was usual in these small thatched cottages there were just three rooms, and when you entered you were right in the kitchen. My dad prided himself on how well he painstakingly had matched the pretty, softly colored, flowered wallpaper that covered the ancient, in many places uneven, walls. Although my mother would put off compliments about the good job with an "ah sure you know John," I know she was proud of it too.

My mom always kept a good turf fire burning by the hob, which was at the opposite end of the kitchen from the door, so the house was very warm and inviting. Usually visitors were hardly in the door when she put the big metal kettle on the crook, and soon it was bubbling ready to make a good warm cup of tae (tea) in the teapot that always sat by the fire. By the time they sat down they were warmed by the dark brew and some slices of buttered soda bread and homemade jam or marmalade. High tea it was not but the hot tea and the luscious sweet jam sure tasted as wonderful as if it were. One of the most special things about Ireland then was the fact that at any hour of the day people took the time to sit down with each other, no matter how busy they were when a visitor showed up on their doorstep, to stop and talk about the goings on in the area. There was a lot of gossip, some fact, some surmised and some I'm sure a figment of overactive imaginative minds. There were some people who shall remain unnamed, who were known as gossips, and their stories over the cup of tae were taken with a grain of salt, as they say.

Just inside, in front of the door by the end of the dresser was the churn. It was a wooden barrel-type structure with wooden slats held together by metal rims. The lid also made of slats or a solid piece of wood, had a hole in the center where the long wooden handle of the dash came through. My mother kept the outside brightly painted, with the slats yellow and the metal rims a bright blue. The doors to the bedrooms were also painted with stripes to match the churn.

After sanitizing the churn by rinsing it out with boiling water, gallons of sweet milk with its thick cream were poured into the churn from where it was stored in crocks. A bit of salt was added and the wooden dash was brought up and down forcefully until the butter formed on the top. Now superstition had it that if someone came in while you are churning the butter, they must take a turn at the dash. If not, when they left they would take the butter with them and you could churn all day but get no butter. The visitor taking the butter would go right home, begin to churn their cow's milk, and get both their and your butter too. The only way to get it back would be to go to their house get a turf from their fire. Then bring it back home and put it in your fire. Then you would resume your churning and your butter would form. There were so many superstitions there at that time.

When churning was finished, the butter floated in big luscious mounds on top of the buttermilk. We removed it to the table to wash it, salt it, and form it into a block, or on special occasions little sweet balls. I remember my mother would put the butter out on a well scrubbed board, and slap it with the butter paddles, turning it all the time, to get all the whey or buttermilk out. Then she formed it into a rectangle, patting it with the patterned side of the paddle so that when finished it had a pretty design on the outside. I loved the taste of that butter, sweet and smooth as silk, on my mother's soda bread. No creamery butter ever tasted that good, and I think what a shame people don't make their own butter anymore.

My mother hated the ragged, scraggly looking gypsies and tinkers who frequently came to our house to beg for food or money or offer to do some work. I really believe that she was scared to death of them. The tinkers repaired pots, pans and porringers. When my dad was a young man he played the tin whistle in a local band and he kept his cap from his uniform. For the benefit of all the gypsies and tinkers who came to the door, she kept my father's band hat prominently displayed on the churn, and when a poor gypsy came to the house, mom was on the attack showing them the hat, pretending to them that it was her husband's policeman's hat and that if they didn't clear off the property she would get him after them. Of course my father wasn't a policeman, but they never waited around long enough to find that out, she was so vicious!

The churn was also the location of our Christmas tree every year. A few days before Christmas, I went out to the ditch near Jimmy Mack's fields, sneaking my father's saw. I picked a beautiful full branch from one of the holly trees that grew there. I dragged it home, set the trunk of the branch into the hole in the top of the churn, and it was ready to decorate. For this I made decorations from the foil paper from my father's cigarette packs, making bells and stars and all kinds of shapes from them. I cut pretty pictures from the Christmas cards we received from distant family and friends in America and England. Decorating my holly tree was a very prickly job but when done it was worth it, and I always thought it was really beautiful. Beauty is in the eyes of the beholder!

# O CHRISTMAS TREE
*School Gyrls Lyrics No Copyright Applied*

O Christmas tree, O Christmas tree,
Thy leaves are green forever,
O Christmas tree, O Christmas tree,
Thy beauty leave thee never.
Thy leaves are green in summer's prime,
Thy leaves are green at Christmas time,
O Christmas tree, O Christmas tree,
Thy leaves are green forever.

Along that same wall was the press. A large closet which my mother had painted blue with yellow trim to match the churn, it contained cups, mugs, plates and dishes on the top shelves, while bags of oaten meal, flour, and other food filled the bottom shelves hidden by doors. All kinds of necessary utensils were stored in the drawers. When my friends came to play, we even used it as a hiding place for hide and seek. We would squeeze into the bottom cabinet and close the door behind us completely out of sight. With the doors closed it was really dark and scary in there, but it was a good place for me to hide and usually the other child would have to give up without finding me.

Along the back wall was one of two tables that my mother kept scrubbed clean with carbolic soap. Leaning up against the wall on that table were her grandmother's willow pattern platters. That was the place of honor in our house and

I knew that I dare not touch them. Above that table was a large picture of Our Lady of Perpetual Help. Also above the table was another of my mother's treasures, a framed picture of the Sacred Heart. After we left Ireland, my Aunt Kathleen took the picture and kept it for my parents. When she passed away recently, my Aunt Veronica and Uncle John sent it to me. It is very old and crumbles when touched but I really am so happy to have it. Under this table was the huge earthenware crock that stored our water supply for drinking and cooking.

I often went to the well all the way on the other side of the road in the meadow and hauled two-gallon buckets of water back up the hill. Well at least I started with two full gallons; but since one of the things I liked to do was twirl around and around faster and faster till the gallons were almost out straight quite often there was a lot less by the time I made it back to the house. For many years the well was just a hole in the ground. It was in the corner of the meadow, a steep slide down and then a climb back to the road.

From what I remember, although the well was on our property, we were not the only family to use that well. Maybe for that reason, at some point the county decided to improve on some wells and ours was one of them. I believe they dug it a bit deeper and then surrounded it with concrete walls and roof. A little entryway with walls and gate kept animals out and a little lip at the edge of the well kept runoff water out. They put concrete steps up to the road. My favorite memory of our well was the fact that in summer raspberries grew wild on either side of the path down to it and I often lingered there to fill up on the delicious, sweet fruit. On return visits to Ireland I tried to find the well from the road, but the path is now completely covered in bushes and brambles. New homes built in recent times have water brought from a nearby well piped into the house so there is no longer a need for those old wells.

On the other side of the window along the back wall was a big old dark wooden settlebed. With its tall back it was a long bench-like seat that could be converted by raising the seat into a bed when needed. It was an old, crude version of a convertible sofa.

The front wall boasted our second scrubbed table. It was used daily and for special occasions covered with brightly colored oilcloth. It was here we ate our meals, where my mother prepared them, where I did my school work, and Mom used it when she cut out my plaid skirts at Christmas. I used it as a base for my in-house play on a rainy day. Mostly I had empty spools and an old box and played going to the creamery on there. On long winter nights we played Checkers or Chutes and Ladders. Occasionally the table was pulled away from the wall and there was an air of excitement in the house as my mother baked and my dad  made ready for the neighbor men who came in for a night of card playing. They became increasingly loud as the night went on and cards were thumped down on the table, with calls of what was trump and lots of other conversations that a little girl would not understand. There was lots of laughter and after the game was over much discussion about how it went and how much better each one could have played. I am sure they never played for more than a penny or two but to them that was high stakes.

On the wall was our entertainment center - a large brown battery-operated radio. It ran on two batteries, a large dry cell which needed replacement very seldom and a wet one that had to be taken into Smith's, the radio shop in town, to be recharged. That was a job because it was made of thick glass, causing it to be very heavy, and it had to be hung on the bicycle handle bars to be carried to town and back. The challenge was not to get any of the acid from it on myself, my clothing or my bike as I transported it. The worst possible thing that could happen was to drop and break it. I just knew that if I did that I would really have to face the music.

It was my father's opinion that the taller the pole used for the antenna to attach to the radio the better the reception. When he put in the radio, my father found the tallest tree in the surrounding area to use as an antenna and attached the wire to it. He dug a big hole in the ground next to the end of the byre and hoisted the trunk with wire attached. He brought the wire through the kitchen window and to the radio. Whether it was the result of the high antenna or not and the fact that we lived on top of a hill, we did get excellent reception on that old radio, and he was always very proud of it!

Because it was the source of all our information, our contact to the outside world, the radio was really of great importance to our everyday lives. Besides hearing news of what was happening in Ireland listening to Radio Erin and BBC, we were kept up to date with the world news. I remember listening to Radio Erin for reports of the uprising in Hungary, especially Budapest, hearing about the tanks rolling down the streets, shooting people. I remember one description of a man standing in the street as a tank came closer and closer, eventually killing him. I tried to picture them, all of this with my own young mind. I knew not what a tank looked like, but I knew they were terrible machines and what was happening to those people was awful and I prayed for them.

On Christmas Eve our radio tracked Santa as he came from the North Pole and passed first over faraway places, gradually getting closer and closer until he was finally in Ireland. Then county by county he got closer. Carefully we put out fruitcake and a cup of milk for the bearded one.

Finally I was just too scared that he would catch me awake so I went off to bed with my parents, shaking in my boots, all the while my mom kept saying she was going to go to the kitchen when he came and pull off his beard. She would laugh. I on the other hand was terrified. Next thing there it was, the hoof sounds on the street outside. My heart pounded so hard I was sure he would hear it when he came into the kitchen. He would make lots of noise as he put the unwrapped presents around the fire with lots of HO HO HOs. We were quiet as mice, although my mother was quivering with the laughter she was holding in. After what seemed like an eternity, we heard the hoofs on the cobbles again and he was gone.

My dad went out to the kitchen first just to be sure he was gone. Then out I came to find new toys, dolls, games, puzzles. One year I even received a doll carriage and new doll. It was like magic! There had to be a Santa! I never imagined that these things could have come from anyone else. No one I knew could afford things like this, least of all my parents. I can't imagine the sacrifices, the things my parents did without, so I could have such a wonderful Christmas every year. They were so good with their way of doing Santa that finally one Christmas Eve when I reached an age too old for Santa they told me where the goodies came from and how our neighbor Jimmy Mack had been playing Santa all those years. He would come and rattle cans and throw stones on the street to make the sound of the sleigh and reindeer. I was devastated. I cried. I didn't know then why I was so sad and upset, but I guess somehow a very special part of my life, a piece of my innocence was gone forever. Years later when our daughters were young we decided to continue the tradition with a friend playing Santa. And now our daughter and her husband do the same with their children and I threaten to go pull the beard off Santa just as my mother did. It is lots of fun and brings back those wonderful Christmas memories again.

Now back to that radio and its importance to my family. I listened to the reports of Pope Pius XII's death and the news of the election of a new pope and my imagination grew. I imagined the cardinals, dressed in their brilliant scarlet robes, as they gathered together and voted to elect a new pope. I remember hearing about the color of the smoke, gray or black, as it rose from the Vatican after each vote by the cardinals. One color would signify that a new pope had been elected, the other that they would have to vote again. Then the anticipation as we waited to find out who the new pope would be.

In a way TV ruins things for children, it shows us the pictures so we don't have to use our imagination. Radio made us grow, expanded our minds as we imagined what we could not see. We had to work a little to picture what was going on. I remember the coronation of Queen Elizabeth II.

It sounded so elegant! So regal! I imagined the gowns and jewels, even her crown, heard the rattle of the carriage wheels and the clop, clop of the horses' hooves on the streets of London as the procession passed by. I felt the excitement of the crowds as they cheered their young princess, and I listened to her young voice as she took her oath and became queen of the British Empire.

Going to sports events was not something that my dad was able to do very frequently, having neither the time nor the money to afford it. He was a real sports enthusiast, however, and he listened to quite a variety of sports on the radio. He would listen to, of course, Gaelic football and rugby. I enjoyed Michael O'Hare's distinctive voice as he called out the plays of football games from Croagh Park in Dublin. Especially when there was a score, his voice roared with excitement. Most of all I remember hearing the boxing matches. I had never seen a boxing match and I tried to visualize the ring and what the announcer meant when he said a boxer was on the ropes. I envisioned some kind of trapeze thing, nothing at all like the actual ropes that surround the ring. I just knew that when they were on the ropes they were in trouble and in danger of a knockout. My imagination got quite a workout with the radio because most of what I heard I had never experienced in my life.

We heard reports of the trouble in the North of Ireland, just a few miles away. Another young man dead, a barracks blown up, a policeman shot. That terror was only miles from our home and I knew some of the people involved as their names were whispered among the adults. Again I prayed! But everything I heard on the radio wasn't bad.

I listened to children's programs. There was the Walton's Irish music program with its theme, "If you feel like singing, do sing an Irish song."

## DANNY BOY
*By Frederic E. Weatherly1848-1929*
*Public Domain*

Oh Danny boy, the pipes, the pipes are calling
From glen to glen and down the mountainside.
The summer's gone and all the roses falling.
'Tis you, 'tis you, must go and I must bide.
But come ye back when summer's in the meadow.
Or when the valley's hushed and white with snow.
'Tis I'll be there in sunshine or in shadow,
Oh Danny boy, oh Danny boy I love you so.

And when you come and all the flowers are dying
If I am dead - as dead I well may be,
Ye'll come and find a place where I am lying.
And kneel and say an Ave there for me;
And I shall hear though soft your tread above me,
And all my grave shall warmer, sweeter be.
For you will bend and tell me that you love me,
And I shall live in peace until you come to me.

# THE ROSE OF ARANMORE

*Sung by Peter McNulty*
*Traditional*

My thoughts to-day, tho' I'm far away,
Dwell on Tir Connel shore;
The salt sea air and the Colleen's fair,
Round lovely greenguigore;
There's a flower there beyond compare,
That I'll cherish evermore;
That blonde Colleen in her gown of green,
She's the Rose of Aranmore.

I've traveled far 'neath the Northern Star,
Since the day I said good-bye;
And seen many maids on the golden glades,
Beneath a tropic sky.
There's a vision in my memories,
I always will adore;
That blonde Colleen in her gown of green,
She's the Rose of Aranmore.

But soon I will return again,
To the scenes I loved so well;
Where many an Irish lad and lass,
Their tales of love did tell;
Those silvery doons and blue lagoons,
Along the Larsons shore.
And that blonde Colleen in her gown of green,
She's the Rose of Aranmore.

# THE BARD OF ARMAGH

*Attributed to Bishop Patrick Donnelly*
*Traditional*

Oh! Listen to the lay of a poor Irish harper,
And scorn not the strings of his old withered hands;
But remember those fingers they once could move sharper,
In raising the merry strains of his dear native land.

It was long before the shamrock, dear isle's lovely emblem,
Was crushed in its beauty by the Saxon's lion paw;
And all the pretty colleens around me would gather,
Call me their bold Phelim Brady, the Bard of Armagh.

How I love to muse on the days of my boyhood.
Though four score and· three years have fled by them;
It's king's sweet reflection that every young joy,
For the merry-hearted boys make the best of old men.

At a fair or a wake I would twist my shillelah,
And trip through a dance with my brogues tied with straw;
There all the pretty maidens around me gather,
Call me their bold Phelim Brady, the Bard of Armagh.

In truth I have wandered this wide world over,
Yet Ireland's my home and a dwelling for me;
And, oh, let the turf that my old bones shall cover,
Be cut from the land that is trod by the free.

And when sergeant death in his cold arms doth embrace,
And lull me to sleep with old Erin-go-bragh;
By the side of my Kathleen, my dear pride, oh, place me,
Then forget Phelim Brady, the Bard of Armagh.

# IF I WERE A BLACKBIRD
*Traditional Irish Song*

I am a young maiden, my story is sad,
For once I was courted by a brave sailin' lad.
He courted me strongly, by night and by day,
Oh, but now he has left me, and sailed far away.

**Chorus**
And if I were a blackbird, I'd whistle and sing,
And I'd follow the vessel my true love sails in,
And on the top riggin' I would there build my nest
And I'd flutter my wings o'er his lily-white breast.

Well, he promised to take me to Donnybrook Fair
And to buy me red ribbons for to tie up my hair,
And, when he'd come home from the ocean so wide,
He'd take me, and make me, his own bonny bride.

Chorus

Now his parents they slight me, and will not agree
That me and my sailor boy married will be
But when he comes home, I will greet him with joy
And I'll take to my heart my dear sailor boy.

Chorus

# THE ANGEL'S WHISPER
*By Samuel Lover 1797 – 1868 Public Domain*
*A superstition of great beauty prevails in Ireland that when a
child smiles in its sleep it is "talking with angels."*

A baby was sleeping,
Its mother was weeping,

For her husband was far on the wild raging sea;
And the tempest was swelling
Round the fisherman's dwelling,
And she cried, "Dermot, darling, oh! come back to me."
Her beads while she number'd,
The baby still slumber'd,
And smiled in her face as she bended her knee;
"Oh blest be that warning,
My child's sleep adorning,
For I know that the angels are whispering with thee."

"And while they are keeping
Bright watch o'er thy sleeping,
Oh, pray to them softly, my baby, with me
And say thou wouldst rather
They'd watch o'er thy father!--
For I know that the angels are whispering with thee."

The dawn of the morning
Saw Dermot returning,
And the wife wept with joy her babe's father to see;
And closely caressing
Her child with a blessing,
Said, "I knew that the angels were whispering with thee."

## THE FOGGY DEW
*By Canon Charles O'Neill 1887-1963*
*Traditional Irish Song*

As down the glen one Easter morn to a city fair rode I,
There armed lines of marching
men in squadrons passed me by.
No pipe did hum, no battle drum

did sound its dread tattoo,
But the Angelus bell o'er the Liffey swell,
rang out through the Foggy Dew.
'Twas England bade our Wild Geese 'Go',
that small nations might be free
But their lonely graves are by Suvla's waves or the fringe of
the great North Sea.
Oh, had they died by Pearse's side,
or fought with Cathal Brugha.
Their names we'd keep where the Fenians sleep,
'neath the shroud of the Foggy Dew.

Right proudly high over Dublin town they
hung out the flag of war.
Twas better to die 'neath an Irish sky
than at Suvla or Sud el Bar;
And from the plains of Royal Meath
strong men came hurrying through,
While Brittania's Huns, with their great big guns, sailed in
through the Foggy Dew.

But the bravest fell and the requiem bell rang
mournfully and clear,
For those who died that Easter tide,
in the springtime of the year;
While the world did gaze with deep amaze,
at those fearless men but few,
Who bore the fight, that freedom's light might
shine through the Foggy Dew.

# THE MOUNTAINS OF MOURNE
*By Percy French 1854-1920*
*Public Domain*

Oh, Mary, this London's a wonderful sight,
With people all working by day and by night.
Sure they don't sow potatoes, nor barley, nor wheat,
But there's gangs of them digging for gold in the street.
At least when I asked them that's what I was told,
So I just took a hand at this digging for gold,
But for all that I found there I might as well be
Where the Mountains of Mourne sweep down to the sea.

I believe that when writing a wish you expressed
As to know how the fine ladies in London were dressed,
Well if you'll believe me, when asked to a ball,
They don't wear no top to their dresses at all,
Oh I've seen them meself and you could not in truth,
Say that if they were bound for a ball or a bath.
Don't be starting such fashions, now, Mary mo chroi,
Where the Mountains of Mourne sweep down to the sea.

I've seen England's king from the top of a bus
And I've never known him, but he means to know us.
And tho' by the Saxon we once were oppressed,
Still I cheered, God forgive me, I cheered with the rest.
And now that he's visited Erin's green shore
We'll be much better friends than we've been heretofore
When we've got all we want, we're as quiet as can be
Where the mountains of Mourne sweep down to the sea.

You remember young Peter O'Loughlin, of course,
Well, now he is here at the head of the force.

I met him today, I was crossing the Strand,
And he stopped the whole street with a wave of his hand.
And there we stood talkin' of days that are gone,
While the whole population of London looked on.
But for all these great powers he's wishful like me,
To be back where the dark Mourne sweeps down to the sea.

There's beautiful girls here, oh never you mind,
With beautiful shapes nature never designed,
And lovely complexions all roses and cream,
But let me remark with regard to the same:
That if of those roses you venture to sip,
The colours might all come away on your lip,
So I'll wait for the wild rose that's waiting for me
In the place where the dark Mourne sweeps down to the sea.

## SLIEVENAMON
*By Charles J Kickham 1828-1882*
*Traditional*

Alone, all alone, by the wave-washed strand.
All alone in a crowded hall.
The hall it is gay and the waves they are grand.
But my heart is not here at all.
It flies far away, by night and by day.
To the time and the joys that are gone.
And I never can forget the sweet maiden I met.
In the valley near Slievenamon.

It was not the grace of her queenly air,
Nor her cheek of the rose's glow.
Nor her soft black eyes, nor her flowing hair.
Nor was it her lily-white brow.
'Twas the soul of truth and of melting ruth,
And the smile of summer's dawn.
That stole my heart away, one mild summer day.
In the valley near Slievenamon.

In the festive hall by the star-watched shore.
My restless spirit cries:
My love, oh my love. Shall I ne'er see you more.
And my land will you e'er uprise.
By night and by day I ever, ever pray.
While lonely my life flows on.
To our flag unrolled and my true love to enfold.
In the valley near Slievenamon.

## THE STUTTERING LOVERS
*Unknown Author – Irish Traditional*

A wee bit over the lea. my lads
A wee bit o'er the green.
The birds went into the poor man's corn.
'Twas feared they'd never be s, s, s, s, s, seen, my lads:
'Twas feared they'd never be seen.

Then out came the bonny wee lass
And she was O! so fair.
And she went into the poor man's corn
To see If the birds were th, th, th, th. th, there, my lads.
To see if the birds were there.

39

And out came the brave young lad
And he was a fisherman's son
And he went into the poor man's corn
To see where the lass had g, g, g, g, g, gone, my lads.
To see where the lass had gone.

He put his arm around her waist
He kissed her cheek and chin
Then out spake the bonny wee lass
"I fear it is a s, s, s, s, s, sin, my lad,
I fear it is a sin."

He kissed her once and he kissed her twice
And he kissed her ten times o'er
'Twas fine to be kissing that bonny wee lass
That never was kissed be f, f, f, f, f, fore, my lads,
That never was kissed before.

## IRISH SOLDIER BOY
*Unknown Author – Irish Traditional*

At a cottage door one Wintry night,
As the snow lay on the ground.
Stood a youthful Irish soldier boy
For the mountains he was bound.
His mother stood beside him saying,
"You'll win, my boy, don't fear,"
With loving arms around his waist
She tied his bandalier.

**Chorus**

Good-bye, God bless you Mother dear,
I hope your heart will pain,
But pray to God your soldier boy
You soon will see again.
And when I'm out on the firing line,
'Twill be a source of joy,
To know that your the mother proud
Of an Irish soldier boy.

When the fighting it was over,
And the Hag of truce was raised,
The leader ordered the fire to cease,
Old Ireland stood amazed.
A Comrade came to her cottage door
With a note from her pride and joy,
Containing the news and sad appeal
Of an Irish soldier boy.

Good-bye, farewell, my mother dear
I'm dying a death so grand,
From wandering scenes and in action's pride
To free my native land.
But I hope we'll meet in heaven above
In the land beyond the sky,
Where you'll always be in company,
With your Irish Soldier Boy.

# OFT, IN THE STILLY NIGHT
*By Thomas Moore 1779-1852*

Oft in the stilly night,
Ere slumber's chain has bound me,
Fond memory brings the light
Of other days around me.
The smiles, the tears of Boyhood's years,
The words of love then spoken;
The eyes that shone now dimin'd and gone,
The cheerful hearts now broken.
Oft in the stilly night,
Ere slumber's chain has bound me,
Fond memory brings the light
Of other days around me.

When I remember all
The friends so linked together,
I've seen around me fall,
Like leaves in wintry weather,
I feel like one who treads alone
Some banquet hall deserted;
Whose lights are fled, whose garlands dead,
And all but he departed.
Thus in the stilly night,
Ere slumber's chains has bound me,
Fond memory brings the light
Of other days around me.

# SING A SONG OF SIXPENCE

*Randolph Caldecott 1846-1886*
*Not in Copyright*

Sing a song of sixpence,
A pocket full of rye;
Four and twenty blackbirds
Baked in a pie.

When the pie was opened,
The birds began to sing;
Was not that a dainty dish,
To set before the king?

The king was in his counting-house
Counting out his money;
The queen was in the parlor
Eating bread and honey;

The maid was in the garden
Hanging out the clothes,
There came a little blackbird,
And snapped off her nose.

# I'LL TELL MY MA

*Traditional*

I'll tell my ma when I go home,
The boys won't leave the girls alone.
They pull my hair, they stole my comb,
But that's all right till I go home.
She is handsome and she is pretty,
She is the belle of Belfast City,

She is courting one, two, three,
Please won't you tell me who is she.

Apoundert Mooney says he loves her,
All the boys are fighting for her,
They rap at the door, they ring the bell,
Saying: 'Oh, my true love, are you well?'
Out she comes as white as snow,
Rings on her fingers, bells on her toes,
Old Johnny Murray says she'll die,
If she doesn't get the fellow with the roving eye.

I listened to children's programs. Till this day, every time I hear "Puff The Magic Dragon," I fly back to my childhood and Ireland. I can see again the laneways of Castletara and imagining Puff and little Jackie Paper all over again. I always imagined myself riding down Teevan's lane with the dappeled sunlight pouring through the trees. I though it sad that Puff could not have lived forever because Jackie Paper grew up. But he does live on in that lane in my heart every time I hear that song.

# THE BLUE TAIL FLY
*Attributed to Dan Emmett*
*Published 1846*

When I was young I used to wait
On my master and hand him his plate;
And pass the bottle when he got dry
And brush away the blue-tail fly.

**Chorus:**

Jimmy crack corn and I don't care,

Jimmy crack corn and I don't care,

Jimmy crack corn and I don't care,

My master's gone away.


Then after dinner he would sleep;

A vigil I would have to keep,

And when he wanted to shut his eye

He told me, "Watch the blue-tail fly."


**Chorus**


One day he rode around the farm,

The flies so numerous they did swarm.

One chanced to bit him on the thigh –

The devil take the blue-tail fly.


**Chorus**


The pony run, he jump and pitch,

He threw my master in the ditch;

He died, and the jury wondered why –

The verdict was the blue-tail fly.

**Chorus**


They laid him 'neath a 'simmon tree,

His epitaph is there to see:

"Beneath this stone I'm forced to lie,

A victim of the blue-tail fly."


**Chorus.**

# HEY DIDDLE DIDDLE
*Randolph Caldecott - 1846 -1886*
*Not in Copyright*

Hey Diddle Diddle
The cat and the fiddle
The cow jumped over the moon
The little dog laughed to see such fun
And the dish ran away with the spoon.

# THERE WAS A CROOKED MAN
*Mother Goose Nursery Rhyme 1780*

There was a crooked man, and he walked a crooked mile
He found a crooked sixpence upon a crooked stile:
He bought a crooked cat, which caught a crooked mouse,
And they all lived together in a little crooked house.

As was the case with all events in Ireland at that time, Walton's Irish Music Hour, sporting events and all major events ended with our national anthem.

# THE SOLDIER'S SONG
*By Peadar Kearney 1883 - 1942*

We'll sing a song, a soldier's song,
With cheering, rousing chorus
As round our blazing fires we throng,
The starry heavens o'er us;
Impatient for the coming fight,
And as we wait in the morning's light,

Here in the silence of the night,
We'll chant a soldier's song.

**Chorus**
Soldiers are we whose lives are pledged to Ireland;
Some have come from a land beyond the wave;
Sworn to be free no more our ancient sireland
Shall shelter the despot or the slave.
To-night we man the Bearna Baoghail,
In Erin's cause, come woe or weal,
'Mid cannon's roar and rifle's peal,
We'll chant a soldier's song.

In valleys green, on towering crag,
Our fathers fought before us.
And conquered 'neath the same old flag
That's proudly floating o'er us.
We're children of a fighting race,
That never yet has known disgrace,
And as we march the foe to face
We'll chant a soldier's song.

**Chorus**

Sons of the Gael, men of the Pale,
The long-watched day is breaking;
The serried ranks of Innisfail
Shall set the tyrant quaking,
Our camp-fires now are burning low,
See, in the East a silvery glow,
Out yonder waits the Saxon foe
So chant a soldier's song.

**Chorus**

# Chapter 3

# The Hob

It has been fifty-one years since I last sat by the hob in our little thatched, mud-walled cabin in Ireland, but if I close my eyes I can still go there in my dreams. Nothing fancy in the generations-old house. The hob was just one wall of the cozy kitchen. The wall sported a painted-on brick pattern on either side of the black, soot-covered center. The hob was very hard and the hotter the fire the harder the hob became, and so came the phrase my dad often said, "harder than the hob of hell." My mother regularly scraped off the shiny, sticky soot buildup to avoid it catching fire from the big hot fire below. The fire itself was piled in the center on the cement floor. Notched crooks hung from a horizontal metal rod built high into the hood of the fireplace. The crooks held the various big black iron pots we used at adjustable levels, as we cooked for the family and the farm animals.

We burned sods of turf (peat), which had such a pungent aroma. In the spring my father and all the neighbor men would go to the bog. Being female precluded my going with them. The boys always got to go. It was really hard work, the turf had to be dug out, put on the bank to dry, cut with a slane, stacked and then brought home with a horse and cart. In some parts of Ireland the turf was transported in woven baskets which were draped over a donkey's back. Single creels were also carried by the men on their own backs as they brought turf home from the bogs.

*A Donkey with Creels and his friend*

*Uncle Patrick with Creel of Turf on his back with*
*Uncles John, and Eugene*

Back then there was no concern about depleting the bogs. The farmers only harvested what they needed for that winter. Now the bogs are being raped by automation and soon will no longer exist. Not many people in Ireland still burn turf, but there is no mistaking as you pass one that does and you get that beautiful smell. At night fresh turf was placed on the fire, then all covered completely with hot ashes to keep the fire alive through the night.

*Hand cut turf ready for burning*

# THE OLD TURF FIRE
*Traditional*

Oh, the old turf fire
And the hearth swept clean,
There is no one so contented
As myself and Paddy Keane;
With the baby in the cradle,
You can hear her grannie say,

"Won't you go to sleep, Alanna,
While I wet your daddy's tay."
Oh, the man that I work for now,
Of noble blood is he.

But sure somehow I'd be telling you,
We never can agree.
He has big towering mansions.
He has castles great and tall;
But I'd not exchange the roof that crowns
My own thatched cottage-hall.
So I've got a little house and lapa
As nate as you could see,
You'd never meet the likes of them
This side of Lisnaskea,
I've no piano in the room,
No pictures on the wall,
But I'm happy and contented
In my little marble hall.

Oh, the old turf fire
What a welcome. now it brings;
As the cricket chirrups gaily,
While the kettle also sings,
And we all join in the chorus
With a merry lifting song,
And the kindly neighbours "droppin' in"
To join the happy throng.
Round the old turf fire

In the morning my mother raked the mound of ashes back to reveal coals and cinders that had stayed hot through the night. New chunks of hand-cut turf, or peat as it is now called, were piled over these coals. Soon wisps of smoke floated up the chimney and that sweet smell of turf filled the room. Before long the kettle added its steam to the smoke as the smell of bacon or sausage and eggs filled the air. On occasion we had rings of black and white puddings, but they frequently were reserved for dinner when we had them. Most days a pot of stir about (porridge) sat at the ready by the fire. Breakfast was soon on the table, but first as it cooked we offered our morning prayers around the fire.

## FRIED IRISH SAUSAGES

1 pound freshly made sausages

½ tablespoon bacon drippings

Prick the sausages well with a fork to prevent them from bursting in the cooking. Melt the bacon drippings in the pan and put the sausages in. Cover the pan with a loose lid. Turn the sausages from time to time until they are well browned. Cook for about 6 minutes. Drain the sausages on absorbent paper.

Serve with fried eggs and bacon.

When frying bacon save the bacon drippings to use as a fat to fry other foods.

In Ireland we ate bacon, sausages and eggs for breakfast or dinner. When used the black and white puddings slices were fried along with the sausages in the pan.

# OLD RECIPE FOR BLACK PUDDING

Servings: 8

1 pound pig's liver

1 ½ pounds unrendered lard, chopped

120 fluid ounces pig's blood

2 pounds breadcrumbs

4 ounces oatmeal

1 medium onion, chopped

1 teaspoon salt

½ teaspoon allspice

Beef casings

Stew liver in boiling salted water until tender. Remove liver and mince. Reserve cooking liquor. Mix all ingredients in large bowl. Stir thoroughly until blended. Fill casings with mixture. Tie off in one-foot loops. Steam for 4 to 5 hours. Leave until cold. Cut into 1/2 inch slices as required and fry in hot fat on both sides until crisped.

I am not at all sure that the blood needed to make this pudding at home would be available today. When I grew up in Ireland we even then bought ours from the butcher, but there were families who butchered a pig and made their own pudding.

An iron crook hung horizontally over the fire with its two vertical sections having holes that held hooks to lower or raise pots according to what was being cooked. Large pots of food for the animals were added to the crook, and the blazing coals began their day's work cooking the food and heating the small house. The various pots sat around the fire awaiting their turn on the crook. We had few pots, yet they were enough to cook everything we needed, a nice big frying pan was essential as were a small and large skillet pot, a large potato pot, the pot oven and a large pot for the animal's food.

Through the day my mother added more turf as needed. The skillet pot often hung on a hook for hours filled with chicken and vegetables for a delicious stew. The fire in an Irish farmhouse never went out night or day. My mother baked delicious soda bread and cakes. Skillfully setting the baking oven in the coals and covering the lid with more hot coals, it became an oven. Roast or stewed chicken, and occasionally roast beef, were cooked in the same manner. Many delicious meals were cooked on that open fire. What a lot of work to bake breads and pies. We only bought bread or pan loaves when we had important company coming. The water kettle and teapot always sat by the fire ready to make a quick cup of tea for anyone who might come to the door. Not to make tea would be considered unwelcoming.

# BACON AND CABBAGE

2 pound slab bacon
1 fresh young cabbage (green)
1 onion
Black pepper
1 tablespoon breadcrumbs
½ tablespoon brown sugar
8 to 10 cloves

Soak the bacon in water for 12 hours. Put in a saucepan and cover well with cold water. Bring slowly to a boil and simmer gently for 1 ½ hours. Turn off the heat and leave the bacon to set in the water while you prepare the cabbage.

# CABBAGE:

Cut in quarters. Wash cabbage well in salted water and rinse in fresh water. Cut out the tough stalks. Plunge cabbage into a pan of fast-boiling water with a skinned onion (this helps to counteract the acrid smell) and boil fast for 5 minutes. Now add 2 to 3 cupfuls of the liquid in which the bacon was cooked. This will salt the cabbage and flavor it. Continue cooking until cabbage is tender but still remains a bit crisp. Do not cook till soggy. Drain well and dust with black pepper,

Skin the bacon if it has skin on. Coat the bacon with the sugar. Stud with cloves and brown under the broiler. Slice and serve with the cabbage.

This is served with potatoes boiled in their jackets and is also delicious with champ.

# CHAMP

## Ingredients
1 ½ pounds cooked potatoes
4 oz scallions
½ cup milk
Salt and pepper
4 large pats butter

Peel the potatoes and boil them in salted water. Drain them well and allow to dry out completely. Meanwhile, trim and wash the scallions. Slice them finely, including the green part, and put them in a saucepan with the milk to simmer gently until soft. Drain the scallions, reserving the milk, and beat them into the potatoes, gradually adding the hot milk until you have a nice fluffy mixture. Season well with salt and pepper and divide between four bowls, shaping each serving into a mound with a dent in the top into which you put the butter. It is eaten by dipping the potato into the melted butter.

Serves 4

One of my favorite meals that my mother made was liver and bacon. I have included a version that bakes the liver after braising. My mother made it completely in the frying pan and is my preferred version.

# BRAISED LIVER AND BACON

## Ingredients

1 large onion
8 slices of lamb's liver
3 tablespoon all-purpose flour seasoned with salt and pepper
1 cup beef broth
1 heaping teaspoon honey
½ teaspoon dried basil
4 thick slices of bacon fried (reserve fat)

Peel and slice the onion. Heat reserved bacon fat in a frying pan and fry the onion until soft. Transfer onion with a slotted spoon to an ovenproof dish large enough to take all the liver in one layer. Dredge liver in seasoned flour, brown lightly in remaining fat in frying pan and lay on top of onions. Mix remainder of seasoned flour with pan juices and mix to a paste over low heat. Add broth and bring to the boil. Add the honey and basil. Bring mixture to a boil, stirring well. Pour around the liver in the dish. Slice bacon in half and place on top of liver. Put dish in a preheated oven at 375° for about 20 minutes.

I also usually set the onions aside on a plate when cooked then I leave the liver in the frying pan and add the other ingredients. Then simmer until liver is tender waiting to place BACON over liver when serving.

Serve with mashed potatoes.

# COLCANNON

## Ingredients
½ cup finely chopped onion, leek or scallion
¼ cup butter
¼ cup milk
1 pound cooked mashed potatoes
1 ½ cups cooked cabbage

Gently fry the onion in melted butter until soft. Add the milk and the well-mashed potatoes and stir until heated through. Chop the cabbage finely and beat into the mixture over a low heat until all the mixture is pale green and fluffy. This dish is an excellent accompaniment for boiled ham.

# BOILED HAM

Soak ham for five to six hours. Cover ham with water in a saucepan. Boil to a boil. Boil for about 2 hours. Ham is cooked when meat separates easily from the bone.

*Mrs. Breiden and my father sitting by the hob*
*are having a good chat. Note the radio on the wall in the*
*background and the pot on the fire covered with coals.*
*My mother must have been baking bread.*
*Toward the top of the picture can be seen the crook that*
*swung out to give better access to the pots over the fire.*

## THE SKILLET POT
### *Traditional*

Did you ever eat Colcannon made from
Lovely pickled cream?
With the flour and scallions blended
Like a picture in a dream.
Did you ever make a hole on top
To hold the melting flake
Of the creamy flav'ry butter that
Your mother used to make?

## Chorus

Yes you did. So you did.
So did he and so did I.
And the more I think about it
Sure the nearer I'm to cry.
Oh, wasn't it the happy days
When troubles we had not
And our mothers made Colcannon
In the little skillet pot.

## Repeat Chorus

Did you ever bring potato cake
In a basket to the school.
Tucked underneath your arm
With your book, your slate and rule.
And when teacher wasn't looking sure a
Great big bite you'd take.
Of the flowery flavoured buttered
Soft and sweet potato cake.

## Chorus

Did you ever go a-courting
As the evening sun went down,
And the moon began a-peeping
From behind the Hill o'Down.
As you wandered down the boreen
Where the leprechaun was seen,
And you whispered loving phrases
To your little fair colleen.

## Chorus

# IRISH SODA BREAD

*Aunt Lillie's Irish Soda Bread for two loafs*
*This recipe for soda bread includes*
*baking instructions for a modern oven.*

4 tablespoons melted butter / margarine

1 cup Raisins

2 teaspoons caraway seeds

3 cups buttermilk

4 eggs slightly beaten

6 cups all purpose flour

2 tablespoons baking powder

2 teaspoons salt

1 teaspoon baking soda

6 tablespoons sugar

Or Splenda - to accommodate today's dieters.

Preheat oven to 350°.

Grease and flour two loaf pans 9 X 5

In a large bowl combine all dry ingredients

In another bowl combine buttermilk, eggs, raisins, caraway seeds & butter

Combine all together and mix well, but do not over mix

Spoon equally into two prepared pans

Sprinkle flour on top to flatten and then with a sharp knife make a cross in the top

Bake for 60 minutes, test, if tester comes out clean remove from pan and allow to cool on wire rack

To have a brown crust sprinkle with a little buttermilk before cooking.

Oh how good the soda bread tasted, fresh and hot from the pan with good fresh homemade butter and sometimes marmalade or homemade plum jam. My mom sometimes made plum jam sweet and spicy when she could get her hands on the plums.

# GINGER MARMALADE

## Ingredients:

2 pounds bitter oranges (Seville type)
2 lemons
1-ounce root ginger
7 pints (140 fluid ounces) water
8 ounces preserved ginger, chopped
7 pounds granulated sugar

## Method:

This recipe makes about 10 pounds of marmalade.

Wash and halve the bitter oranges and lemons. Squeeze out the juice and seeds. Strain the juice into a bowl and tie the pulp, seeds (pips) and root ginger together in a piece of muslin or doubled/tripled cheesecloth. Shred peel to the desired thickness and put peel and juice in a pan with the water and the bag of pulp and seeds. Simmer gently for 1 1/2 to 2 hours, or until the peel is quite soft. Remove the bag of pulp (squeeze over the pan as you do) and add the preserved ginger. Measure liquid, add sugar and stir over low heat until dissolved. Boil rapidly to setting point, then store in sterilized jars or pots.

Thinking back, that hob was the single most important spot in our everyday life. It was sitting around that fire that I learned songs, my morals were formed, and I learned my lessons and learned my prayers.

My dad's chair kept guard by the hob with its open fire on the parlor wall of the kitchen. His chair was our one comfortable chair and I loved to sit in it either by myself or on his lap as he told stories or sang songs or gave out a recitation, of which he had many. It was a big black leather chair with a high back. In spite of the fact that it was the worse for the wear, guests who visited our home were ushered to sit in my father's chair. Especially if the priest came, he was always guided to my father's chair. My mother's chair was plainer and I had a three-legged stool. When other company came, we used the straight backed wooden kitchen chairs for them.

In the evening after the sun went to sleep and all the animals were in bed, my mother lit the oil lamp on the wall by the old battery radio. We gathered around the now more gentle fire to say our evening prayers. With our backs to the fire, we, on our knees, rested our elbows on our chairs while our backs and the soles of our shoes were roasted by the fire. It was my father's responsibility to "give out" the rosary and he always ended it with "Meditating on these mysteries may we imitate what they contain and obtain what they promise through Christ our Lord, Amen." This was followed by The

Litany of The Blessed Virgin Mary. I can still in my mind hear my father leading the rosary.

## LITANY OF THE BLESSED VIRGIN

**LORD, have mercy on us.**

*Christ, have mercy on us.*

**Lord, have mercy on us.**

*Christ, have mercy on us.*

**Christ, hear us.**

*Christ, graciously hear us.*

**God the Father of heaven,** *have mercy on us*

**God the Son, Redeemer of the world**,

*have mercy on us.*

**God the Holy Ghost**, *have mercy on us.*

**Holy Trinity, one God**, *have mercy on us.*

**Holy Mary,** *Pray for us.*

**Holy Mother of God,** *Pray for us.*

**Holy Virgin of Virgins,** *Pray for us.*

**Mother of Christ,** *Pray for us.*

**Mother of divine grace,** *Pray for us.*

**Mother most pure,** *Pray for us.*

**Mother most chaste,** *Pray for us.*

**Mother inviolate,** *Pray for us.*

**Mother undefiled,** *Pray for us.*

**Mother most amiable,** *Pray for us.*

**Mother most admirable,** *Pray for us.*

**Mother of good counsel,** *Pray for us.*

**Mother of our Creator,** *Pray for us.*

**Mother of our Redeemer,** *Pray for us.*

**Virgin most prudent,** *Pray for us.*

**Virgin most venerable,** *Pray for us.*

**Virgin most renowned,** *Pray for us.*

**Virgin most powerful,** *Pray for us.*

**Virgin most merciful,** *Pray for us.*

**Virgin most faithful,** *Pray for us.*

**Mirror of Justice,** *Pray for us.*

**Seat of wisdom,** *Pray for us.*

**Cause of our joy,** *Pray for us.*

**Spiritual vessel,** *Pray for us.*

**Vessel of honour,** *Pray for us.*

**Singular vessel of devotion,** *Pray for us.*

**Mystical rose,** *Pray for us.*

**Tower of David,** *Pray for us.*

**Tower of ivory,** *Pray for us.*

**House of gold,** *Pray for us.*

**Ark of the Covenant,** *Pray for us.*

**Gate of Heaven,** *Pray for us.*

**Morning Star,** *Pray for us.*

**Health of the weak,** *Pray for us*

**Refuge of sinners,** *Pray for us.*

**Comforter of the afflicted,** *Pray for us.*

**Help of Christians,** *Pray for us.*

**Queen of angels,** *Pray for us.*

**Queen of patriarchs,** *Pray for us.*

**Queen of prophets,** *Pray for us.*

**Queen of apostles,** *Pray for us.*

**Queen of martyrs,** *Pray for us.*

**Queen of confessors,** *Pray for us.*

**Queen of virgins,** *Pray for us.*

**Queen of all saints,** *Pray for us.*

**Queen conceived without original sin,** *Pray for us.*

**Queen assumed into Heaven,** *Pray for us.*

**Queen of the most Holy Rosary,** *Pray for us.*

**Queen of peace,** *Pray for us.*


**Lamb of God, who takest away the sins of the world**, *spare us, O Lord.*

**Lamb of God, who takest away the sins of the world**, *graciously hear us, O Lord.*

**Lamb of God, who takest away the sins of the world,** *have mercy on us.*


## Pray for us, O holy Mother of God.

*That we may be made worthy of the promises of Christ.*

Of course it always ended with prayers for the dead, "And may the souls of the faithful departed, through the mercy of God. rest in peace. Amen."

But I remember many times when my mother, exhausted from the day's work and relaxed from the warmth of the fire, would fall asleep as she knelt and responses were not quite what they should be. Then there were the nights when, in the middle of the rosary, my mother and I got the giggles. Oh, how angry my father would get and that only made us laugh more. Amazingly, as my dad spent his last two years ill, very confused and not remembering too much of anything, he always remembered his rosary and fingered the beads in his hands.

Afterward was a quiet time to make plans and just have fun together. We played games such as Snakes and Ladders and Checkers, or, since my father was an avid reader he liked to sit in his big old chair and read a book while my mother sat knitting nearby in her chair. Meanwhile I played with my dolls or sat on my three-legged stool reading one of my favorite books.

However not all nights were like that, and without TV the Irish had found a way to amuse themselves on those long winter nights. After all the chores were done neighbors came a ceilieing, as we called it in Cavan. I always loved those evenings as the unplanned gatherings formed a semicircle seated on wooden kitchen chairs around the fire, warming those gathered from the frost outside. At first the local news and gossip was shared, politics discussed and sometimes argued. Very often the ongoing undeclared war in the North of Ireland, or the troubles as it was called, and those who took part in it was a big topic of discussion. Soon the mood of the evening changed and, all revived by a good cup of tea with soda bread and jam, the group was ready for some fun. Singing Irish folk songs and traditional Irish music followed. My father played the flute and a neighbor played my accordion while others sang along. Quite often a dance was enjoyed as the merriment continued.

Then gradually it died down as did the fire's now hot glowing embers. It was time for my favorite part of the evening, cuddled up in my mother's lap, Gazing into the small flickering tongues of fire from the glowing coals, I was ready to listen to all those stories of ghosts and fairies. Each person tried to outdo the other. I huddled closer to my mother as my eyes grew heavier.

# A MOTHER'S LOVE'S A BLESSING

*Thomas Peter Keenan 1866-1927*

As an Irish boy was leaving
Leaving his native home
Crossing the broad Atlantic
Once more he wished to roam
And as he was leaving his mother
And walking all the day
He threw his arms around his head
And these were the words he said.

**Chorus**

A mother's love is a blessing
No matter where you roam
Keep her while she's living,
You'll miss her when she's gone.
Love her as in childhood
Tho' feeble old and gray
For you'll never miss a mother's love
'Till she is buried beneath the clay.

And, as the years go onward,
I'll settle down in life,
And meet a nice young Irish girl
And ask her to be my wife.
And as the kids grow older
And climb around my knee,
I'll teach them the very same lesson,
As my mother -- she taught to me.

**Chorus**

I'm sure I would never have wanted to go to sleep alone in my room had it not been for the fact that I soon fell sound asleep on my mother's lap and was lifted up and laid in my bed by my Dad. The laughter and the stories continued into the night. Eventually, having been good hosts to their neighbors and enjoying their company, my dad put out the dog for the night while my mother put fresh turf on the fire. She piled on all the ashes from the evening over the fresh coals. All around the hob was quiet as they blew out the lamp on their way to bed. The hob was ready for the next morning.

# Chapter 4

# The Parlor

The parlor or the big room as it was called was the largest room in the house. It was one step up from the kitchen, behind the fireplace. The parlor doubled as my parents' bedroom. It, like our kitchen, had a concrete floor. It contained a chest of drawers that sat in front of the window. This was covered with a lacy cloth and dressed with statues of the Blessed Mother, the Sacred Heart, the Infant of Prague and Blessed Martin. My mother treasured these. The statues were wedding gifts given to my parents by friends in 1943 and were so important to them. The statue of the Sacred Heart stood about two feet tall. Each May my mom brought the statue of Mary to the kitchen and placed it in the window. She gathered the wild flowers that grew along the lane and made an altar to the Blessed Mother. It was there she prayed and said her novena to The Blessed Mother every day as she did for all of her life.

One day as I played alone in the house I decided to hide in my parents' bedroom and chose one of the dresser drawers as a perfect place to hide. As I got in, the chest tilted and came to rest on the drawer where I was hiding. All the statues tumbled, the Sacred Heart ending up in the drawer with me. I crawled out of there as fast as I could. I didn't wait to see where the other statues were and ran to the fields and hid in a ditch under briars. If I broke a statue my mother would have my hide.

As darkness approached and having found what I had done, my parents began to search for me, going through the fields and calling my name. Several times they passed within feet of me but never saw me I was so well hidden and so quiet. Now I can only imagine how terrified they must have been. I'm sure they thought I had fallen into the flax hole or been taken by a stranger. Finally my fear of the dark got the best of me and I made for home, there to find that all statues had survived and I was only in trouble for running away and hiding. The statues were among the few things my parents brought with them to America when we left Ireland. Those statues graced a small altar in her bedroom until my mother died. Upon her death the statue of the Sacred Heart found its new home in our bedroom. The statue of the Infant we placed in her casket when she died and he is with her through eternity.

A big dark wooden wardrobe stood to attention in one corner of the room. It housed our good clothes, most of which my Aunt Helen sent us from America. Because she usually wrote to us telling us to expect a package, we watched for Mr. Woods, the mailman, every day until it finally arrived. Oh how we looked forward to those packages and the surprises they contained. I thought the clothes, mostly my cousins hand me downs, were the most beautiful in the world and they always smelled so good. Occasionally she bought a new outfit for me and I felt like a princess. My aunt made me the best dressed child in the parish. There was the time she sent me a long beautiful night dress with small blue flowers all over it and ruffles at the neck and cuffs and down the bodice. When the May crowning time came to Ballyhaise, I wanted to wear the long dress. My poor mother had a terrible time talking me out of it. I was four years old then and had just started Ballyhaise School that spring. I could not understand why I should not wear it and was absolutely heartbroken that I couldn't show off that beautiful dress.

The front of the wardrobe had a full length mirror and I spent many hours in front of it practicing and perfecting my Irish dance steps. I wanted to have them just right! So hour after hour I worked at it, one two three, hop two three, etc.

Because the parlor served a dual purpose, we had a beautiful mahogany table surrounded by heavy high-backed chairs and usually it had clothes and other things piled high on it. It was pushed up against the end wall of the house, but when we had really special company and ate in the parlor, my parents' bed was pushed back from the center of the room where it normally stood. The table took its place out in the center of the room and the beautiful, oil burning parlor lamp was put in the middle of it and lit. With a well starched and ironed Irish linen tablecloth covering the rich mahogany wood it all seemed so very elegant then. At times like that for sure we would have ham and tomatoes and a pan loaf of bread, and my mother would make potato salad and we would have fresh lettuce from the garden. Dessert was a wonderful trifle made with layers of cake soaked in brandy, Jello, fruit and Bird's custard all topped with fresh whipped cream. All of this was such a special treat. I still love the taste of deli ham and tomato sandwiches and the memories they evoke.

For many years, until I was about five or six, my bed was also in that room. It was against the wall behind the hob. That wall also had a fireplace though I don't believe my parents ever put a fire in it. At any rate I do not remember one. My mother had a habit of stuffing clothing and rags to be washed in it. That room too was papered with pretty flowered wallpaper. Heavy wool blankets and quilts covered the beds to keep us warm during the cold damp nights.

# Chapter 5

# My Bedroom

My room was the lower room, the room at the other end of the kitchen. It was smaller. It had a dirt floor, but it was pressed solid from years of use by many, many generations of feet. I had a little single bed there and a small table that was my dressing table where I kept all my little special trinkets, pretty empty perfume bottles, and pretty pieces of glass. I still have the little silver shoe from Ted and Nell Reilly's wedding cake. I had a bureau for my clothes. The other half of the room stored the oats and grain for feeding the animals during the winter, with big burlap bags stacked high on top of each other. I also stored my bicycle in my room resting against the sacks of oats and animal food. The mice really liked to find their way into my room and sometimes I would see one scurry between the sacks of grain looking for a meal. Poor little things their life was usually cut short by the traps my father set for them.

In the summer, because of twilight, I usually went to bed in the daylight. I didn't want to close my eyes while it was still bright outside so I would sit in my bed and read or play until darkness fell. Occasionally someone came a ceileing (visiting) after we were in bed and I would lie there very quietly until they were gone, not wanting them to know that I was still awake. I still get that warm cozy feeling if I get to go to bed before dark. I remember snuggling down under the wool blankets, rough yet comfy, feather ticks or eiderdowns and feather pillows. Even summer nights were cool. As I lay in bed I often thought of the poem we learned in school.

## BED IN SUMMER
*Robert Louis Stevenson*

In winter I get up at night
And dress by yellow candlelight.
In summer, quite the other way,
I have to go to bed by day.

I have to go to bed and see
The birds still hopping on the tree,
Or hear the grown-up people's feet
Still going past me in the street.

And does it not seem hard to you,
When all the sky is clear and blue,
And I should like so much to play,
To have to go to bed by day?

In winter when the winds howled and the moon climbed high and bright as daylight we needed some extra heat in bed. We didn't have the luxury of a heating pad or even a hot water bottle so each night before we went to bed my mother would heat iron pot lids until they were very hot in the coals of the turf fire, wrap them in brown paper, and put them between the bed covers. When we climbed into bed it was all snugly and warm and I would push it down between my feet. I loved to sit in my bed on winter nights and look at the moonlit sky, and the front street and hill beyond that seemed to be transformed by the moonlight.

Quite often in summer my cousins who lived in Belfast and Dublin came to stay with us for a few weeks. When Kathleen Breslin came she slept at the top of the bed while I had to sleep at the bottom. I think it was because she had a problem with her eyes and wore a patch over one of them that it always seemed my parents favored Kathleen, and I really resented her seemingly preferential treatment. It was many years later when Kathleen visited us in the U.S. that I got to know her and that we became closer. It makes me a little angry with my parents that they didn't see how they were ruining my relationship with my cousin.

When my cousin Eileen came down from Dublin it was a totally different matter. She and I were close in age and had so much fun together. She was treated just like I was and we slept together at the top of the bed and would stay up until all hours giggling and laughing. I hated to see her go home to Dublin at the end of the summer. It was at times like those that I wished I had a brother or sister like everybody else.

It seems to me that my mother had a warped sense of humor at times. When Eileen and I were out in the fields playing, she would dress up in my dad's old clothes and with a hat pulled down over her face she was not recognizable from a distance. She would come toward us, head down, shoulders bent, sounding threatening. Eileen and I were scared to death and would run for the house and safety. Of course the one thing we needed was to have my mother there to comfort us and assure us that we were safe but she was not there. In a few minutes she would return smiling and giggling to find us crying in fear. She never told us it was her, but at some time as we got older we caught on. Once we did it was no longer fun for her and she stopped doing that. I never understood why she did that or how she found it funny.

*My father snapped this picture of my mother dressed up to scare Eileen and I*

*My cousin Eileen Clarke and me in center on our hill looking toward Ballyhaise before Hannigans house was built*

*Monica by the half door*

*My beloved dog Tiny and me outside the front door of our
house in convent school uniform 1958*

I happened to be home from school sick, the day that Rose Reilly returned to the US and she came down to my room to say goodbye to me. I really loved her and hated to see her go. It was a very sad day for me. Little did I know that in just a few short years I would see her again in New York. While that was not a happy sick day, usually days home in bed sick were fun. I would gather my toys around me and play all day long.

# THE LAND OF COUNTERPANE
*Robert Louis Stevenson*

When I was sick and lay abed,
I had two pillows at my head,
And all my toys beside me lay
To keep me happy all the day.

And sometimes for an hour or so
I watched my leaden soldiers go,
With different uniforms and drills,
Among the bedclothes, through the hills;

And sometimes sent my ships in fleets
All up and down among the sheets;
Or brought my trees and houses out,
And planted cities all about.

I was the giant great and still

That sits upon the pillow-hill,

And sees before him, dale and plain,

The pleasant land of counterpane.


Under our beds we stored the "poe" or piss pot to be used during the night, rather than going out in the often cold, damp night. My mother would empty the poe in the morning if it had been used during the night. As has always been her way she did everything in a hurry, and that is how it happened that one morning she rushed out the door, poe in hand, turned it to splash its contents toward the dunghill and all too late emptied it all over the priest, who had come onto the street. He was making a surprise visit. It was a real surprise for both of them. Poor Fr. Hunt and can you imagine my mother's embarrassment?

Our house had a window in each room in the front wall. They were large enough to allow light to enter, but not so large to make the house drafty or allow in the winter chill. When I was little, my dad broke through a small window in the back of the kitchen and the warm afternoon sun poured through it. We needed that extra light because one of my mother's passions was flowers and she had so many in the front kitchen window that very little light came through it. My mother, who always loved curtains, kept pretty white Irish lace ones on these windows. They were well starched and bright. My mother kept that house immaculately clean. She was always a very good housekeeper.

When I was very little, actually until I was about twelve years old, we didn't have electricity. When it became available we got it installed right away. Unlike many of our neighbors, who were afraid it would burn their houses down, we acquired electric light, but then only in the kitchen. One large wall plug provided electric for a brand new electric radio, which was the only electric appliance we had. We lived so simply that we never saw a need for anything more, nor could we have afforded it even if we did. No curling irons or blow dryers. My mom used rags to set my unruly curly blonde hair. Our iron was a large iron box with a handle and heavy removable bars that were put in the fire until fiery red then lifted out with tongs and put into the iron. While it was very heavy it really did do a pretty good job of taking out the wrinkles. No TV, never even heard of it, just one bare light bupound hanging from a wire in the middle of the kitchen ceiling and our radio. Life was good. We had all we could possibly need and my parents were proud of what they had.

# Chapter 6

# Outside The House

Outside the house was white washed frequently and my dad kept the roof gold with fresh thatch. He was an expert thatcher and kept the roof in perfect condition so that we never had a leak. I don't know how many layers of thatch were on the roof but it was very thick. It required that every few years as too much thatch accumulated he removed some of the old layers and re thatched the entire roof. In fall after all the oats and hay was in the haggard and the potatoes in their mounds he proceeded to thatch the roof. After wetting down bundles of straw he stuck pieces of wood into the existing roof. He then took smaller sections of the wet straw up onto the roof and rested it on the pieces of wood along with lengths of pliable sticks called scallops, which he had pared into pointed ends. Along with these he carried up a mallet and thatching rake. He would take a measure of straw, fold it in half, and secure it in place with a loop of a sally rod. Then he twisted it and secured it with at least one more now u shaped rod, pounding them into the existing roof with the mallet. Starting at the bottom he continued this one section at a time, overlapping the rows of thatch until the entire roof was covered and golden. As he completed each section he trimmed the jagged pieces overhanging the existing roof. It seemed to sparkle in the sun. The only rods that showed were a row about a foot from the edge that held the ends of the bottom layer in place and a row at the peak to hold the top layer in place against the wind. After the whole area was thatched it was washed down with a substance that prevented seeds from growing.

*First Communion picture outside our front door April 1952
showing the row of scallops on the roof*

The outside of the house was surrounded by flowers, dahlias, gladiolus, fuchsias and the most beautiful of all the roses. My mother always prided herself on how lovely her flowers looked. The area close to the house was a riot of color and beautiful perfumes. Ours truly was the little old mud cabin on the hill.

# THE LITTLE OLD MUD CABIN ON THE HILL

*Eddie Coyle / S. Gaffney - Traditional*

Go sell the pig and the cow and all,

And we'll take you far away,

For your dear old parents

You must leave behind.

Go and seek your fortune far away

In a land across the sea,

For in Paddy's land it's poverty you'll find.

Those were the words my mother spake

As I left old Ireland.

And the sad farewell is in my memory still.

As I placed that bundle on my back,

And I left for ever more,

From yon little old mud cabin on the hill.

Oh, for the roof was thatched with yellow straw,

And the walls were white as snow.

And the turf fire boiled the pot, I see it still.

Old Ireland's engraven in my heart,

It's the place where I was born,

In that little old thatched cabin on the hill.

I still can see the turf fire

With my mother by its side.

My dear old father sitting by her side,

His pipe is lit and the smoke ascends,

And they're thinking of the time

When they sent their darling boy across the tide.

No more I'll see them dancing on yon kitchen floor

To the music of the bagpipes loud and shrill.

No more I'll see the happy times

That we had in days of yore,

In yon little old mud cabin on the hill.

Oh, for the roof was thatched with yellow straw,

And the walls were white as snow.

And the turf fire boiled the pot, I see it still.

Old Ireland's engraven in my heart,

It's the place where I was born,

In the little old mud cabin on the hill.

# Chapter 7

# Returning To Fairtown

## BORN IN IRELAND
*Traditional*

I was born here in Ireland
But a foreign land called me away
Now I've come back to see my hometown
And my friends of yesterday
Gone are the old folks friendly faces
And the friends I used to know
So many things have changed in Ireland
Since I left it long ago

Life in that home with our little family was very happy and memories were so beautiful. As I grew older I wanted to take my family there. In August 1986, at the urging and encouragement of my husband, we made the decision to return to Ireland with our then twelve- and fourteen-year-old daughters. With much anticipation I looked forward to showing the girls the house where I was born, where I played and learned to pray, this place that had been so much a part of who I had become. I could hardly contain my excitement as we climbed the now overgrown hilly laneway to the house. This was where, as a child, I picked wild strawberries and primroses.

The trees and bushes were so overgrown that I hardly recognized where I was when we came into a clearing that had once been our yard. It was now a quagmire of mud that swallowed my wellingtons, the knee high rubber boots I was wearing, and held onto them when I pulled my feet from the muck. I had not thought what happens to a thatched roof, mud wall cabin when there is no fire in it to keep it dry and no one wants to maintain it anymore. I stood there in disbelief and utter grief, for the house I'd come so far to see, to touch, was no more, nothing but a sea of mud to greet me.

The grove of evergreens that were young when I was young had grown tall, but there was now no house for them to protect from the cold north wind, just a mound of dirt covered with rushes in one corner of the sea of mud. Not a trace. I felt as though my heart was being ripped from my chest, a pain so palpable that the wrenching sobs came from deep within my soul. I'd come home to show, to touch and see, but there was nothing left. I can still taste that bitter emptiness and sadness as I stood there.

I searched for any small clue to our lives there, anything that could connect me to that lovely happy home and childhood. But there was nothing. So I picked up five small stones, each one as gently and carefully as a mother would her newborn baby, and held them close as the tears flowed down my cheeks. Maybe it was a part of my home. Anyway it was a part of my land. More than anything on this trip I wanted to see that house, to go inside.

Earlier I felt such excitement and anticipation as we drove down the Cootehill Road. At the bottom of the lane by the road was a beautiful tall tree and as I approached our farm I looked for that tree, which was a sure marker for our lane. I think it was the tallest tree I've ever seen, but now it was no longer there. The gate which hung from the post at the other side of the lane had been latched to that tree. Many times I opened it and swung on that gate, much to my father's aggravation. Now there were just two posts with a cold metal gate between.

Later that day I found a Bovril bottle at the now abandoned home of our neighbor John "The Redfellow" Reilly and his sister who I called "Aunt Rose". I placed the five stones gently in the small brown bottle and there they have rested ever since.

On returning home to America, I placed my treasure, more valuable to me than gold, by the kitchen sink. They are a daily reminder of all the wonderful and tough times life in Ireland held in the 1950s. They bring sweet memories of growing up in a time without TV or telephones or electricity or running water, of a simple time when life was centered on family and friends and God was at the heart of it all.

# LIFE IN AN IRISH COTTAGE
*Unknown*

With its simple roof of thatch;
Just a cottage in old Ireland,
With its chickens and its farmyard,
And its green potato patch.
Just a shrine of joyful childhood.
That we'll carry where'er fortune
In a land away from home.
That's why, after years of exile,
We Irish cross the foam.
To see our aged mother
And our other friends at home.
And when we've traveled o'er the sea
Just to gaze at it once more,
Our hearts will find with gladness
As we stroll up to the door.
And when we kiss our mother
And clasp her to our breast,
Our voice will ring with laughter
For the one that we love best.
And when the summer shadows fall,
And our daily work is done,
We can gather at the crossroads
And have our fill of fun.
And on the winter evenings
When the sun is sinking low
We can listen to our fathers
Telling tales of long ago.

Or on a Sunday morning
When the dew is on the grass
We may see the lark ascending
As we stroll along to Mass.
This is just an Irish cottage
With its simple roof of thatch,
But no matter where you wander
You'll never find its match.

Sometimes I take the five small stones from their resting place and hold them gently in my hand. I know that they are a constant reminder of who I am. They are an inspiration from a time when work was hard and play was free and values guided life. I hold them, for they are all I have now of that time that formed me. I will never forget the sadness of that day. The many times that I have returned to Ireland I have never returned to that spot where the house once stood.

# Chapter 8

# The Fields

As we wandered the fields, surrounding the house, so many memories rushed back.

## THE GARDEN BEHIND THE BYRE

In the garden behind the byre was where I had my swing, between two large pine trees. I loved to swing high as I could and am reminded of the poem "The Swing". After seeing the circus when it came to town I pretended to be a trapeze artist gliding through the air, sometimes even standing on the seat. Unfortunately for me I usually ended up getting a bit out of control and ending up in a pile on the ground, which was not so bad because it was covered with the richest green grass I have ever seen. I wonder if I remember how green it was because of all the times I saw it up close as I landed face first.

## THE SWING
### By Robert Louis Stevenson

How do you like to go up in a swing,
Up in the air so blue?
Oh, I do think it the pleasantest thing
Ever a child can do!

Up in the air and over the wall,
Till I can see so wide,
Rivers and trees and cattle and all
Over the countryside.

Till I look down on the garden green,
Down on the roof so brown,
Up in the air I go flying again,
Up in the air and down.


I also had my babby house there, made with broken pieces of pottery and odds and ends. One Christmas Santa brought me a real china tea set with cups and saucers. I was ever so thrilled! I played with my dolls there, and when my friends Vera or Annie came we had wonderful make believe tea parties with mud pies decorated with daisies and sweet peas. Maybe that's why until this day I love when Joe decorates a cake with vines of sweet peas all over it. My tea was dalkin seeds, but I thought it was all very elegant. Vera had her babby house in the rocks near her house and the rocks were her table. Mine was the soft green grass.

This garden was also known as the haggard because this was where we stored the hay and straw from the oats for the winter. It was where the thrasher was used when it came to remove the oats from the straw and chaff. In the early years Eddie Reilly would come with the thrasher. A large meitheal (group of men from surrounding farms) came and helped bring in the oats, while others tended the thrasher, filled bags with oats, and piled the straw securely for the winter, as all the while the chaff blew all around like a golden snowstorm. It was a really busy day and the women all came also to help with the food in the kitchen cooking and serving the men. When the day was over there was a great sense of accomplishment and thankfulness for the harvest. The next day this was repeated at another farm and so on until all the farmers had their grains and straw secured for the winter. I can recall my father keeping track of which men he owed a day's work to for their help.

The magpies occupied the tops of the large pine trees. It was a good vantage point for them to see the little field mice that made their homes in the warm reeks of hay and straw. They were beautiful, noisy birds with a penchant for swooping down and grabbing the unspecting mice. But since they did the same with the baby chickens who followed the old hens as they pecked the ground for seeds from the hay and oats my mother spent lots of energy chasing them away from near the house. Waving her arms wildly and throwing stones at them only sent them away for a little while. Before we knew it as soon as she left the haggard the magpies returned to their lookout waiting for supper.

Even worse were the hawks that silently winged their way toward the haggard and before even the watchful magpies could move they swooped down and snatched their prey and were silently gone. I'm sure that there were many times the poor magpies were blamed for the crimes of the unperceived hawk.

Magpies were harbingers of all kinds of messages and in a culture of superstition they were always counted when they appeared. Why? This rhyme will tell.

> One for sorrow
> Two for joy
> Three for a girl
> Four for a boy
> Five for silver
> Six for gold
> Seven for a story never to be told

No matter what magpies were bad news! My father told this story: One day he and his father were out in the field digging potatoes when a lone magpie landed on the blade of my grandfather's shovel. They attempted to chase it away but it returned again and again refusing to be gone. The very next day the family received word that my father's eighteen year old sister Katie, who had immigrated to New York, had died accidentally. Coincidence? One for sorrow!

## POTATOES

As we walked through the fields I remembered the year we planted the potatoes in the field near Ted Reilly's. That was the year the potato crop rotted because of too much rain. The weeds grew faster than the potatoes, and we had to go out daily on our hands and knees, weeding by hand acres of potatoes. I helped before and after school, even taking off from school. I watched the other children go the old road to school and I was already out in the field weeding. In spite of all our hard work we still lost most of the crop that year. It was soon after that we came to America. I truly believe that the failure of the potato crop on which we depended so much instigated my aunt's suggestion that we leave and emigrate to America.

As spring approached, while we sat by the fire at night my parents spent the evening cutting in half the seed potatoes we saved from the previous year, making sure both sections had eyes. In spring Eugene Reilly came with the tractor and plough to dig the fresh earth. It was now time to take the manure from the dunghill out to the field in the horse drawn cart. My parents then spread the manure from the dunghill on the drills and again a meitheal of men came to drop the seed potatoes, which my parents had already cut, on the manure. A tractor covered over the potatoes with a drill machine. I helped with dropping potatoes and while it was back breaking work I enjoyed it. It was fun, a lot of stories were exchanged by the grown ups, and the day went fast. The potatoes were tended carefully by my dad. Several times as they grew he sprayed them with a mixture of bluestone and washing soda to keep away the blight. What joy to see them pop up through the earth and grow thick and tall until they eventually produced little blue flowers with yellow centers.

Soon my mother and I would sneak out to the field, go down a row and dig out a plant. If the potatoes were big enough we had new potatoes for dinner that night. There is no flavor quite like that. Buttered new potatoes, skins and all! That was always an exciting meal. My dad was proud of what had been produced. Of course if what we pulled were still too small we packed them back and left them for another day with a warning from my mother, "Don't tell Daddy." He would be very angry we picked potatoes before they were ready.

## NEW POTATOES

Heat enough water to cover potatoes to boiling.
Add a teaspoon of salt to the water.
Meanwhile wash potatoes thoroughly with a soft brush, do not scrub potatoes.
Add to boiling water and cook on medium until skins are split and potatoes are fork tender.
To serve: Drain potatoes and toss with fresh butter.
Sometimes I also add finely chopped parsley.

## IRISH POTATO SOUP

2 tablespoons butter
2 medium onions
3 large potatoes, peeled

5 cups milk
1 clove garlic, crushed
Salt and pepper
1 sprig thyme
1 bay leaf
1 bunch parsley  tied together
Chopped chives to garnish

Melt the butter in a heavy pan. Add the thinly sliced onions and potatoes. Toss well in the butter. Sautee over low heat until softened but not browned. Now add the milk and all the other ingredients except for chives. Simmer for a half-hour. Discard the thyme, bay leaf, and parsley and sieve the soup. Reheat. To serve sprinkle with chopped chives.

Some time after we had been sampling the new potatoes the meitheal came back, as did the tractor with the digger. It dug out all the potatoes, sending them spinning like little missiles all over the field. The men followed, picking potatoes into buckets and putting them in long heaps. For the next few days my father was busy covering the heaps with a deep layer of straw and then a deep layer of dirt to save them from the winter frost. We sold some of our potatoes in town or down at the creamery, some we used for food for the animals and our own use in the house, and most importantly some we saved to use for seed for the next year. Potatoes were such an important crop for the Irish family that a failed crop would be a disaster, leaving man and animals hungry and with no seed for the next year.

Without the tractor and digger and drill, my father dug the field with a horse drawn plough and then made wide ridges for the potatoes to be planted three abreast with a shovel. He dug them out in the same way. It was very labor intensive work back then.

## THE POTATO

We have a loyal little friend
the potato smooth and round.
And seldom does it fail to lend,
a dish that's good and sound.
Oh! Truly tis a friend in need
tho treated with disdain.
A most essential food indeed
that fully earns its fame,
They say Sir Walter Raleigh
(So it's generally agreed)
Implanted in our valleys fair
The first prolific seed.
There sprang from out the fertile soil
(At least that's what we're told)
With eager care and earnest toil
A crop a hundred fold.

Oh! they've got Royal Standards now
They've Queens with gracious manners
And Royal Kings, the least highbrow
Who mix with Arran Banners.

But there's many a fine variety
That claim no regal fame
Just as good society
As those that flaunt the name.

Please God today, let come what may
Our farmers will plant more
Of these tubers which are bound to stay
Stark hunger from our shore.
So let us call them what we may
Be it spuds or pomme de terre
They are a vital food today
In which we all must share.

The tractor and digger were only used in later years before we left Ireland; but I remember when farmers put the potatoes in ridges, each one dug by hand. The ridges were about 3 feet wide and maybe 12 inches high with 3 potato plants across. The area between ridges was wide enough for a man to walk so he could check the crop and spray the plants when necessary. The sprayer was a large, heavy metal cylinder that was carried on the back with a long hose and nozzle. I can only imagine how heavy it was when filled with the liquid that was being sprayed. What back breaking work going up and down the rows spraying back and forth on either side, all the while carrying this load on your back! All the work putting the potatoes in, making the ridges, maintaining them and when mature, digging them out was done with just a spade.

# GARDEN WHERE THE PRATIES GROW

*Johnny Patterson 1840-1889*
*Publis Domain*

Have' you ever been in love, boys,
did you ever feel the pain?
I'd rather be in jail, I would, than be in love again;
Tho' the girl I love was beautiful, I'd have you all to know
That I met her in the garden where the praties grow.

**Chorus**
She was just the sort of creature that nature did intend
To walk straight thro' the world without the Grecian bend;
Nor did she wear a chignon I'd have you all to know
That I met her in the garden where the praties grow.

She was singing an ould Irish song,
called, "Gra gal machree,"
Oh! says I, what a wife she'd make for an Irish boy like me:
I was on important business, but I did not like to go.
And leave the girl in the garden where the praties grow.

Says I, "My lovely fair maid, I hope you'll pardon me!'
But she wasnt like those city girls,
that would say, "You're making free!"
She answered right modestly, and curtsied very low,
Saying,"You're welcome to the garden
where the praties grow."

Says I, "My lovely darling, I'm tired of single life,
And if you have no objection, I'll make you my dear wife."
Says she, "I'll ask my parents and tomorrow
I'll let you know,

If you meet me in the garden where the praties grow!"

Now her parents they consented and we're
blessed with children three
Two girls like their mammy, and a boy the image of me;
I'll train up the children in the way they oughta go.
But I'll ner forget the garden where the praties grow.


Usually my parents planted their vegetable garden in one corner of the field where we had the potatoes. Rows of green cabbage stood alongside beetroot and carrots and scallions. We grew turnips and parsnips. Sweet peas climbed a trellis of sticks and strings guarding green leeks and onions beneath.

# IRISH PEAS

3 pounds peas in the pod
1 teaspoon sugar
Boiling salted water
1 sprig mint
2 teaspoons butter
Strain Salt and pepper


Remove fresh peas from the pods.
Put into a pan of boiling salted water with the mint and
sugar. Boil gently until tender, about 5 to 7 minutes.,
shake lightly in butter, salt and pepper.
Delicious!

# MASHED TURNIPS

1 ½ to 2 pounds yellow turnip

Boiling salted water

½ tablespoon butter

Salt and pepper

Peel the turnip. Cut it into 1-inch slices. Drop into a pan of boiling salted water. When tender, drain very thoroughly and return the pot to the heat to allow the turnips to dry off. Mash to a fine pulp. Add the butter, salt and pepper to your taste and heat all together.

# ONION SOUP

4 large onions thinly sliced

1 ½ tablespoons butter

1 ½ tablespoons flour

2 cups scalded milk

1 bay leaf

2 cups Chicken stock

½ teaspoon powdered mace

Salt and pepper

2 egg yolks

½ cup evaporated milk or cream

Add the bay leaf to the milk and heat to scalding. Sautee the thinly sliced onions in the butter until translucent. Shake the flour into the onions and stir well to absorb the butter. Remove the bay leaf. Gradually add the scalded milk being careful that the soup doesn't lump! Now add the chicken stock and seasonings. Simmer until the onions are cooked.
Beat the egg yolks and evaporated milk (or cream) together. Put them in the bottom of a tureen and gradually add the hot soup as you whisk.

# THE FIELD BEHIND THE BYRE

When we went to the field at the back of the byre, so many memories came, but most of all I remember the story of the lone bush, that to this day graces the middle of the field.

The story goes that my grandfather decided that the bush was a nuisance and had to go, so he and my dad dug it out one fine day. The next morning when they went out the bush was back in place, not a sod of dirt disturbed. They blamed my grandmother, but she said lone bushes are fairy bushes and the little people did it and besides it's bad luck to disturb a lone bush. But they didn't listen and dug it out again, with the same results. After the third time digging it out, they stayed by the bush all night and saw nothing; but when the sun came up in the morning, the bush was back as it had always been. They'd neither seen nor heard anything, and after that they never touched it again. We Irish have a healthy respect for the spirits and little people. They say many people suffered terribly as a result of cutting down lone bushes and disturbing old forts which dotted the land. I was always a bit afraid of passing through that field alone. I always felt a presence I never could explain. How could I now explain to my American family my reverence for this bush as we posed for a picture by it? I prayed the fairies didn't mind.

*The gnarly lone bush*

# THE FAIRY TREE

*Mary Isabel Leslie 1899 - 1978*
*Pen name Temple Lane & Jean Herbert*

At moonrise round the thorn tree
The Little People play,
And men and women passing,
All turn their heads away.
From break of dawn till moonrise
Alone it stands on high,
With twisted twigs for branches,
Across the eastern sky.

They tell you dead men hung there,
Its black and bitter fruit

To guard the buried treasure
Round which it twines its root.
They tell you Cromwell hung them,
But that could never be.
He'd be in dread like others
To touch the fairy tree.

But Katie Ryan saw there
In some sweet dream she had
The Blessed Son of Mary,
And all His face was sad.
She dreamt she heard Him saying,
"Why should they be afraid,
When from a branch or thorn tree
The crown I wore was made?"

All night around the thorn tree
The Little People play,
And men and women passing
All turn their heads away,
But if your heart's a child's heart
And if your eyes are clean,
You'll never fear the thorn tree
That grows beyond Clogheen.

# THE LEPRACHAUN
*Robert Dwyer Joyce 1830 - 1883*

In a shady nook one moonlight night
A leprachaun I spied;
With scarlet cap and coat of green,
A cruskeen by his side.

'Twas tick tack tick, his hammer went
Upon a weeny shoe,
And I laughed to think of a purse of gold,
But the fairy was laughing, too!

With tip-toe step and beating heart,
Quite softly I drew nigh,
There was mischief in his merry face,
A twinkle in his eye.
He hammer'd and sang with tiny voice,
And drank his mountain dew;
And I laughed to think he was caught at last,
But the fairy was laughing, too!

As quick as thought I seized the elf,
"Your fairy purse!" I cried,
"The purse," he said "is in her hand,
That lady at your side!"
I turned to look; the elf was off!
Then what was I to do?
Oh! I laughed to think what a fool I'd been,
And the fairy was laughing, too!

## THE FAR FIELD BY JIMMY MACK'S

Passing through the gap into the field next to Jimmy
Mack's fields, I remembered lots of crops in this field, but
most of all I remembered the plum trees along Mack's ditch.
When the plums were ripe, they were sweet and juicy, but I
usually started testing them when they were greenish and

sour. Till this day a slightly tart plum can transport me back 5,000 miles and 40 years. That field also had a ditch that in spring was filled with big juicy strawberries. I'd sit there and eat till I'd had my fill and then bring the remainder home for strawberries with sugar and fresh cream later in the day. What a treat!

There were lots of briars or brambles in the ditch, too, and they produced luscious blackberries. My mother and I collected the juicy berries and she would make the most delicious blackberry jam and pies with them. Collecting blackberries was what we were doing one day when a plane came overhead, swooping so low it seemed to almost touch the ground. We ran for our lives and hid in the ditch until it was long gone. Recently an American pilot was talking on TV about being in Europe and how he and other pilots amused themselves by swooping low over the farms in Ireland and England and watching the people run and hide. The war had just recently ended and we were still afraid of those planes. It was anything but fun for us.

# BLACKBERRY PIE

1 recipe standard pastry crust
1 pound blackberries
3 oz sugar
3 oz flour
½ teaspoon cinnamon
1 oz butter or margarine

Pick over and hull the blackberries. Mix together the sugar, flour and cinnamon. Sprinkle this mixture over the blackberries and stir gently until they are well blended. Line an ungreased pie pan with half of the pastry, roll to 1/8 inch thick. Pour the fruit into the pie shell and dot with butter. Cover with pastry. Bake in a $450^0$ oven for 10 minutes, then reduce the heat to $350^0$ and continue baking until the pie is golden brown, about 40 minutes in all.

# BLACKBERRY & APPLE JAM

2 pounds of peeled and cored cooking apple

11 cups of blackberries

11cups of sugar

¾ cup water

## Instructions

Slice the apples and stew them with about 200 ml of water. Mash the stewed apples to a pulp. Cook the berries until they are soft. Put the berries in a wide stainless steel pot or pan. Add the apple pulp, Add the sugar. Stir over a gentle heat until the sugar is dissolved. Bring the mixture to a rapid boil for about 20 minutes. Test the mixture for a set; if it works, leave to cool for about 15 minutes then pour into sterilized jars and seal immediately.

I added the juice of a small lemon and a package of pectin then boiled for another five or ten minutes, which worked much better.

To test for a set cool three or four small plates in the freezer. pour a teaspoon of the mix onto the plate and allow it to cool down, then push it with your finger. If it wrinkles it is set! If not continue cooking until it tests done.

# HOMEMADE BLACKBERRY JAM

2 pound. blackberries

2 pound. sugar

Wash berries and place in preserving pan, using some of the redder berries as well as the ripe dark berries. Crush the berries. Stir over gentle heat until mixture boils, boil for 30 minutes, stirring often so that the jam does not stick. Add sugar stirring again until boiling. Stir over a gentle heat until the sugar has completely dissolved. Bring the berries up to the boil then boil hard until the jam reaches setting point. Check the setting point every ten minutes, although it may take up to half an hour to reach setting point. To test the setting point, remove the pan from the heat. Take your saucer from the freezer and place a drop of jam onto the cold plate. After a few seconds push the jam with your finger. If the jam surface wrinkles then it has reached setting point and is ready. If it slides about as a liquid, then it hasn't reached setting point and should be returned to the heat and boiled for a few more minutes before testing again. When setting point has been reached, turn off the heat. Skim off any scum on the surface of the jam with a large spoon. Let the jam cool and thicken in the pan for ten minutes, so that the strawberries don't all sink to the bottom in the jam jars. Stir the jam; ladle it into the sterilized jars. Use a wide mouth funnel, if you have one, to avoid spilling too much jam. Cover with a lid while still hot, label and store in a cool, dark place.

# PLUM JAM

## Ingredients:

juice of 1 lemon

5 cups of sugar

2 1/2 pounds of pitted plums

**Directions:**

Wash, pit and cut the plums into quarters then peel, combine everything in a pot along with lemon juice and the sugar. At this point, cook for 20 minute on a very low flame, until the plums are mushy. Once the plums are all mushy you can pass everything through a food mill to make it smooth, but if you like fruit chunks, avoid this step and let it simmer until nice and thick. Simmer the mixture on a low flame for 30 minute or until it thickens, skim the jam while simmering, remove any foam that rises to the surface or the jam will be cloudy. To know when the jam is ready, dip a teaspoon into the mixture and let a drop fall on a tilted plate. If it doesn't run, the jam is ready, otherwise continue cooking until ready. When jam is ready take a few sterilized jars and use a large mouth funnel to fill them. When the jar is full put the lid on, seal tightly, turn it upside down and let it cool to create the vacuum.

# PLUM JAM ROLY POLY
*(serves 4-6)*

5½ oz self-rising flour, sifted

3 oz suet chopped into meal

3½ fl oz cold water

pinch salt

5 tablespoon plum jam (or raspberry, damson)

**Method**

Preheat the oven to 400°. Mix the sifted flour, suet, and salt together in a large bowl. Add enough water to make a soft, but not sticky dough. Knead lightly on a lightly floured board for a few minutes before rolling out to a ½ in thickness and a rough 8 in square shape. Spread a thick layer of jam over one side of the dough, leaving ½ in border, which you dampen with a little water. Roll up loosely, pinching the ends together as you go to stop the jam escaping. Place the roll on a large lightly buttered piece of parchment paper, sealed edge down. Join the ends of the paper and make a pleated join along the top to allow for the pudding to expand, twist the ends like a sweet (candy) wrapper. Put the pudding into a large loaf tin or a brownie tin. Fill a roasting tin with boiling water and place on the bottom rack of the oven. Then put the roly poly on the top rack for 35-40 minutes. Serve a single thick slice, with homemade custard.

# BAKED CUSTARD

2 eggs

2 ½ cups milk

2 egg yolks

2 tablespoons sugar

1 teaspoon butter

Beat the eggs and egg yolks with sugar. Scald the milk and pour on the egg mixture while beating. Pour into individual buttered dishes or one large dish. Dot top with the butter. Stand the dishes in a larger dish containing 1 inch of water and bake at 350° until firm in the center.

# THE FIELD NEXT TO THE FIELD AT THE BACK OF THE HOUSE.

I recall having hay there and I would break branches off the ash bushes. They had small branches on either side of the main one. I'd trim them and make stick people, put a dress on them and line them up about a cock of hay and play school. I pretended to teach them their sums, asked them their spelling, and when I didn't get the right answer like the master in school I gave them a good slap with a stick. Sometimes these stick people became my dance partners and we would dance around the field. Oh the imagination! I was an only child and didn't have any other children who lived close by, other than the Clancy's who they were all boys and wanted nothing to do with a girl. That would be sissy! So I had to make my own fun. The farm animals were my friends and often my playmates too.

## THE GARDEN BEHIND THE HOUSE

The garden between the house and the field at the back was one of my favorite places to play. I loved to plant things and spent hours digging and planting bushes from slips of existing bushes. The pine trees were smaller then and I played among them.

The lower end of the garden was usually my bathroom area. Without any type of outhouse it provided my dalkin leaves for cleansing. At one time we had a nasty rooster. He was vicious and just when I settled in my favorite bathroom spot, he came sneaking up behind me and pecked away on my bottom. I ran to the house screaming. I always checked to see where he was after that before I settled myself.

This garden had some gooseberry and current bushes and when they ripened they were really delicious.

# GOOSEBERRY JAM

7 pounds gooseberries
7 pounds sugar
a teacup of water

Top and tail the gooseberries and wash them. Put the gooseberries and the sugar in a large pot with water. Stir well until the sugar is all dissolved. Then let this mixture boil for about 30 minutes, stirring and skimming frequently. Pour into sterilized jam pots (jars) and let cool

# GOOSEBERRY PIE

### Crust

1 ¼ cups flour
¾ teaspoon salt
6 oz butter or margarine
2 tablespoons water

### Filling

1 pound gooseberries

¾ cup sugar

¼ cup tablespoons water

1/8 cup flour (25g)

1/8 teaspoon salt

½ teaspoon cinnamon

½ teaspoon ground cloves

½ teaspoon nutmeg

Sift the flour with the salt. Cut the butter into the flour until the particles are the size of large peas. Sprinkle with water, a tablespoon at a time, and mix lightly with a fork until all the flour is moistened. Gather the dough together with your fingers so that it leaves the sides of the bowl clean, and press firmly into a ball. Divide into two parts, one slightly larger than the other. Line a pie dish with the smaller portion and brush with melted butter.

Cook the gooseberries in ½ cup of sugar and water until tender. Combine the remaining ¼ cup sugar with the flour, salt and spices. Stir into cooked fruit and cool.

Cover with the rest of the pastry, making slits in the pastry. Bake in hot oven for 40-45 minutes at 425°.

# BLACKCURRANT JAM

2 pounds blackcurrants (washed, topped & tailed)

2 pounds sugar

1 cup water

Place your prepared fruit into a large saucepan or preserving pan with the water. Bring to boiling point then simmer gently for 20 minutes. Add the sugar and boil for about 30 minutes from the time the jam re-boils or until a little almost immediately sets when tested on a cold plate. Towards the end, the jam must be stirred continuously to prevent it boiling over or sticking to the bottom of the pan.

Pour into sterilized pots, cover and label. Store in a cool dry place.

The garden also had a good crop of nettles in another corner and if you were not careful you could get stung by them. There again the dalkin leaf came in handy, you rubbed it on the sting and you had to say, "Dalkin in and dalkin out, take the sting of the nettle out." I never tried it without the words but it did the job.

There was a spot in that garden that was special to me. Religion was important to me, especially the Blessed Mother. We in Ireland were very devoted to her. She had appeared so close by in Knock Co. Mayo, in Fatima and Lourdes. As an innocent little child I prayed to her often and planted a little area just for her in case she wanted a place to appear in Cavan. I went there often and hoped one day she might grace the special spot I'd prepared for her appearance. It was strange standing in that spot again thirty years later. I'm still devoted to her, but I've lost that childish hope I had back then and that too is sad.

This was also the garden where my mother hung the wash. She scrubbed the clothes on a washboard and then rinsed and hung them out on the line to dry. When almost dry she brought them in all rolled up and ironed them. One of my neat finds on our trip to Ireland was my great grandmother's pressing iron. It was a small solid iron which was placed entirely in the fire. It was thrown out in one of the gardens at my Aunt Kathleen's. I think it's a family treasure.

There were hedges all around this garden but the hedge at the bottom of this garden had the sweetest smelling wild roses growing in it and cascading over all the other bushes. No beautiful rose smelled sweeter than they and I could stay beneath its canopy for ages just drinking in the aroma.

# THE FIELDS ON MACK'S SIDE OF THE LANE

The upper of two fields between the house and the road on Mack's side was often used for grazing the cows. We didn't have a bull, only the larger farms had one. When breeding time came, dad put a tether around the cow's head and led her to the Hannigans, the farm next to us. As the years went by and artificial insemination became popular, the vet came in a van and artificially inseminated the cow. Then we watched and waited as she became heavy with calf. Rose Reilly, John's sister, came home to Ireland to live after living many, many years in the States. When she heard the vet was coming to inseminate the cow, she couldn't figure how he was going to get the bull into his car to bring it to their house. Rose very soon realized she was not cut out for farm life and after about two years returned to America.

When her time for delivery came the cow was brought into the byre and a neighbor called on to help my father with the delivery in case the cow needed assistance. At the first sounds, my mother and I were chased to a neighbor's until the calf arrived. Ladies did not belong around a calving cow. The baby calf was always so sweet, a little wobbly at first, but funny and cute. At first they nursed from their mothers but soon we weaned them, teaching them to drink by putting their mother's milk in a bucket and putting our hand in fingers up so they could suck on our fingers.

As slow and quiet as the cows were, the calves loved to kick up their heels and play and run through the fields. I was always sad to see them sold when they grew older, but occasionally we kept a female and raised her as our cow or at least until she was a heifer and had her first calf. Then dad would walk her into town on the fair day and sell her, hopefully getting the price he wanted, though quite often the buyer offered less than he requested. Then usually a third person known to both intervened and suggested they split the difference. This was acceptable to both because what my father asked was more than he expected to get. Then the luck penny, usually a few shillings, was paid. It was traditional to give the person buying the animal a small portion of the price as a token of good luck and confirmation that the animal was really as presented.

Fair days always seemed like fun for the men. It usually ended with a few pints in McDonalds, with buyers and sellers drinking to each others health. I remember my dad coming home in a great mood and recounting all the day's happenings to my mother and bringing sweets and biscuits (cookies) for me. I envied the young boys who could go to the fair with their fathers; little girls had to stay home.

This was also the field that had the ditch we crossed to go visit the Macks. I loved to go to the Macks and every time my mother took me there as soon as we walked in the door I would start to whine that I was hungry. They always seemed to have a special treat. My poor embarrassed mother would try to shush me but I was always very persistent. After several of these scenes she decided to put an end to this awkward situation by handing me my favorite snack, a piece of bread with butter and sugar on it, just before we got to the door. Surely now I would not ask for food. But she was wrong! Within minutes I was whining, with the bread still in my hand, that I was hungry and wanted something to eat. Mary Mack was so kind and understood though my mother was now more embarrassed than ever.

While our home had cement floors in the kitchen and parlor many of the mud cabins had mud floors throughout. Through generations of feet they were packed tightly, clean and dry. Such was the case at the Macks and I was always fascinated by a single bowl-shaped indent in the floor near the table. When Mary served a cup of tea she took the jug of milk and poured a little into the indent for the cat, a built in cat dish! It just seemed the most natural thing. Speaking of milk, we farmers depended on each other a great deal back then. We borrowed from each other, considering being generous in sharing with each other to be what we should do. So it was that if our cows were dry, not producing milk, then neighbors supplied us with whatever we needed and of course the favor was returned when they needed it. I mention this now because I remember many a gallon of milk passing over the ditch to Macks, going both ways. They were always good neighbors.

In Ireland back then there was always a shortcut through the fields to where you wanted to go. And you didn't need to ask permission to go through a field to get to a destination. When you lived there you knew the short cuts through the gaps and over the ditches. Today it seems nobody walks anywhere anymore. Everyone has cars. It was fun back then to go through the fields whether it was to church or school or to visit a neighbor. We were sure to meet someone on the way and stop to bid the time of day.

# THE FLAX HOLE FIELD

The field closest to the road near Macks had a flax hole. The last few years we lived on the farm we didn't have flax, but I remember a time when flax was a very important product of our farm. It was a lot of work, planting it, tending it, and when it became tall with sweet small blue blossoms it was cut and dried and then bundled. The bundles were drowned in the flax hole, a very large, rectangular hole in the ground several feet deep and filled with water from an underground spring. After some weeks in there, it was carefully removed with a grape. Then spread out on the stubble to dry. Once dry it was once again bundled and hauled to the flax mill by horse and cart where it was sold to make the then famous Irish linen.

When I was very little my mother always worried that I would fall into the flax hole if I went too near it, so she told me of creatures that were in there and when I wasn't looking would throw stones in to frighten me. She never was a good aim and one day missed the hole when she threw a large rock, hitting my dad on the head and knocking him out cold.

Worrying about me and the flax hole was valid. For a small child it was a fascinating place with the frogs who liked to spawn there. They were fun to watch and their croaking could be heard from afar. I enjoyed seeing the tadpoles as they grew and matured. My mother warned never to touch the frogs or tadpoles because they would cause warts. To this day I will not touch a frog!

*My dad John Argue throwing flax sheaves into the flax hole by the Cootehill Rd 1949*

That field was also home for many blackthorn bushes that were covered with sweet white blossoms in spring. As I walked past the thorny hedge, I remembered how many times my dad cut a cudgel or a shillelagh from those bushes. Many American visitors were given one as a souvenir through the years. He was proud of them. Along the hedge on the other side of that field were many primroses and bluebells. I love the sweet scent of the primroses and we used them every spring on the May altar we erected on the churn in the kitchen. We would place the statue of Our Lady on a clean cloth on the churn and surround it with primroses and bluebells. It was a beautiful devotion to our Blessed Mother, a devotion which I've carried with me to my family. Of course I don't have the churn!

Another May tradition which I have continued with our daughters was the May bush. The evening of April 30th we would go out and find a beautiful thorny whin bush in full bloom, cut it and bring it home, or I would use one close to the house. I'd gather flowers from the laneways, fields and ditches, place a saucer under the bush, and then scatter the flowers all about the bush, always partially covering the saucer. Next morning as soon as I woke up I rushed to dress and ran out to find what treasure would have been left. I would find several small coins, sixpence, half pennies, three penny bits, a couple of shillings, a virtual treasure for a little girl who had so little. That was my May bush. With no whins available in America we us a forsythia bush, placing the flowers beneath them.

If we ran out of primroses in that field there were lots more lining the lane to the house which separates the fields next to Macks from the upper and lower bush fields on the other side. Although I have tried almost ever year I have never been successful growing primroses in my American garden, but I do enjoy their scent in little pots for a few weeks in the spring.

# PRIMROSE TIME IN CAVAN
## RECITATION
*Shaun O'Nolan - Traditional*

It was primrose time in Cavan, I thought I was in heaven
When I heard the cuckoo calling and the skylark sing his lay.
I espied a little mother as primrose she did gather
To beautify her altar for the station the next day.
Says I God save you kindly, says she God save you stranger
Come in and have a cup of tea and make yourself at home.
I've been cleanin', scrubbing, white-washing and rubbin'
For its primrose time in Cavan and
the childers coming home.
When I walked into that kitchen. Oh wasn't it bewitchin'
As I saw the big turf fire, and heard the kittle sing
She says what would you be takin',
some duck eggs and bacon.
They were only laid this mornin' and are fit for any king.
Says I, I don't feel hungry, says she, I don't believe you.
You must have walked from Kingscourt,
or maybe from Stradone.
Would you like a goat's milk pancake
or a piece or two of boxtee.
You know the childer loved it when they were all at home.
Says she, you are a stranger,
but your clothes looks like a Yankee.
I said you guessed it rightly; I'm from the U. S. A.
Then her angel face did brighten,
and her handshake did tighten.
Oh, it must have been God sent you, around the road to-day.
In America I have seven, there's two more up in heaven.

Last June their father joined them and left me all alone,
But I am not a cryin, or in God's face a flyin,
For it's primrose time in Cavan,
and the childers comin' home.
There's the cradle thy were rocked in,
there's the heart stone that they played on;
And there's the little altar where I thaught them how to pray.
There's the school books and the fiddles
and the book with all the riddles.
They keep me from being lonesome
while the childer is away.
She says wasthore you're cryin', and I was I'm not denying,
I never shall forget her until my dying day.
This night I'll pray God bless her
May angel's lips caress her
For it's Primrose time in Cavan three thousand miles away.

# THE LANE

I recall too how I was afraid of the gypsies who traveled the roads and how I used to rush through the gate at the bottom of the lane when I saw them coming. I'd quickly hide. I must have been afraid they would steal me. They always seemed to have lots of children and on occasion my mother told me that they took naughty children as a way to make me behave. They had beautiful horses and brightly colored caravans, but often they were dirty and their clothes tattered. Once when I was coming home from school by the mountain road, Mary Ellen Brady and the other children told

Sean Rudden and me that there were gypsies in the rocks, the way we usually went home. Because we were so afraid we went home another way, a long distance out of our way. It took so long and it began to get dark and we were frightened. Our parents who had been searching for us were hysterical with worry when we got home. They thought we were lost or in a flax hole. I'm not sure what happened to Sean that night, but I got a good spanking and never deviated from the accepted route again.

Sean Rudden didn't have to worry about the route to and from school very much. He didn't go very often and when he did it was after a big fight. His dad would drag him kicking and biting and screaming off to school. His mother was a gentle woman who didn't like that and would follow crying, "John don't kill him for God's sake," while the father threatened death. It was quite a show. After a while they just gave up and he never went to school again.

Going up the lane there was a small well along the side, actually it was more of a stream, where the cows came to drink. Even in summer that little stream kept producing water. On a more recent trip to Ireland I was told a very sad story about that spot. It seems during the great famine there had been a large well there and my great grandfather either drowned or committed suicide in the well. No one really knows for sure but the well was filled in after that. To this day, even in the hottest weather, the water still flows. I went to the spot after I heard the story and said a prayer for him. May God grant him eternal rest.

There were lots of watercress and sorrel plants growing in the little stream and they had a very interesting flavor, kind of sour and tangy. My mother told me that people in the city sometimes ate them along with dandelion leaves as part of a meal. I could not imagine that.

All along the lane were more wild strawberry plants. I ate all I could of them and then picked the rest to take home and have later with cream. My mother was delighted when I came home with hands full of berries. There were lots of strawberries at some areas along the Cootehill Road and if I brought home enough of them she liked to make strawberry jam.

# STRAWBERRY JAM

## Ingredients:
2 pound 3oz strawberries
2 pound 3oz granulated sugar
½ lemon, juice only
(Substitute Raspberries in this recipe to make Raspberry Jam)

## Directions:
The day before you wish to make the jam, hull and halve the strawberries. Check for soft spots (which must be removed) and discard any berries with bruises or that are overripe. Place the strawberries into a large bowl with 18oz of the sugar. Turn carefully to mix and coat well, then cover and place into the fridge overnight. The next day, place a saucer into the freezer to chill - you'll need this when you

come to test the setting point of the jam. Pour the strawberries, their juice and any residual sugary juices into a very large pan or preserving pan, remembering that the mixture will rise as it boils, and add the remaining 18oz sugar and the lemon juice. Stir over a gentle heat until the sugar has completely dissolved. Bring the strawberries up to the boil then boil hard until the jam reaches setting point. Check the setting point every ten minutes, although it may take up to half an hour to reach setting point. To test the setting point, remove the pan from the heat. Take your saucer from the freezer and place a drop of jam onto the cold plate. After a few seconds push the jam with your finger. If the jam surface wrinkles then it has reached setting point and is ready. If it slides about as a liquid, then it hasn't reached setting point and should be returned to the heat and boiled for a few more minutes before testing again. When setting point has been reached, turn off the heat. Skim off any scum on the surface of the jam with a large spoon. Let the jam cool and thicken in the pan for ten minutes, so that the strawberries don't all sink to the bottom in the jam jars. Stir the jam; ladle it into the sterilized jars. Use a wide mouth funnel, if you have one, to avoid spilling too much jam. Cover with a lid while still hot, label and store in a cool, dark place.

There was a spot in that lane with a big indentation in the ditch. You can still see the roots of the trees, but now it is just beginning to grow over with grass. It seems many years ago there was a terrible thunderstorm and the horse got very scared and ran off. My dad was bringing him back past that spot in the lane when lightning struck there. Dirt and stones went flying in all directions. The horse took off, but my father now terrified ran for the house as fast as his legs could carry him, letting the horse fend for himself. He loved to tell that story and always claimed that it was the horse that drew the lightning. It was believed that animals drew lightning and that you should not be near them in a thunderstorm.

The lane had such a steep hill and when I learned to ride my bike my mother warned me never to ride down the hill. I was not going to listen to her; after all she never rode a bike so how could she know? Down the lane I went going faster and faster with stones spinning out from beneath my wheels, clicking against each other and hitting the ditches with a thud. I nearly never got the bike stopped at the bottom. My father as a young lad was less fortunate. He failed to stop, went right across the road and ended up head over heels and bike into the meadow the other side of the road. My mom tried very hard to learn to ride, but somehow she could never keep her balance. She would sneak my father's bike when he was busy in the fields. When I got a new bicycle dad told her he'd buy her one too if she learned to ride. She really went at it in earnest, borrowing mine every time I wasn't home. She'd take it up on John Reilly's pass and try time and time again. She always ended up in the briars and I'd have punctured tires. Luckily my father kept a well stocked box of tire patches and repair parts for the bikes and she kept him busy. She never did learn to ride a bike.

*The lane going up to our house*

# THE LITTLE LANES OF IRELAND
*Unknown*

The little lanes of Ireland are crooked, old and wise,
They like to hide their happiness from cold and curious eyes.
They know it is a secret that is not learned in years,
But comes to you who strolls and strives with
laughter, toil and tears.

The little lanes of Ireland are always left behind
By you who on the highway a fortune go to find,
Yet when in dusk and glare your dreams and you must part,
Some little, happy far-off lane is fragrant to your heart.

The little lanes of Ireland are rather hard to find.
Their over-hanging hedges are often close and kind.
And hidden in their leafy bowers is joy so rich and rare,
You never can forget them, if you've ever wandered there.

The little lanes of Ireland are holy through the land,
With angels in their silences for you who understand,
And when you walk and worship there
you will wonder how you dare
O God must love the little lanes, to put such beauty there.

# THE LOWER BUSH FIELD

On the other side of the lane were the upper bush field and the lower bush field. The lower field was the one by the road and as I grew older I kept the hedge along the road very well trimmed. I knew what time of day the young men went to work or school and it was convenient to trim the hedge then, but I always kept it high enough so I could hide behind it if the gypsies came. The back ditch of that field had bilberry plants. John Ash and I played together and often spent time stuffing bilberries in our mouths. We often arrived home with blue mouths and blue fingers, but they were oh so good. Sometimes I collected the bilberries and my mother served them swimming in fresh cream. That field had a really steep hill with a flat area just before reaching the lane. I loved to roll down the hill. Starting at the top and rolling over and over, I could go all the way to the lane.

Standing at the top of that hill we could see for miles around. What a view from there! We could see the mountain with its purple heather, the beautiful hills and valleys all the way to Ballyhaise. On a clear day we can see the church steeple in Ballyhaise. I wished, as I stood there as an adult, that I could build a house there with lots of windows and enjoy the beauty of my surroundings like living in the center of a postcard. That field, like the vacant spot where the house once stood, for some reason, makes my heart ache with loneliness and longing.

The field at the back of that one, my own field bought from the Shields family years ago, brought back a memory of making hay. After the hay was cut with a scythe and left to dry in swats the work began. I recall being up and out in the hay field very early in the morning, before bicycles passed going to work in town, turning the swats over with a rake back and forth across the field. After a few days the swats were raked into rows and then collected by hand into laps, which were then allowed to sit another week or two to dry some more At that point they were collected into cocks or large mounds, about 5 to 6 feet high. To keep the hay in its place on the cock, my father would have me help him twist hay ropes. He would get a piece of stick from a nearby tree and wrap a piece of hay around it then as I turned the stick he fed more hay into it. We would continue this until the hay rope was long enough to reach from the base at one side to the base at the other with a bit extra to anchor it to the cock. Each cock got two ropes crisscrossed over the tops. As I stood there thinking of making hay, I thought I heard the sweet distant sound of the Angelus bell as it rang out calling all the farmers to stop their work to pray. I remember seeing the men in the fields as they took off their hats or caps, held them in their hands as they stood heads reverently bent and prayed.

# THE ANGELUS

V. The Angel of the Lord declared unto Mary.
R. And she conceived of the Holy Ghost. *Hail Mary! Etc.*
V. Behold the handmaid of the Lord.
R. Be it done unto me according to Thy word.
*Hail Mary! Etc*
V. And the word was made flesh.
R. And dwelt amongst us. *Hail Mary! Etc*
V. Pray for us, O holy Mother of God.
R. That we may be made worthy of the promise of Christ.

*Let us pray*
Pour forth, we beseech Thee, O Lord, Thy grace into our
hearts, that we, to whom the incarnation of Christ, Thy Son,
was made known by the message of an angel, may, by His
passion and cross, be brought to the glory of His
resurrection: through the same Christ our Lord. Amen.
May the divine assistance remain always with us.
May the souls of the faithful departed, through the mercy of
God, rest in peace.

A sign of the cross and their backbreaking work

began again. Somehow they seemed renewed and refreshed

by their prayers. Three times a day the bells rang out, 6 am,

12 noon and 6 pm. Each time, no matter how busy, everyone

stopped to pray.

The cocks stayed in the fields for several weeks once

dry were quite rain proof. Then one day my dad arranged a

meitheal to bring in the hay. Two horses were harnessed up

with a long chain that was placed around the base of the cock

and they pulled it back to the haggard. In later years Eugene

Reilly came with the tractor and hay lift and brought the

cocks into the garden in back of the byre, where it was gathered and stacked into very large hay stacks or reeks. I loved to ride on top of the hay cock while it was being brought in. I also liked to play on top of the hay stacks as the men tossed forkful after forkful of hay on top. When it grew really tall I slid down the side into my father's waiting arms. The most delightful part of working with the hay was that beautiful sweet scent.

# THE HAYLOFT
*Robert Louis Stevenson*

Through all the pleasant meadow side
The grass grew shoulder-high,
Till the shining scythes went far and wide
And cut it down to dry.

These green and sweetly smelling drops
They led in wagons home;
And they piled them here in mountaintops
For mountaineers to roam.

Here is Mount Clear, Mount Rusty-Nail,
Mount Eagle and Mount High;
The mice that in these mountains dwell,
No happier are than I!

O what a joy to clamber there,
O what a place to play,
With the sweet, the dim, the dusty air,
The happy hills of hay.

One of the things I really enjoyed when helping with the hay in the field was afternoon tea. My mother would bring a tray with cups of tea, soda bread, sometimes egg sandwiches out to the field. We'd sit often in silence, in the cool grass near the ditch looking out over the sweet smelling field of hay as our small terrier chased rabbits or searched for burrows. Sometimes stretching out on the soft grass as lazy white clouds wafted slowly overhead, we were at peace. I can still remember the taste of that tea. No high tea in Buckingham Palace ever tasted better. It had a flavor all its own and our hearts had a peace that today is so elusive. Growing in the ditch right behind where we enjoyed our tea were wild cherry bushes, and when the birds didn't get the ripe fruit before I did they were deliciously sweet. If we were lucky enough we were able to collect enough sweet cherries to make a pie or cake.

## CHERRY CAKE

4 oz butter or margarine
6 oz castor sugar
3 eggs
12 oz flour
4 oz sliced citron
8 oz washed and dried and pitted cherries
1 teaspoon baking powder
¼ teaspoon salt
4 tablespoons cold water

Cream the butter and sugar, and add the unbeaten eggs, one by one, beating well after each addition. Mix about 3 tablespoons of the flour with the citron and the cherries. Sift the remainder of the flour with the baking powder and salt. Add the flour, alternately with cold water, to the creamed mixture, then mix in the fruit. Turn into a greased and floured tin. Bake 2 ½ hours in a slow oven at 325°.

# THE HILL

In front of our house at the top of the lane was a field where I spent lots of time. It was "The Hill." It sloped down to the lane on one side and to the fields we called Shields on the other. There was a gap closed by a big gate that went onto the hill from the street and by the gap on the street side was a well. We used the water from it for washing dishes, bathing and shampooing, everything except drinking and cooking. The cows stopped by there for a refreshing drink as they made their way to and from the nearby byre with my father always urging them on.

The hill also had a well just a few feet from the gate on the other side of the hedge and the cows and horses enjoyed many drinks from it too. In the evening it seemed to be the gathering place for the cows as they waited to go in for milking. They were sweet docile animals, not too bright but usually friendly. I never got to milk a cow, but I always wanted to. We usually had three or four cows and each had their own names. One was named Polly; the other names evade my memory. They had their own personalities as well. My dad picked up his three-legged stool and bucket and milked the cows twice a day by hand. Some liked to be milked and stood there patiently, perfectly still. Others hated it and my dad had to be careful how he placed the stool when he sat down or the cow might kick the bucket, sending him, the stool and the bucket of milk all over the byre. Or they swished their long tails in his face, with blinding accuracy over the eyes. Milking was not always fun. If all else failed and he worried too much about the hooves and tail, around came the head complete with horns and they could really hurt and send a man toppling, again wearing the milk and bucket.

## THE COW
*Robert Louis Stephenson*

The friendly cow all red and white,
I love with all my heart:
She gives me cream with all her might,
To eat with apple-tart.

She wanders lowing here and there,
And yet she cannot stray,
All in the pleasant open air,
The pleasant light of day;

And blown by all the winds that pass
And wet with all the showers,
She walks among the meadow grass
And eats the meadow flowers.

The goat was even worse to milk. It seemed everything moved even faster, hooves and horns, but at least there was no tail to worry about. Dad didn't like the goat. My grandfather, James Clarke, gave it to me when it was a tiny kid and so very cute, but it grew and eventually produced kids of its own, which I brought in to Shurdens and sold. I hated to part with them. They were such sweet little animals, but my dad said that one goat was enough since they ate the bark off the trees and young sprouts from bushes. However our goat was really good and usually ate only grass. Maybe that was because she was fed the same food as the cows, as well as the grass she grazed on. Someone said goat's milk was good for me and would make my hair beautiful, so I tried it, but only once! It was very strong, an awful taste! It tasted as bad as the goat smelled which was pretty nasty. I decided I'd rather have ugly hair than drink that stuff.

The hill was where I played a lot with my constant companions, my dogs. Tiny was a white and tan wired haired terrier. Later Cora, a Kerry blue collie, came into my life. My aunt Mollie and her son Tom were going to America to live, so they gave me this beautiful dog. I loved her! She was a loyal companion until the day I left Ireland. Those dogs waited every day at the road for me until I came home from school. There they greeted me with tails wagging, running ahead of me to the house. They knew that soon I would join them out on the hill running and playing with them again.

My father was a small, wiry, man who prided himself on his athletic ability. He enjoyed having races on the hill and we would start at the top and run toward the house. He always beat me no matter how fast I ran. I remember one day Kathleen Reilly (Brady) came over and she challenged him to a race. Now Kathleen was very fast and at first it seemed she might beat him, but at the end he sprinted past her and remained the champion of the hill!!

In the winter I enjoyed playing in the rushes. Between them there often were puddles where I would find on very cold days what I as a young child thought were the most beautiful patterned pieces of glass. I would pick them up very carefully, they seemed to break so easily, and hide them. They were so beautiful and I wanted to save them. They were always gone when I returned days later. I often wondered if the fairies took them. I'm not sure when I realized the patterned glass was really ice.

As we walked around the hill I thought about the day when I was little and went to play. I didn't know that the nasty old sow was loose and on the hill also. Boy, she took after me, chasing me around and around. I could never get enough ahead of her to open the gate and escape from her nasty snout. Finally my mother rescued me, responding to my terrified screams. But not all sows are nasty. We even had one that was quite friendly and I liked to climb on her back and ride her like a pony. Did you ever ride a pig? Their hair is very rough and bristly, but it didn't stop me.

My father knew how much I enjoyed the baby or suckling pigs, so when he cleaned the pigsty he would put the sow out on the hill closing the gate securely. Then when he put in the fresh straw he would give me time to play with the babies. They were the most delightful, playful, cuddly creatures, soft and sweet and gentle. I loved how they poked me with their rubbery pink little noses when I sat down in the fresh straw. I hated to see them grow up and the day I hated the most was the day they took them to McCarran's to be slaughtered. We usually took the runt of the litter into the house and bottle fed him until he became large enough to survive outside. We referred to him as the pet pig and indeed he was that. Because he had spent his early weeks being raised by us he never bonded with his mother and acted more like a dog than a pig, following us around and wanting attention. But all too soon when he had been fattened up he too had to go and was either taken to the fair or to McCarran's to be sold. There he would be butchered into bacon, sausages, chops and roasts.

The hill was also the place where I could corner the horse and climb up onto the ditch and then onto her back. She was a huge workhorse, our Fanny, but gentle and I loved to ride her. When we had cousins from the city come to visit Dad would put the collar around the horse's neck and while he held the reins gave everybody rides. Everybody always loved it. I remember on one occasion our cousins the Smiths from Glasgow, Scotland came on holiday and were thrilled when my Dad gave the adults a ride on the horse.

*Grandfather James Clarke, my father and me on the hill looking toward the mountain*

*Monica on the hill showing Hannigan's field with cocks of hay before their new house was built*

*Paddy Freelan gets a ride on Fanny*

From the hill I looked toward Hannigan's lane and I thought of my first day of school. I was four years old when my mother brought me down to Hannigan's one morning all dressed up with a school bag almost as big as I was. Evelyn Hannigan was older and I was entrusted to her care to take me to school. I loved Evelyn and off I went very happily with her. I remember very little about the school but I do remember all the fun I had. As the spring rolled into summer on our walks home from school we picked strawberries and gooseberries along the way and lots of flowers, wild roses and woodbines and my favorite, lilacs. Evelyn finished

Ballyhaise School that summer and in the fall I started Castletara National School.

*My first day of school, Evelyn Hannigan, her sister and my mother and me*

# SHIELD'S FIELDS

Walking through the muddy gap at the other side of the Hill into Shields' other two fields, I remember when we bought them. I remember that we used those two fields usually to graze the cows. But we always had to beat them to the furthest part of the fields in the early morning and there in the grass we would find delicate white mushrooms with tender pink undersides that looked like little accordion bellows. We would gather them up and take them back to the house, where my mother set them upside down on the hot coals with a light shake of salt in the center. They were delectable as we drank the juice from the center and ate the tender flesh. I can still taste them. If we were lucky enough to find a large number of mushrooms in the morning then my mother would cut them up and simmer them in milk and make a delicious soup.

## Mom's Fresh Mushroom Soup

2 cups of fresh mushrooms
3 cups warm milk
1 cup heavy cream
Salt and pepper to taste

Clean and chop the mushrooms and add to warm milk. Simmer on low about 30 minutes. Do not boil! Stir in fresh cream. Add salt and pepper to taste.

When she made this soup my mother skimmed cream from the top of the fresh milk before it went to the creamery.

I have been able to almost duplicate the taste of the mushrooms roasted on the coals by placing cleaned mushrooms upside down on a glass pie plate, sprinkling them with a little salt, and microwaving them for about a minute or until juice forms in the center. Almost as tasty as those so long ago.

At the very far side of that field was a babbling stream which separated our farm from Jerry Flood's. Standing there I wondered what ever happened to Jerry. He lived alone in that house ever since his sister Mary married Jemmy Mack. He liked to fix things, patch porringers, kettles, etc.

Thinking of fixing things now my mind wanders to the gypsies again. I remembered how they came to the house to beg for money or food and some of them fixed things. We called them tinkers. They put new handles on pots and porringers and fixed holes in pots. Usually when we saw the gypsies coming we closed and locked the doors and didn't answer their knock when they came, except for one.

He was from Mayo, and he was an especially nice man and never asked for handouts. Always wanted to do a job for the money we gave him. My parents always gave him something to do, welcomed him in and gave him something to eat and drink. These people were interesting and I wish I'd grown up a little less afraid of them. I wish I had been able to talk with them, to understand them and their wandering ways. It was much later I realized that the pieces of rags that they always left behind were not left because they were sloppy and untidy, but rather they were a sign to other gypsies, traveling people, about this spot where they had camped. If it was friendly, etc., were all indicated by the color of the rags left behind on the trees. I wish I could remember what color the rags were that were left by our meadow and what the rags told about us.

# THE WHISTLIN' GYPSY ROVER
*Traditional*

The gypsy rover carne over the hill,
Down through the valley so shady.
He whistled and he sang till the green woods rang,
And he won the heart of a lady,

**Chorus:**
Howdy-do, howdy-do-da-day,
Howdy-do, howdy-day,
He whistled and he sang till the green woods rang,
And he won the heart of a lady.

She left her father's castle gate,
She left her own true lover,
She left her servants and her estate,
To follow the gypsy rover.

**Chorus**

Her father saddled up his fastest steed
Roamed the valleys allover,
He sought his daughter at great speed,
And the whistlin' gypsy rover.

### Chorus

He carne at last to a mansion fine,
Down by the river Clady,
And there was music and there was wine
For the gypsy and his lady.

### Chorus

'He is no gypsy, father', said she,
'But lord of these lands all over,
And I shall stay till my dying day,
With my whistlin' gypsy rover.'

### Chorus

Speaking of rags reminds me of the time my rag doll became very dirty and my mother decided to wash it for me. She removed all the rags and washed them, and it looked like a gypsy camp when she set them out to dry.

There was a man who came occasionally to visit. We thought of him as a beggerman but he was always well dressed and somehow now as I look back I'm not so sure he was. He was dumb, couldn't speak, and we called him "The Dummy." He used sign language and made unrecognizable sounds to try to communicate with us. Each time he came to our house my parents gave him some money and quickly shooed him away; or if they saw him coming we hid, were quiet as mice and wouldn't answer the door. I often wondered who he really was, where he came from and if he really came to get money. He certainly was very different from any other beggerman who came around. It was not that we thought less of him but at that time he was different and we didn't understand his disability. In a way I guess my parents were afraid of what they didn't understand.

If we saw him on the road I was sent running to the neighbors to alert them that this man was in the area so that they could also avoid answering the door if he were to come to their houses. I always took the short cut through the fields so I never worried that I might meet him.

# THE BEGGARMAN'S SONG
*Unknown*

I am a little beggarman, and begging I have been.
For three score years this little Isle of Green.
I'm known along the Liffey from the Basin to the Zoo.
And everybody calls me by the name of Johnny Dhu.
Of all trades a going, sure the begging is the best.
For when a man is tired he can sit him down and rest.
He can beg his dinner, he has nothing else to do.
But to slip around the corner with his ould rigadoo.

I slept in a barn one night in Currabawn,
A shocking wet night it was but I slept until the dawn;
There was holes in the roof and
the rain drops coming through,
And the rats and the cats were all playing tink-a-boo,
Who did I waken but the woman of the house,
With her white spotted apron and her fine gingham blouse;
She began to get excited and all I said was "Boo,
Sure don't be afraid at all, tis only Johnny Dhu."

I met a little girl when a walking out one day,
"Good morrow, little flaxen-haired girl, I did say;
"Good morrow, little beggarman, and how do you do?
With your rags and your tags and your ould rigadoo."
I'll buy a pair of leggin's, and a collar and a tie,
And a nice young lady I'll. go courting by and-bye;
I'll buy a pair of goggles and I'll colour them with blue,
And an ould fashioned lady will make her too.

So all along the high road with my bag upon my back,
Over the fields with my bulgin' heavy sack;
With holes in my shoes and my toes a peeping through.
Singing skill a malick adoodle with my ould rigadoo,
O! I must be going to bed, for it's getting late at night.
The fire's all raked and now 'tis out the light;
For now you've heard the story of my ould rigadoo,
So goodbye and God be with you, from ould Johnny Dhu.

Walking around these fields I remember how I made frequent trips to visit Mrs. Shields and Annie, her daughter. They were relatively new in the area, but they were accepted and well liked. As a child I learned to crochet and make Irish lace from Mrs. Shields. She seemed like a very old lady and she had the "shakes." I presume it was Parkinson's.

In spite of her shaking hands, she made the most beautiful lace I've ever seen, priest's vestments, gloves, scarves for furniture, hankies, all kinds of lovely things. When we came to America she made a pair of gloves for me, which I still have. Her fingers moved so fast. I was and am to this day in awe of her talent. I wonder if she ever realized the beautiful gift that God had given her. I learned to make a little of the fragile lace. I wish I had learned to do more. We sat and talked as my young steady fingers struggled to form the stitches that the old woman's knarled, shaky hands made so easily and quickly. How easy it is for an art like that to be lost from one generation to another. I don't ever remember her daughter picking up a crochet needle. Perhaps she did.

As I think of these ladies I remember how they always made a cup of tea when I came to visit and there was always sweet cake to eat. Every visit was a tea party. I loved going to their home and for many years heard from Annie at Christmas time.

# THE FIELD BY JOHN REILLY'S LANE

That field on the way to John Reilly's, or as he was locally known the red fellow, was most often used to graze the cows, but I remember the year we had the oats there. Planting oats was quite a job especially in the early years of my growing up when all the work was done by horses. First the ground was plowed by horse and pushed plough one score at a time. Then when the field was all turned over my dad would change the plow for a harrow and go up and down and then back and forth in a grid pattern until all the clods of dirt were broken. Then he scattered the seeds and harrowed the field again so the seeds were covered. Through the summer the oats grew tall and as fall approached it turned to gold. For so many years my dad cut it with a scythe and then he gathered and tied it into sheaves. These were gathered three or four together into stooks, tops resting against each other, bottoms separated into a triangle to allow air to circulate and dry the sheaves. They were secured at the top with a straw rope. After several weeks when they were completely dry they were gathered into rucks and eventually brought in on a lift before threshing day when the grain was separated from the straw. Early on threshing day Eugene Reilly arrived towing the big machine behind the tractor. Pretty soon it was all set up and the men took their positions around it. Two men took their places on the top while others threw stooks up to one who handed to the other who fed them into the thresher. Meanwhile more men collected the threshed straw and pitched it to others who proceeded to build a tall reek. Still more men collected the grain into burlap bags as it poured from the groaning machine. All this performed in a swirling cloud of chaff that surrounded the work area like snow. It was a beehive of activity!

In later years all of this was done with a tractor, very quickly. Eugene Reilly took his plow, which made several furrows at a time, and went from farm to farm. Then later he returned to each to harrow while the men spread the seeds. Later at the end of the summer he came back with a combine Harvester, which cut the oats, thrashed it separating the grain and the straw and bundled the straw, all at one time. That was an amazing accomplishment and made the farmer's work so much easier.

Some of the oats was sold at the mill while some was crushed for food for the farm animals and some more milled into flour. An amount was kept whole to feed hungry chickens and fatten turkeys. Of course we had to save enough to provide seed for the following year's crop.

# Chapter 9

# Shantemon Mountain

As I stood at the crest of "The Hill" I looked around. The view from there is spectacular, and toward the north is Ballyhaise with its tall church spire. We could even see miles beyond there, so many miles in all directions, except to the right where Shantemon Mountain is located. When I was growing up that mountain was really beautiful, purple with heather and yellow with whins. I loved to climb the rocky surface and pick the tender bilberries that grew wild all over its face. I'd climb high up to the five finger stones at the summit. The story goes that an ancient Irish giant sitting on Sleighlah Mountain took the five stones, put them on his five fingers and threw them, landing so many miles away on Shantemon. It was fun climbing on the tall high stones, all of which, except for the pinkie were taller than me. The sides were straight up. The view from the mountain is absolutely beautiful. I loved it and could spend hours up there. I liked to take sandwiches, to have a picnic there was getting away from it all.

*Monica sitting on one of the finger stones on the mountain*

*My parents and me on the hill with the mountain in the
background*

As I looked toward the mountain it has really changed. It has been planted with trees for the most part and the beautiful heather and whins are gone from the greater part of the mountain, now covered with tall trees. Later in our visit we climbed the mountain, going up along the fence separating the forest area from the wild. It was raining and the climb was steep and slippery, but I was determined to take my family to see the finger stones and see the view from on top of them, have my American daughters climb them as I did.

There were a few blueberries along the way, but when we reached the top, finding the stones was another matter. Finally we turned into the woods and walked among the tall trees, then all at once we were in a small clearing and there in the forest were those stones. They looked deserted, like people didn't enjoy them anymore and the view from there; well the only view was the surrounding trees. It was pouring rain and my heart sank deeper than the drops that fell from the sky. You can't go home again!

*The finger stones surrounded by trees*

We went to the natural side of the mountain. From there we could see Shantemonn Lake, nestled among the patchwork of fields, glistening in the sun and all the farms around. Many now deserted, but others still have their families there. My Grandfather's farm, The Boylan's, Ted Reilly's, John Reilly's, Annie Miney's. All of them hold so many memories, even our own old farm, there it was, the grove where the house had been and there was the hill. Thank God I could still see it from the mountain.

On a more recent visit to Ireland I was delighted to find that the trees are gone and the billberries, whins and heather are slowly returning and of course that wonderful view is back too. A few fences make it a bit difficult to move around at the top but I am filled with joy that it has become more like the beautiful mountain that I remember and love. I can see Castletara Church again and Castletara School and the Cootehill Road with many new houses along it and all the farms again. It is more as I remembered it and I can see for miles and it is beautiful! I feel at home there and I am forever drawn to that spot.

*Shantemon Lake from the Mountain*

*View from the mountain*

*View from the mountain*

I remember one time when I was young we looked toward the hill and from beyond it saw thick black smoke billowing toward the sky. We ran out toward the top of the hill and reaching it first my dad yelled, "The mountain is on fire." Flames and smoke crawled across the front of the mountain. It was a pretty scary thing because there were homes and farms right in the path of the flames. I just remember how upset he was as he ran toward the burning mountain. It was up to the surrounding farmers to extinguish the blaze.

# Chapter 10

# Driving To Town

## AUNT MOLLIE

The ride toward town was a flood of memories. Going past where my Aunt Mollie lived brought to life so many wonderful memories. When I think of Aunt Mollie I immediately see a tall, stately and beautiful woman. She had a way of standing in front of the fire, cigarette in hand. She would take a puff, fill her cheeks with the smoke and slowly let it out through her pursed lips. She had an elegant way I can't ever forget. I wanted to be just like her and when people said I was a bit like Mollie Argue I was proud as punch. She worked hard raising her family alone. I know at times it was really tough for her but she was a survivor. Before her death she was in a nursing home for many years, but as fragile as she became, even then, she was still a survivor.

*Aunt Mollie*

I love to sew and like to design the things I make. Aunt Mollie sewed for me when I was a little girl. I remember her making pretty dresses. She'd pin it on and sew it. She made me feel special! I remember the old Singer pedal machine where she sat to make so many lovely things. She always gave me scraps of material to make doll clothes and that was one of my favorite pastimes. Once, like I had seen Mollie do with fabric, I cut out a dress with a pleated skirt using the Sunday newspaper and taped it together. I was so very proud of it as I showed it to Aunt Mollie, who was delighted with my effort and praised me abundantly. My mother on the other hand was much less impressed.

In front of her house Aunt Mollie planted a flower garden filled with dahlias, carnations, roses, all kinds of flowers. Most of all I remember her dahlias. They were taller than any I have ever seen and so many colors; red, deep burgundy, yellow and snow white with creamy centers. Some were red with petals tipped with white. They were so beautiful! Each one was larger than the next. That lovely garden is gone now, but its memory is very much alive in my heart.

My heart was filled with homesickness as I passed where her home once was. I wish I could stop there and go through her front door just once more and see her standing by the fireplace once again holding a cigarette between two fingers, puffing out her cheeks before the smoke swirled gracefully from her pursed lips. She was such an elegant lady.

Across the road from her gate was the Clancy's house. Mrs. Clancy died at a very young age, leaving behind a large family of very active boys. Most of the neighbors thought they were a bunch of hooligans, but in retrospect they were just lively young boys. I wonder where all of them are now.

# DONAGHUES

Just up the road past Aunt Mollie's lane a new home was built by the Donaghues when I was a little girl. They had a new baby, just a few months old it seems to me when Christmas time came. Now I had never seen a real Christmas tree in a home. The only one I had ever seen had been by the town hall in Cavan and I was in awe of that. When I heard that this family had a tree I could not wait to go visit and see it, so one day I paid Mrs. Donaghue a visit. She was very nice, gave me tea and sweet cake, and then I asked if I could please see the tree. She took me into the drawing room. Wow! There it was, huge with real decorations. It even had lights. I was wide eyed, amazed, awed by it. I wanted to see it light up and asked as a shy timid seven or eight year old girl might dare if I could please see the lights turned on. I was crushed when she said "No," they wanted their months old baby to be the first to see it lit on Christmas morning. I just wanted to burst into tears.

She could never know how sad and disappointed she made me feel that day. Somewhere inside of me on my way home I resolved that someday I would have a real Christmas tree, not just a holly branch, with real ornaments, not ones made from foil cigarette wrappers and last year's Christmas cards, and I would have lots of lights and I would turn them on whenever I wanted to. Little she knew how that day she changed Christmas for me forever.

## THE BREIDENS

A short way up the road past Rudden's Lane is the Breidens. My family was always friends with them. They were richer than most of the other neighbors. They even had a car! Mrs. Breiden was a lovely lady with a unique voice. We spent many evenings visiting with them, but I was always a bit uneasy there because from listening to some neighbors I thought they were supposed to be different because they were Protestant. In Ireland at that time Protestants were not so readily accepted, and although they were nice people there were some real bad attitudes toward them.

They had a son Bob who was quite a guy. He immigrated to the United States along with my cousin Bunnie, Mollie's daughter, and many other young neighbors. Bob was a great story teller and came to visit my parents frequently before he left Ireland. After he moved to the United States he always came to visit when he came back to Ireland. He was an interesting person who seemed to live an interesting life.

But like I said before, Bob was Protestant and in school I'd learned that anyone who wasn't Catholic would not go to heaven. They would go to hell when they died or at best end up in purgatory, but never see the face of God in heaven. So one day while Bob sat talking away on my dad's big old chair in the kitchen I stood up behind him on the step going up into the parlor and using some holy water I solemnly sprinkled it on his head and baptized him in the name of the Father, the Son and the Holy Spirit. He was so busy talking that he never knew it. I liked him, he was special, kind, a really nice guy and I wanted to ensure his eternal salvation. Bob was a staunch Protestant; I wonder what he would think if he knew I baptized him Catholic. Religion was so simple then!

# Chapter 11

# Sprees

In our part of Ireland when visitors came home from the US or England we would have a big party called a spree. Actually while they were home many neighbors would have a spree. It was always an opportunity for fun. Even though we were poor everyone liked to have a good time. This was a real opportunity to escape the hard work and drudgery of everyday life. At the sprees there was always lots of food; ham, loaf bread, lettuce, tomatoes, roast chicken, salads and the stout flowed freely for the men, port wine for the ladies.

We were never at a loss for entertainment; someone usually brought an accordion or melodeon, a mouth organ or violin. My dad played a flute or tin whistle and we all danced the night away. That's how we passed down our traditional folk dances; the stack of barley, sweets of May, the fling, the walls of Limerick, or maybe a set dance, where you spun around at a dizzying speed. As the night progressed and spirits soared various people were called on to sing; "Noreen Baun," "The Green Glens of Antrim," "Rose of Tralee," "Valley of Knockanure," "The Croppy Boy," "Danny Boy," "The Stuttering Lovers," "Kevin Barry," "If I Were a

Blackbird," Doran's Ass," "Courtin' in the Kitchen," or "Whack Fall the Diddle.". My cousin Tom always was called on to sing "The Valley of Knockanure." Bunnie and Peggy sang together, the voices of angels. My dad usually sang one of his "Come all ya's," a silly slightly naughty song made up about some local event!

Quite often as the individual sang their song, they got ahead of themselves in the words and the wrong line was sung at which point the singer waved an arm and said, "Ah shur I just went all through it." Acting as though he wanted to quit there was much encouragement from all to continue, where upon the singer capitulated and started over this time completing it perfectly to a rousing applause.

Mrs. Rudden usually sang "The Rose of Tralee" in a very nasal tone. I remember one spree when my Aunt Helen and Uncle Mike were here from America and he sang "By the Bright Silver Light of the Moon." He had a beautiful voice and I wish I could have heard it more. I always wanted to sing but my mother would never let me, always saying "shush you can't sing."

# THE BRIGHT SILVERY LIGHT OF THE MOON
### *The Silver Moon – J. W. Turner 1850*

As I strayed from my cot at the close of the day,
About the beginning of June,
By a Jessamine shade I espied a fair maid,
And she sadly complained to the moon;

172

**Chorus**
"Roll on, silvery moon, guide the traveler on his way,
While the nightingale sings its full tune;
But never again with my lover I'll stray
By the bright silvery light of the moon."

"As the hart on the mountain my lover was brave,
And so handsome, so manly, to view;
So kind, so sincere, and he loved me so dear,
No love was ever more true
But now he is dead and gone to his lone bed,
Cut down like a rose in full bloom;
He has fallen asleep, and I am left to weep
By the bright silvery light of the moon.

**Chorus**
"For he died for his country, my sweetheart so true,
For Ireland he gave his Young life;
He fell with our heroes, when mourners were few,
Mid the rifle-fire, cannon, and strife.
And his brothers-in-arms, 'neath that bright Easter sun,
Fought and prayed that the dawn would come soon-
'Gainst the fierce, foreign, foe, till the Vict'ry was won
By the sweet silvery light of the moon."

**Chorus**
O, never again can my heart beat with joy.
My lost one I hope to meet soon.
And kind friends will weep, o'er the grave where we sleep,
By the bright silvery light of the moon.

# THE ROSE OF TRALEE
*William P. Mulchinock 1820 - 1864*

The pale moon was rising above the green mountains,
The sun was declining beneath the blue sea,
When I stray'd with my love to the pure crystal fountain
That stands in the beautiful vale of Tralee.

She was lovely and fair as the rose of the summer,
Yet 'twas not her beauty alone that won me,
Oh, no, 'twas the truth in her eyes ever beaming
That made me love Mary the Rose of Tralee.

The cool shades of ev'ning their mantle were spreading
And Mary, all smiling, was lis'ning to me,
The moon through the valley her pale rays were shedding
When I won the heart of the Rose of Tralee.

Tho' lovely and fair as the rose of the summer,
Yet 'twas not her beauty alone that won me,
Oh, no, 'twas the truth in her eyes ever beaming
That made me love Mary the Rose of Tralee.

# DAWN ON THE IRISH COAST

("The Exile Returns")
*John Locke 1847 - 1889*

Th'anam an Dhia! but there it is
The dawn on the hills of Ireland!
God's angels lifting the night's black veil
From the fair, sweet face of my sireland!
Ireland, isn't it grand you look
Like a bride in her rich adornin'!
And with all the pent-up love of my heart
I bid you the top O the mornin'!
This one brief hour pays lavishly back
For many a year of mourning;
I'd almost venture another flight,
There's so much joy returning
Watching out for the hallowed shore
All other attractions scornin';
Ireland! can't you hear me shout?
I bid you the top o' the mornin'!
Ho, ho! upon Cliodhna's shelving strand
The surges are grandly beating,

And Kerry is pushing her headlands out
To give us the kingly greeting;
In to the shore the sea birds fly
On pinions that know no dropping,
And out from the cliffs, with welcomes charged,
A million of waves come trooping.
Oh, kindly, generous Irish land,
So real and fair and loving!
No wonder the wandering Celt should think
And dream of you in his roving!
The alien home may have gems and gold,
Dark shadows may never have gloamed it;
But the heart will sigh for the absent land
Where the love-light first illumined it.
And doesn't old Cove look grand out there,
Watching the wild waves motion,
Leaning her back up against the hills,
And the tips of her toes in the ocean!
I wonder I don't hear Shandon's bells-
Ah! maybe their chiming's over,
For it's many a year since I began
The life of a Western rover.
For thirty summers, a stoir mo chroidhe.
The hills I now feast my eyes on
Were never seen, save when they rose
On memory's dim horizon.
Even so, it was grand and fair they seemed
In the vision spread before me;
But dreams are dreams, and my eyes would open
To see Texas' sky still o'er me.
And often upon the Texan plains,
When the day and the chase were over,
My thoughts would fly o'er the weary wave,
And around the coast-line hover;
And a prayer would rise that some future day
All danger and doubting scornin'
I might help to win for my native land
The light of Young Liberty's mornin'!

Now fuller and clearer the coast line shows
Was ever a scene so splendid!
I feel the breath of the Munster breeze;
Thank God that my exile's ended!
Old scenes, old songs, old friends again,
The vale and cot I was born in--
O Ireland! up from my heart of hearts
I bid you top o' the mornin'!

# MASTER MCGRATH

*(Lord Lurgan's great greyhound, which won the Waterloo
Cup in 1868, 1869 and in 1871)
James Custer ~ 1880*

Eighteen-sixty-eight being the date of the year,
Those Waterloo sportsmen did grandly appear,
To gain the great prizes and bear them away-
Never counting on Ireland and Master McGrath.
On the 12th of December, that day of renown,
McGrath and his trainer they left Lurgan town;
John Walsh was the trainer, and soon they got o'er,
For the very next day they touched great England's shore.
And when they arrived there in big London town,
Those great English sportsmen, they all gathered roun'-
And one of those gentlemen gave a "Ha! ha!"
With "Is that the great dog you call Master McGrath?"
And one of those gentlemen standing around
Says, "I don't care a damn for your Irish greyhound;"
And another he laughs with a great "Ha! ha! ha!
We'll soon humble the pride of your Master McGrath."
Then Lord Lurgan steps forward and, says, "Gentlemen,
Is there any among ye has money to spen'-
For ye noble of England I don't give a straw-
Here's five thousand to one on my Master McGrath."
Her master and keeper all close by her side;
They have let her away and the crowd cried "Hurrah'"
For the pride of all England -- and Master McGrath.
And Roose stood uncovered, the great English pride,

Her master and keeper all close by her side;
They have let her away and her the crowd cried "Hurrah"
For the pride of all England -- and Master McGrath.
McGrath he looked up and he wagged his ould tail,
And he winked at his lordship to know he'd not fail.
Then he jumped on the hare's back and held up his paw-
Give three cheers for ould Ireland and Master McGrath.

# THE OLD BOG ROAD
*Teresa Brayton 1868 - 1943*

My feet are here on Broadway this blessed harvestmorn,
But oh, the ache that's in thim for the sod where I was born;
My weary hands are blistered from toil in cold and heat,
And 'tis oh to swing a scythe to-day
Through fields of Irish wheat.
Had I my choice to journey back or own a king's abode,
'Tis soon I'd see the hawthorn tree on the old bog road.
Whin I was young and innocent, my mind was ill at ease
Through dhramin' of America and gold beyond seas;
Och sarra take their money, but 'tis hard to get that same--
And what's the whole world to a man
whin no one speaks his name!
I've had my day, and here I am with buildin' bricks for load,
A long three thousand miles away from the old bog road.
My mother died last springtime,
Whin Ireland's fields were green,
The neighbours said her wakin' was the finest ever seen;
There were snowdrops
And primroses piled up around her bed,
And Ferns church was crowded
When her funeral Mass was said.
And here was I on Broadway, with buildin' bricks for load,
When they carried out her coffin from the old bog road.
There was a dancing girl at home who used to walk.
With me,
Her eyes were soft and sorrowful,
Like moonbeams on the sea;

Her name was Mary Dwyer---but that was long ago,
And the ways of God are wiser
Than the things a man may know.
She died the year I left her, but with buildin' bricks for load;
I'd best forget the times we met on the old bog road.
Och, life's a weary puzzle, past finding out by man,
I take the day for what it's worth, and do the best I can;
Since no one cares a rush for me, what need to make a moan
I go my way and draw my pay and smoke my pipe alone,
Each human heart must know its grief,
Though bitter be the load,
So God be with old Ireland and the old bog road.

## TEDDY O'NEAL

*(A corrupt version of this sweet and plaintive old song is
heard too often.. It makes the song a gross caricature of Irish
life. This is the correct version.)*
*Unknown*

I dreamt but last night, och! bad cess to my dreaming,
I'd die if I thought 'twould come truly to pass;
I dreamt, while the tears down my pillow were streaming,
That Teddy was courting another fair lass.
Och didn't I wake with the weeping and wailing,
The pain of the thought was too deep to conceal;
My mother cried: "Nora, child! What is your ailing?"
But all I could answer was "Teddy O'Neal."

I've seen the old cabin beyond the wee boreen,
I've seen the old crossroads where we used to dance;
I've rambled the lanes where he called me his storeen,
And my girlish heartfelt the thrill of romance.
But now all around is so sad and so dreary,
All dark and all silent, no piper, no reel;
Not even the sun through the casement shines cheery,
Since I lost my heart's darling boy, Teddy' O'Neal!

Shall I ever forget when the big ship was ready,

And the moment was come for my love to depart;
How I sobbed like a child: "Och! Goodbye to you, Teddy"
With a tear on my cheek and a stone in my heart.
He said 'twas to better his fate he went roving,
But what would be gold to the joy I should feel-
If he'd only come back to me, tender and loving,
Still poor, yet my own darling Teddy O'Neal.

# KEVIN BARRY

*Died for Ireland, November 1st, 1920*
*Unknown*

In Mountjoy one Monday morning,
High upon the gallows tree,
Kevin Barry gave his young life
For the cause of liberty.
But a lad of eighteen summers,
Yet no one can deny
As he walked to death that morning
He proudly held his head on high.

### Chorus
Another martyr for old Ireland,
Another murder for the Crown,
Whose brutal laws may kill the Irish,
But can't keep their spirit down.
Lads like Barry are no cowards,
From the foe they will not fly,
Lads like Barry will free Ireland,
For her sake they'll live and die.

Just before he faced the hangman,
In his dreary prison cell,
British soldiers tortured Barry,
Just because he wouldn't tell.
The name of all his brave companions,
And other things they wished to know,
"Turn informer or we'll kill you,"

179

Kevin Barry answered "No."

**Chorus**

Calmly standing at "attention,"
While he bade his last farewell.
To his broken hearted mother,
Whose grief no one can tell,
For the cause he proudly cherished,
This sad parting had to be;
Then to death walked softly smiling,
That old Ireland might be free.

**Chorus**

# PAID O'DONOGHUE
*Patrick Archer 1861 - 1919*

The Yeos are in Dunshaughlin
And the Hessians in Dunreagh;
And spread thro' fair Moynalty
Were the fenribles of Reagh.
While Roden's godless troopers
Ranged from Screen to Mullachoo,
When hammered were the pikeheads
First by Paid O'Donoghue.

Young Paid, he was as brave a boy
As ever hammer swung,
And the finest hurler that you'd find
The lads of Meath among;
And when the wrestling match was o'er
No man could boast he threw
The dark young Smith of Currogha
Young Paid O'Donoghue.

So Padraig lived a happy life
And gaily sang each day.
Beside his ringing anvil some sweet old Irish lay;

Or roamed light-heartedly at eve
Thro' the woods at lone Kipoundrue,
With her who'd given her
Pure heart's love to Paid O'Donoghue:

But ninety-eight's dark season came
And Irish hearts were sore;
The pitch-cap and triangle
The patient folks outwore;
The blacksmith thought of Ireland
And found he'd work to do;
"I'll forge some steel for freedom,"
Said Paid O'Donoghue.

Tho' the Yeos were in Dunshaughlin
And the Hessians in Dunreagh,
Tho spread thro' fair Moynalty
Were the fencibles of Reagh;
Tho' Roden's godless troopers ranged
From Screen to Mullachoo,
The pike-heads keen were hammered
Out by Paid O'Donoghue.

And so in Currogha each night
Was heard the anvil's ring,
While scouting on the roadways
Were Hugh and Phelim King.
With Gillies Mat, and Duffy's Pat,
And Mickey Gilsenan. too,
While in the forge for Ireland
Worked young Paid O'Donoghue.

But a traitor crept among them,
And the secret soon was sold
To the captain of the Yoeman
For the ready Saxon gold;
And a troop burst out one evening
From the woods of dark Kipoundrue,
And soon a rebel prisoner bound,
Was Paid O'Donoghue.

Now Padraig Og, pray fervently,
Your earthly course has run;
The captain he has sworn you'll
Not see to-marrow's sun.
The muskets they are ready,
And each yeoman's aim is true;
Death stands beside thy shoulder,
Young Paid O'Donoghue.

"Down on your knees,
You rebel dog," the yeoman captain roared
As high above his helmet's crest
He waived his gleaming sword.
"Down on your knees to meet your doom,
Such is the rebel's due;"
But straight as pike-shaft
'Fore him stood bold Paid O'Donoghue.

And there upon the roadway
Where in childhood he had played,
Before the cruel yeoman
He stood quite undismayed--
"I kneel but to my God above,
I ne'er shall bow to you;
You can shoot me as I'm standing,"
Said Paid O'Donoghue.

The captain gazed in wonder,
Then lowered his keen-edged blade,
"A rebel bold is this", he said,
"Tis fitting to degrade,
Here, man!" he cried, "unbind him,
My charger needs a shoe;
The King shall have a workman
In this Paid O'Donoghue."
Now to the forge young Paid
Has gone the yeoman guard the door
And soon the ponderous bellows
Is heard to snort and roar;

The captain stands with rein in hand
While Padraig fits the shoe,
And when 'tis on full short
The shrift he'll give O'Donoghue.

The last strong nail is firmly clenched,
The captain's horse is shod!
Now rebel bold, thy hour hath come,
Prepare to meet thy God!
But why holds he the horse's hoof,
There's no more work to do?
Why clenches he the hammer so,
Young Paid O'Donoghue.

A leap! a roar! A smothered groan!
The captain drops the rein,
And sinks to earth with hammerhead
Sunk deeply in his brain;
And lightly in the saddle fast
Racing towards Kipoundrue
Upon the captain's charger sits
Bold Paid O'Donoghue.

A volley from the pistols,
A rush of horses feet--
"He's gone and none can capture
The captain's charger fleet;
And on the night wind backwards
Comes a mocking loud "Halloo!"
That tells the yeoman they have lost
Young Paid O'Donoghue

# THE CROPPY BOY
*(A Ballad ... of 98)*
*Carroll Malone 1845*
*Unknown – Earliest Date 1798*

"Good men and true; in this house who dwell,
To a stranger bouchal, I pray you tell,
Is the priest at home or may he be seen?
I would speak a word with Father Green."
"The priest's at home, boy, and may be seen;
'Tis easy speaking with Father Green;
But you must wait till I go and see
If the holy father alone may be."

The youth has entered an empty hall
What a lonely sound has his light foot fall!
And the gloomy chamber's chill and bare
With a vested priest in a lonely chair;
The youth has knelt to tell his sins,
"Nomine Dei," the youth begins,
At "Mea culpa," he beats his breast,
And in broken murmurs he speaks the rest

At the siege of Ross did my father fall.
And at Gorey my loving brothers all,
I alone am left of my name and race
I will go to Wexford and take their place
I cursed three times since last Easter Day-
At Mass-time once I went to play;
I passed the churchyard one day in haste
And forgot to pray for my mother's rest

"I bear no hate against living thing,
But I love my country above my King,
Now, Father! bless me and let me go,
To die, if God has ordained it so."
The priest said naught, but a rustling noise
Made the youth look up in wild surprise
The robes were off, and in scarlet there

184

Sat a Yeoman Captain with fiery glare.
With fiery glare and with fury hoarse,
Instead of a blessing he breathed a curse-
"Twas a good thought, boy, to come here and shrive
For one short hour is your time to live.
Upon yon river three tenders float.
The priest's in one-if he isn't shot
We hold this house for our lord and King,
And, amen, say I, may all traitors swing!"

At Geneva Barracks that young man died,
And at Passage they have his body laid,
Good people, who live in peace and joy,
Breathe a prayer, shed a tear for the Crappy Boy.

# A BUCKET OF THE MOUNTAIN DEW
*Traditional Irish Song*

On yonder hill there's a darlin' little still
With the smoke curling up to the sky;
By the smoke and the smell you can plainly tell
There's potheen, my lads, close by.

**Chorus**
Sure it fills the air with an perfume rare,
And betwixt both me and you,
As home you roll, you can take a bowl,
Or a bucket of the mountain dew.

Now away with the pills that cure all ills,
Be ye heathen, or Christian, or Jew;
Take off your coat and grease your throat
With a bucket of the Mountain-dew

**Chorus**

Oh, peelers all, from Donegal,
Sligo and Leitrum too,
Will all ring a bell if they ever get a smell
Or a drop of the mountain-dew.

**Chorus**

Now learned men who use the pen
Have written the praises high
Of that rare poten from the "Isle of green
That's made from wheat and Rye

**Chorus**

Let grasses grow and waters flow,
In their good old Irish way;
But give me enough of the good old stuff,
That is made near Galway Bay.

**Chorus**

# BOOLAVOGUE

*Patrick Joseph McCall*
*Traditional Irish Song*

At Boolavogue as the sun was setting,
O'er the bright May meadows of Shelmalier
A rebel hand set the heather blazing,
And brought the neighbours from far and near,
Then Father Murphy from old Kilcormack
Spurred up the rock with a warning cry:
"Arm. arm," he cried, "for I've come to lead you,
For Ireland's freedom we'll fight or die!"

He led us 'gainst the coming soldiers,
And the cowardly yeoman we put to flight,
'Twas at the Harrow the boys Of Wexford
Showed Bookey's regiment how men could fight;
Look out for hirelings, King George of England,
Search every kingdom where breathes a slave,
For Father Murphy of County Wexford,
Sweeps o'er the land like a mighty wave.

We took Camolin and Enniscorthy,
And Wexford storming drove out our foes,
'Twas at Slieve Coilte our pikes were reeking
With the crimson blood of the beaten Yeos.
At Tubberneering and Ballyellis,
Full many a Hessian lay in his gore,
Ah! Father Murphy had aid come over,
The Green Flag floated from shore to shore!

At Vinegar Hill, o'er the pleasant Slaney,
Our heroes vainly stood back to back.
And the Yeos at Tullow took Father Murphy,
And burnt his body upon a rack.
God grant you glory, brave Father Murphy,
And open Heaven to all your men,
The cause that called you may call tomorrow,
In another fight for the Green again.

# THE WILD COLONIAL BOY

*Traditional Irish Song*

There was a wild colonial boy,
Jack Dougan was his name.
He was born and bred in Ireland
In a place called Castlemaine.
He was his father's only son,
His mother's pride and joy,
And dearly did his parents love
The wild colonial boy.

At the early age of sixteen years
He left his native home.
And to Australia's sunny shores
He was inclined to roam.
He robbed the rich and helped the poor.
He stabbed James McEvoy.
A terror to Australia was
the wild colonial boy.

One morning on the prairie while
Jack Dugan rode along,
Listening to a mockingbird
Singing its mocking song.
Up jumped three troopers fierce and wild,
Kelly, Davis and Fitzroy.
The all set out to capture him,
The wild colonial boy.

"Surrender now Jack Dugan,
For we are three to one.
Surrender in the Queen's name,
For you're a plundering son."
Jack drew to pistols from his side
And proudly held them high.
"I'll fight but not surrender," cried
The wild colonial boy.

He fired a shot at Kelly
Which brought him to the ground.
He fired a shot at Davis
Which felled him at the sound.
But a bullet pierced his brave young heart
From the pistol of Fitzroy,
And that is how they captured him,
The wild colonial boy.

# THE VALLEY OF KNOCKANURE
*Traditional Irish Song*

You may boast and speak about Easter week
or the heroes of ninety eight,
Of the Fenian men who roamed the glen
to victory or defeat.
The men who died on the scaffold high
were outlawed on the moor.
They were the men who fought and fell
in the valley of Knockanure.

There was Walsh and Lyons and Dalton,
boys, they were young and in their pride,
In every house in every town
they were always side by side,
The Republic bold they did uphold
though outlawed on the moor,
And side by side they bravely died
in the Valley of Knockanure.

'Twas on a summer's evening those
our heroes did lie down.
They were waiting on a brief despatch
to come from Tralee town.
It wasn't long till Lyons came on sayin'
"time's not mine nor yours,
Look out my boys we're surrounded
in the valley of Knockanure."

Young Dalton grabbed a rifle
which stood by Walsh's side.
He gazed across the valley
and along the mountain side.
In the glen where armed men
with rifles fired galore,
There were Dalton, Dan and the Black and Tans
in the valley of Knockanure.

One shot from Dalton's rifle
sent a machine gun out of play.
He turned to young Lyons and said
"Now try and get away.
Keep wide of rocks, keep close to nooks,
and cross by dreary moor
Walsh and I will fight till we die
in the valley of Knockanure.

The summer sun was sinking fast
O'er Kerry by the sea.

The pale moon it was rising way off beyond Tralee.
The twinkling stars they in the heavens above
shone out on the dreary moor,
The banshee cried, when our heroes died
on the valley of Knockanure.

How will we tell their mothers
the loss of their darling sons.
It might have been home they died
but God's will must be done
They chose to die by the mountain high
Way out by the dreary moor.
And the wild birds fly where their bodies lie,
In the valley of Knockanure.

# DOONAREE

*Words by "Emor"*
*Ellish Boland 1955*

If you ever go to Ireland:
I'm sure you will agree,
To take the road from Dublin town,
Way down to Doonaree;
And when you find the Wishing Well,
Beyond the chestnut tree,
In ,a shady nook by a winding brook,
Will you make-this wish for me?

**Chorus**
Oh, to be in Doonaree,
With the sweetheart I once knew,
To stroll in the shade of the leafy glade,
Where the Rhododendrons grew;
To sit with my love on the bridge above,
The rippling waterfall,
To go back home, never more to roam,
Is my dearest wish of all.

And if you take the hilly path,
To the wood where bluebells grow,
Where we as barefoot children played,
So many years ago;
You'll find the slumb'ring castle there,
Entwined in memory,
Beneath the spell of the wishing well.
Will you make this wish for me?

**Chorus**

# THE BLACK VELVET BAND
*Traditional Irish Song*
*Unknown – Earliest 1854*

Twas in the town of Tralee
apprentice to trade I was bound.
With a-plenty of bright amusement
to see the days go round.
Till misfortune and trouble came over me,
which caused me to stray from my land,
Far away from my friends and relations,
to follow the Black Velvet Band.

**Chorus**
Her eyes they shone like diamonds,
you'd think she was queen of the land.
With her hair thrown over her shoulder,
tied up with a black velvet band.

As I went walking down broadway,
not intending to stay very long.
I met with a frolicsome damsel as she came tripping along.
She was both fair and handsome,
Her neck it was just like a swans
And her hair it hung over her shoulder,
Tied up with a black velvet band
**Chorus**

191

I took a stroll with this pretty fair maid,
When a gentleman's passing us by
Well I knew she meant the doing of him,
By the look in her roughish black eye
A goldwatch she pulled out of his pocket
and slipped it right into my hand
On the very first day that I met her,
bad luck to the black velvet band.

**Chorus**

Before the judge and the jury
the both of us had to appear,
And a gentleman swore to the jewellery
the case against us was clear.
For seven years transportation right
unto Van Dieman's Land,
Far away from my friends and relations,
to follow her Black Velvet Band.

**Chorus**

Oh all you brave young Irish lads,
a warning take by me.
Beware of the pretty young damsels
that are knocking around in Tralee.
They'll treat you to whiskey and porter,
until you're unable to stand.
And before you have time for to leave them,
you are unto Van Dieman's Land.

**Chorus**

# GENTLE MOTHER

*Traditional Irish*

By the side of a clear crystal fountain
There stands a lonely churchyard closely by,
There's a tombstone decorated with primroses,
In the memory of a loved one passed away.

### Chorus

Shall I ne'er see you more Gentle Mother,
In the fields where the wild flowers grow,
Gathering flowers as they grow among the wild woods,
And I cherish 'twas no trouble unto you.

Some children take a liking to their parents,
While some others fill their mothers' hearts with pain,
But some day they will be sorry for their blindness,
When crying will not take her back again.

### Chorus

Shall I ne'er see you more Gentle Mother,
In the fields where the wild flowers grow,
I am sorry for the loss I can't recover,
'Neath yon' willow lies my Gentle Mother's love,

# NOREEN BAWN
*Traditional Irish*

There's a glen in old Tir Conaill
There's a cottage in that glen
Where once there dwelt a maiden
Who inspired the hearts of men
She was winsome, hale and hearty
Shy and graceful as a fawn
And the Neighbors loved the widow's
Handsome daughter Noreen Bawn

Till one day arrived a letter
With her passage paid to go
To the land of the Missouri
Where the Mississippi flows
She said goodbye to Erin
And next morning at the dawn
The poor widow broken-hearted
Parted with her Noreen Bawn

Many years the widow waited
Till one evening at the door
Came a gentle looking lady
Costly were the clothes she wore
Saying, "Mother, don't you know me?
I have only caught a cold."
Yet those scarlet spots appearing
Upon her cheeks the story told

There's a graveyard in Tir Conaill,
Where the flowers sadly wave,
There's a broken hearted mother
Leaning o'er a lonely grave
"My Noreen", she is saying
"I'm lonesome since you're gone,
"Tis the curse of emigration
Leaves you here, my Noreen Bawn."

Fair lads and gentle maidens
Ponder well before you go
From your humble homes in Ireland
What's beyond you do not know
Whether gold or whether silver
When your health and strength are gone
When you think of immigrating
Wouldn't you think of Noreen Bawn

While Noreen Bawn was a very popular song at sprees, it was not sung at parties or going away sprees for those young people who were leaving the poverty of Ireland and going to America, England or in some cases far off Australia for the first time. That would be considered inappropriate because it would add to the sadness of the occasion. At one time these parties were even referred to as wakes because quite often it would be many years, if ever until the families were reunited.

As I gather these songs and as I sing again the words to myself I realize that sprees were much more than what they seemed to be, a chance to get together and have fun. They were lessons in history, told stories of heroes who gave everything for Ireland. They told of times of sadness, of immigration and loss and times of joy. They passed on the richness of who we were as a people, at times sad but strong, filled with hope and triumph in adversity, resilient under repression and always indestructible. Sprees gave us lessons of who we were in our stories, songs, recitations, music, even in our traditional dancing.

Sprees gave me an opportunity to do my step dancing. I loved that!! Dancing was the love of my life. My dad was a good dancer and at sprees or any occasion where there was music he was the first one out on the floor. As often as not I was his partner because my mother seemed to only enjoy a waltz with him. He knew all the dances well and very energetically performed them every chance he got. I guess that's where I got my love of dancing.

Anyway the partying would go on all night long. Occasionally young people, couples, sneaked out for a little rendezvous in the hay shed or out back of the house.

Of course none of the houses had bathrooms and when nature called we had to go outside in the dark. I remember the night we were at a spree at my Aunt Mollie's. A few of us girls went outside to heed the call, and in the dark in order to find our way walked close to the house, too close, because the well was right by the end of the house. All at once, splash, one of the girls fell in. It was so funny! We all laughed. I still laugh when I think about that night.

The nineteen fifties was also a time when there was a renewal of Irish traditional music and dance. There was renewed pride in the newly free state.

*Mary and Jemmy Mack at a spree in our home*

*Kathleen Reilly Brady, Rose Reilly, Mary Argue, Mary Flood
Mack, Kathleen Clarke, Aunt Molly Argue Smith, Unknown,
Margaret Brady at a spree in our house*

*The men at the spree, Granfather James Clarke, James Brady holding Pete Reilly, Jemmy Mack, Tom Smith, John Argue, Pat Lee, Ted Reilly, Jim Costello, and me.*

*Jim Costello, Pat Lee, Ted Reilly*
*Mary & Jemmy Mack*

# Chapter 12

# Going Ceiling

As I grew up, one of the fun things was the custom of going a ceiling to neighbors. With no TV, we had lots of time to spend having fun with people! Summer brought twilight and people visited each other's homes unannounced. Usually they exchanged stories and folklore by the fire as they drank tea and ate soda bread or whatever little treat might be available.

Quite often the night started off with current events and happenings in the area. They talked about politics, Fianna Fail versus Fin Gael, and the state of the country. My father and his peers were borne soon after the turn of the century and so they remembered the British occupation and spoke of the black and tans and their cruelty toward the Irish. They remembered the uprising at the GPO in Dublin and its aftermath. They remembered when Ireland was divided to end the British occupation of the twenty-six counties. The stories of that time and the songs of that time were all that they grew up with and passed on. Inevitably as the night progressed the talk turned to less serious conversation, ghost stories and the little people, fairies and banshees.

One of the places my family went on a ceili was Ruddens. Sean, as I've said, was an only child like me, unusual for an Irish family. His parents were good people, but he really ran their lives. Our parents were friends and spent many evenings together; therefore, Sean and I spent much time playing together, mostly hide and seek in the closets, behind the crocks, churns, etc. We did have lots of fun, but mostly we listened to the jokes and stories our fathers told while our mothers exchanged gossip. Mrs. Rudden often made boxty, potato bread that my father loved when made well. Unfortunately Mrs. Rudden's was a bit doughy and slathered with butter and jam. My mother always worried about what my dad ate because he had a stomach ulcer, so she was really worried about Mrs. Rudden's boxty until on the way home he showed her pockets full of the greasy cake. He had slipped the boxty into his pockets when the Ruddens were looking the other way. This was his way to avoid offending them if it wasn't eaten and seemingly enjoyed. I always enjoyed it and it never bothered my young stomach.

As the old rhyme goes,
"Boxty on the griddle,
Boxty in the pan
The wee one in the middle,
Is for Mary Ann.
Boxty on the griddle,
Boxty in the pan

If you don't eat Boxty,
You'll never get a man!"

# BOXTY
2 large raw potatoes shredded

2 cups mashed potatoes

½ teaspoon salt

1 teaspoon baking soda

½ cup flour

1 teaspoon. caraway seeds (optional)

Shred raw potatoes and allow to sit for a few minutes then drain. Mix all ingredients together in a large bowl. Put into greased and floured bread pan. Bake about 40 minutes at 350°. Slice and fry slices in bacon fat.

I remember James McCaffrey, Mick Kelly, Jimmy McAvinue, Mick Melligan, Hugh Reilly and the Ruddens came regularly to our house on Friday night, and the jokes and ghost stories were told and retold. I remember sitting on my mother's lap by the open turf fire and listening to these stories.

James McCaffrey and Mick Melligan told the story of the night they were coming home from ceiling. After exchanging many ghost stories, which I'm sure were very much on their minds, all at once they heard chains rattle behind them. They stopped to look back and the chains rattling stopped. In the dark night they could see nothing so they continued, as did the rattling chains. When the men stopped so did the chains. For miles they were followed. When they reached James McCaffrey's lane they decided that he, because the house was only a few hundred feet away, would wait by the road, while Mick continued on to his house. Mick would whistle until he reached his lane and then stop, at which time they would go to their respective houses. Well he started to walk, but so did the chain noise. Now James, never known for his bravery, took off for his house, never looking back as the chains followed. He hardly slept that night, but by the morning light there was his ghost, a goat that had broken free and dragged its chain along on the ground. So much for "brave" men.

Then there were the stories about Black Magic. My father told the story about the night a group of people were at a neighbor's house and someone there said he could make a turf move and dance around the floor. Of course he was dared to do that, and finally he was coaxed into doing it. As the story goes, the turf started to move all around the kitchen and the men began to jump on tables and chairs to get away from it, knowing its power came from the devil! When asked to stop it the man said he could not do so, but if anyone there could say the prayer after Mass, the "De Profundis," then it would stop. It was said and the turf lay still. Because so many acts of black magic were being performed, and also to rid the land of evil spirits, that prayer had been added at the end of Mass in Ireland.

# DE PROFUNDIS, PSALM 130

*(Prayer for the Dead)*

"Out of the depths I cry to you, O Lord;
Lord, hear my voice!
Let your ears be attentive
To my voice in supplication:
If You, O Lord, mark iniquities,
Lord who can stand?
But with You is forgiveness,
That You may be revered.
More than sentinels wait for the dawn,
Let Israel wait for the Lord.
For with the Lord is kindness,
Wand with Him is plenteous redemption;
And He will redeem Israel
From all their iniquities."

My father, rest his soul, detailed the bright moonlight night he was riding his bicycle home late from town. As he road by Shurdens he saw a large black dog in the road. Just then a car came down the road; he yelled at the dog, but it never moved. The car hit it squarely. There was no noise; however, and when my dad jumped from his bike to investigate, sure the dog was dead, but there was no dog anywhere on the road, or in the ditch, anywhere. He got back on his bike and continued on his way, but as he went he broke out in a cold sweat and by the time he reached Jimmy Smith's by the road he felt faint. He stopped and knocked on the door in spite of the late hour, and when they answered the door, they bade him come in and have a wee whiskey.

Jimmy Smith said,"you've seen something and you are not the first nor will you be the last to stop here after seeing something."

Then there was the story of the old woman who lived in the rocks, that sometime after she died, people coming home from their ceiling at night would see her sitting in a chair in the rocks. They asked the priest what to do and he asked if anyone had talked to the ghost. Of course no one had, everyone was too frightened, but the priest reassured them that she would not harm them. Because she appeared quite regularly, the priest and the people went to the rocks and there, sure enough, was the old lady. The priest went forward to talk to her. After a few minutes he came back and assured the people she would never be seen again. The priest explained that when she died she owed a few shillings to someone and never got a chance to pay it back, and so she kept coming back until he talked to her. He promised to pay her debt and she appeared no more.

But then there were the "ghost" happenings that were manmade. Like the night Hugh Reilly was coming home from a ceili at his brother John's. Now he had to walk a plank over a ditch between fields. My father, who wasn't up to much good, when he heard him coming, hid in the ditch under the plank. Just as poor old Hugh came down the plank, my father grabbed him, scaring him half to death. Hugh, not a young man, ran for his life and my father had a great laugh at his expense.

Then there was the time an old man died. Now he had spent most of his past few years sitting in a chair and had died there but some time passed before he was found. His body was forever in a sitting position. For the wake, the man laying him out put two big bricks over his knees to flatten them. Some of the "good boys," as my father referred to them, found an opportunity for some fun and put string around the bricks and ran it along the floor to the window and outside. They tied old tin cans to a goat and had her by the window. As the wake progressed the men were in the kitchen having a few drinks and the women were sitting with the corpse praying. The "boys" decided it was time. One pulled on the strings, pulling the bricks from the corpse's knees, while another hit the goat, who made quite a racket by the window. The force of the dead man's knees springing back into place brought him to a straight-up sitting position. The poor women were sure the devil himself had come to life and they took off like rabbits.

Throughout Ireland and especially in Cavan there are many old buried circular forts, or as they were known when I grew up a home for the little people. There was one on my Aunt Mollie's farm.

I remember when I was quite young visiting a family with my parents. They had one of these forts on their property and were amazed by the interest shown it by some people who I'm sure were archaeologists. They had started digging and had found the remains of several bodies. The farmer didn't quite understand what all the excitement was all about. As far as he was concerned it was a fairy's fort and that was it. He took us out to show us the fort. At that time there was an apple orchard within the fort. He showed us around and while we were there picking some delicious apples and enjoying them there was a rustling in the bushes. We all took off out of there as fast as we could. It was probably just a bird in the thick hedge, but in Ireland you never knew where the little people might be.

My father also told the story about the night he was going from one house to another and he stepped into a certain hill in front of a house. I can't recall now who it belonged to. Anyway all at once he kept walking, but could not get off the hill. He could see the light in the house but could not get any closer no matter how hard he tried. Finally after yelling for ages, another visitor to the house heard him.

The man of the house stood and whistled by the door as the other man took my father off the hill, lantern in hand. The next morning when they looked out, there was a circle about 12 feet in diameter where my father had walked around and around and around for so long. He had been stuck on a fairy ring and without the whistling of the other man and light from the lantern he would have remained on the hill, walking until the dawn's first light. According to the owner of the hill my father was not the first one stuck there. Others had haplessly walked into the fairy ring and walked till they dropped down exhausted, only to be found sound asleep the next morning by the farmer.

Ireland - the land of spirits! I remember when Hugh Reilly died. I was so sad, I really liked him. He was such a nice old man. But I was more than sad, I was also scared and a bit excited too, as at the wake I watched and waited for the banshee to arrive from the mountain. I had never seen one and I hoped this would be my opportunity because so many acts of black magic were being performed. A banshee was a small fairy woman who lived in the mountain, and mourned certain families. When someone from that family died, weeping, she would come down from the mountain through the fields and stop outside the window where the dead person was laid out, wailing all the while. Then return to her abode in the rocks among heather and grouse. I never did get to see or hear the banshee that night as I struggled to stay awake. Now I am not saying she did not come when I dozed off. I just never heard her. I was afraid, however, that when we left the wake in the wee hours of the morning we might run smack dab into her on the way across the fields. I was at the same time disappointed and relieved when we reached home and I had neither seen nor heard her. Maybe it was the "De Profundis" that kept her away.

# HOW OFT HAS THE BANSHEE CRIED

*Thomas Moore 1779 - 1852*

How oft has the Banshee cried!
How oft has death untied
Bright links that Glory wove,
Sweet bonds entwined by Love!
Peace to each manly soul that sleepeth;
Rest to each faithful eye that weepeth;
Long may the fair and brave
Sigh o'er the hero's grave!

We're fallen on evil days!
Star after star decays,
Every bright name that shed
Light o'er the land is fled.
Dark falls the tear of him that mourneth
Lost joy, or hope that ne'er retumeth:
But brightly flows the tear
Wept o'er a hero's bier.

Quenched are our beacon lights-
Thou, of the Hundred Fights!
Thou, on whose burning tongue
Truth, peace and freedom hung!
Both mute-but long as valor shineth,
Or mercy's soul at war repineth,
So long shall Erin's pride
Tell how they lived and died.

And so the stories would go on and on. By the end of
the evening I was scared to death and wondered if there were
any ghosts lurking outside my bedroom window.

# Chapter 13

# Riding Bicycles

When I was growing up, a bicycle was the major means of transportation in Ireland. All the young people and most of the adults rode bikes wherever they went. Both men and the young women who worked rode their bikes to their place of employment. Even the Garda Siochana, Irish police force, rode on bicycles as they performed their duties. On a Summer Sunday evening country roads were thick with swarms of bicycles as all the young adults made their way to the local carnivals. For the teens going to the tech school in the town, St Patrick's College and Loretto College bikes were their mode of travel. Those who worked in town depended on the bicycle to get there on time.

For many years, actually all her life, my mother tried but never learned to ride a bike. She would sneak my father's bike and later mine up the pass going to John "The Red Fellow" Reilly's. The only success she had was in getting punctures in the tires. Later my bike suffered the same fate. Luckily my dad kept a good supply of bike repair materials in the house and he would repair whatever she or I had managed to do to the bike. He kept both his and my bike well oiled and in good working condition. Parts for bike repair were readily available in most stores and every man knew well how to care for the bicycles in his household. What my mother needed was a bicycle built for two, or better yet one of those now available tricycles made for adults.

# DAISY BELL
## (A BICYCLE BUILT FOR TWO)
*Harry Dacre, 1860 - 1922*

Daisy, Daisy,
Give me your answer do! I'm half crazy,
All for the love of you!
It won't be a stylish marriage,
I can't afford a carriage
But you'll look sweet upon the seat
Of a bicycle made for two.

I could not wait to learn to ride, and the summer that I reached the ripe old age of ten my cousin Bunnie came home from America, and bought a good used bike so she could get around. She offered to teach me to ride. I was so excited but I also remember how angry I was when my parents wanted her to also teach my cousin Kathleen. Kathleen came from Belfast to visit every summer and I always thought my parents favored her. I was jealous; after all, Bunnie was my cousin and she was teaching me to ride.

Up and down the Cootehill Road in front of our lane we went until I was able to balance reasonably well on my own. I learned pretty quickly. I think Bunnie had a bit too much confidence in me because the following week she was going to visit friend's way down by Redhills and invited me to go along. I used her bike while she borrowed another. Unfortunately Bunnie over estimated my ability and at Ballyhaise Cross, when it came time to turn, I didn't. I went straight into the ditch. We realized right then and there that I was not going to make it all the way, and I returned home pushing the bike most of the way with my ego wounded.

*July 1955, the day I learned to ride a bike*

When Bunnie returned to America she gave me her bike. I practiced my riding and eventually got really good. Once I learned to ride well I became a great help to my mother. On Saturday mornings I rode into town, usually carrying several dozen eggs, in a bag hung from the handlebars, to sell at McDonalds. The eggs were on one side and on the other side was the wet battery for the radio to be charged at Smiths shop. After I sold the eggs I bought the few groceries we needed and did any other necessary errands. My mother always let me spend a couple of pence buying one or two bananas in Hickey's. That was a real treat. After picking up the wet battery for the radio and loading my handlebars with it and my carrier on back with groceries, I'd start home, making one more stop at Ownie Cusach's at the cross, where I bought my final treat, banana ice cream between crisp thin wafers. Usually I bought one for me, which I ate right away, and another I'd have them wrap for my mother. Then there was no time to waste on the ride home.

Once I learned to ride reasonably well my parents expected that I would ride to school. I was so delighted that I hardly slept the night before the first time. All was fine and I had no problem with the bike but there was another problem. I was the only child riding to school and some of the other children made fun of me, so much so that I really never wanted to take the bike to school again. That was a problem because I could never tell my parents about the harassment and could never come up with another excuse for not riding to school. I considered only taking the bike part of the way and hiding it somewhere so I could continue on foot and retrieve it on the way home. However I was too scared that someone would find it, maybe gypsies, and steal it. The trouble I would be in then would be much worse than the teasing of the other children.

Riding a bike also gave me lots of freedom and I really enjoyed it! My friend Annie Flatley and I rode all over. We would go as fast as we could with the wind in our hair singing, "When the red, red robin comes bob, bob, bobin' along." One of our favorite things to do was hang around Ballyhaise Cross at the end of her lane on Sunday afternoons. It was then that all the area young adult boys, Michael Flatley, Sean Prior, the Coyles and others gathered at the cross to play skittles, a game similar to bowling. Pieces of wood standing on end are used instead of pins and a long stick is spun across the ground to knock down the standing ones. We spent lots of energy bugging the boys; but when we finally got their attention, we would take off on the bikes again, going as fast as we could until we could no longer see them behind us. Then we hid behind a hedge until they had passed by.

When I started the Convent school, my father bought me a brand new bike. Because I'd be riding back and forth to town everyday, he wanted my bike to be the safest it could be. It was like buying a new car today. It was bright and shiny and new. At that time in Ireland getting anything new, especially if you were a child, seldom happened and a new bike was really special. Now I wonder how my parents afforded it and what they had to sacrifice so I could have it.

Then there was the day I was coming home from school and Michael Flatley and some other boys from St. Patrick's College were behind me as I rode home. I wanted to show off, as 13-year-old girls do. I was riding with hands on hips and as I came past my Aunt Mollie's lane the road was a little hilly and banked, and I put my feet on the handlebars. "Look Ma, no hands, no feet," a trick rider! I was so talented! Next thing I knew I hit a rut and I was flying through the air, landing in the briars and nettles. There I was in a crumbled mess under my bike, but the hurt from scrapes and nettle stings was nothing to the hurt my ego experienced as the boys sped by, laughing uncontrollably. I was so embarrassed! Then I had to go home and explain to my mother why I had blood all over me and my white uniform blouse. I stretched the truth. I simply told her I fell off my bike. Not the complete story but there was always confession to seek forgiveness for white lies.

# Chapter 14

# Friends

I had many acquaintances while growing up in Ireland, but only a few really close friends. Living on farms that were long distances apart made it difficult for children to get together. One of my first real friends was Vera Charters, who lived with her Aunt Mollie and Uncle Paddy Tully along the old road near the quarry. We played dolls and baby house together. Her baby house was in the rocks near her house. I remember her house was really beautiful and she always had nice clothes and lovely things. Vera had long, shiny, black hair that was poker straight, so much prettier than my curly, blonde locks.

My family and the Rooneys were always friends, and Mary Rooney and I played together often. My mother enjoyed visiting with Mrs. Rooney, and it gave Mary and me lots of opportunity to play together.

Later when we went to the Convent School, Mary Ellen Brady and I became friends. She was a fun person, the eldest of three Brady children, with Christie a younger brother and Theresa her little sister. We had fun riding to and from school together, and because we were the only ones from Castletara, we shared a special bond as we went to school with the "town" kids and girls from other areas.

Through all the years one friend always was and still is my closest friend. I can't remember a time when Annie Flatley and I were not friends. I remember visiting her house in Drumoohan. She had a huge family and that seemed like so much fun to me. I loved to go to her home! There were older and younger children there, always someone to play with. When her mother moved to the States she left Annie in charge of the family. She was about eleven years old then. Of course like so many Irish children she had to quit school to cook and clean and help around the farm, and take care of her younger brother, Sean, who was only two years old and still in nappies. What a job for a little girl! But Annie did it. She cleaned house, helped on the farm and cooked all the meals. She baked the best soda bread in the world! Might I add, there was no electricity at that time, so all the cooking for both family and animals she did on an open fire. Yet with all this work she still found time to be my friend and we did have many good times together. Today, she and I enjoy reminiscing about our time growing up and all the fun we had so long ago.

When we were children her sister Kathleen became so very ill and I remember how worried everyone was, especially Annie. Thank God, after many months Kathleen began to recuperate and the whole parish heaved a sigh of relief. As I said Annie and I remain friends and to this day she can still make me laugh and like when we were children we can still share OUR secrets. When she came to America, a year after I did, she went back to school, starting 9th grade. Having been out of school for a few years that took guts! She worked hard in school and graduated. I really admire her! She has always been my inspiration.

*Annie's First Communion Picture*

# Chapter 15

# Halloween

Halloween, or Hollow Eve as we called it, was rich in tradition. There was always something magical about that evening, All Souls evening. Usually some neighbors came a calling and we played games. My father had many games. In one he put a halfpenny on the forehead of an unsuspecting player. He would push it really hard, and then the player had to nod his or her head to knock it off. The first time each nod counted the number of years until the person got married, usually the halfpenny came off with one or two nods. Then he pushed it on again. He pushed really hard. This time each nod was another child the person would have. Of course that number was really high due to the fact that my father, after pushing so hard, slipped the penny into the palm of his hand. When an unbelievable number was reached he simply flipped it onto the floor. It was fun. As the number climbed, the harder the person worked to remove it.

Another of the favorite games he loved to play required a chair in the center of the floor, front legs resting on the floor, back of the chair and legs level, parallel to the floor. After testing the distance, he placed a pan of water containing a half penny on the floor near the chair. The object of the game was to lift the coin out of the water while tilting upside down on the chair back. Now certain people had an added problem with bowel gas and once turned upside down out it came! There was much laughter at and encouragement for the individual. As I said, he loved to play games and the one that caused the most embarrassment for the poor unsuspecting participants was "Kiss the Blarney Stone." He told everyone that he had a piece of the famous stone and that if they wanted he would let them kiss it, blindfolded of course. He would have, however, many people brave enough to play go into another room and would bring them out one at a time, blindfolded! His helper escorted the poor soul to a spot in the room and he told them to bend over to prepare to kiss the stone. They were obviously startled when they kissed a hairy piece of warm flesh, the helper's arm; but when they quickly removed their blindfold they saw not the arm but my dad pretending to hurriedly pull up his pants. At this the whole room erupted in laughter. The poor, red-faced player was then urged to sit and watch the next unsuspecting soul. At which point they saw that an arm was what they had indeed kissed. And so it continued! These games he didn't just play at Halloween but any time a get together was really going strong and he thought it ready for them, especially if there was someone there who had never seen them before, a new victim! We always played some children's games too and I always enjoyed them. I remember bobbing for apples in a big old tub of water. One of my favorites involved hanging an apple on a long string from the rafters in the kitchen, and with hands tied behind our backs we took turns trying to catch it in our teeth and take a bite out of the apple. Try it! Not easy! Once you captured an apple you got to eat it. That was so much fun.

Halloween also meant special foods, fruit, nuts, the best hazel nuts in the world! To this day hazel nuts are my all time favorites. We always had a Barn Brack for Halloween. It was a sweet yeast bread and in a purchased Barn Brack was hidden a ring wrapped in paper. Tradition goes that the person who got the ring in their cut of bread would get married within the year. It was great fun speculating who the spouse might be. Lots of teasing and joking ensued. Although my Aunt Kathleen occasionally made the sweet bread, ours was store bought.

## AUNT KATHLEEN'S BARM BRACK

1 oz package of yeast
½ cup sugar
½ cup butter
1 cup Warm milk
2 Eggs well beaten
1 pound all purpose flour
½ teaspoon salt

1 cup raisins

1 cup sultanas

½ cup currants

½ cup mixed candied peel (optional)

cold tea

Marinate fruit and peel in cold tea, overnight if possible Place finger temperature milk in medium bowl, add yeast and stir to dissolve. Add salt and butter cut up in chunks and stir to melt Add beaten eggs and sugar. Gradually add flour and mix to soft dough. Drain fruit and add, mixing thoroughly. Continue to add flour until mixture leaves sides of bowl. Turn out on floured board and knead for five minutes. Place mixture in greased 9" cake tin, with 3" sides. Cover with cloth and let rise until mixture has doubled in bulk. Bake at 375o for 1 hour. Ten minutes before done, brush with a little egg beaten with water for glaze

Usually after the games and the tea and brack things settled down, and as we sat around the turf fire the ghost stories began. Occasionally during the evening the festivities were interrupted by small groups of older children dressed up with blackened faces among them were Winnie Breiden and Tessie Manterson. They entertained, were given fruit and off they went to the next house. I never got to do that, my parents didn't allow, it but I did want to and I envied the children who did.

# Chapter 16

# Lent

Lent was one of my favorite times of the year. It was a time we spent many hours in church.

The Tuesday before Lent began was known in Ireland as Shrove or Pancake Tuesday. The evening meal on that day was pancakes. I remember how delicious they were smothered with fresh homemade butter and sugar, a treat that we seldom had.

## MY MOTHER'S PANCAKES

1 pound flour
½ teaspoon salt
1 teaspoon baking soda
2 eggs
Buttermilk

Sift together flour, salt and baking soda. Lightly beat eggs and add to well in center of flour. Mix well. Beat in enough buttermilk to make a thick batter. Drop by ¼ cupfuls onto greased pan and fry until golden, turn and fry until golden on second side. Smother with butter and sugar.

# POTATO PANCAKES

3 eggs
1 teaspoon salt
1 tablespoon sugar
3 cups milk
2 cups flour
1 tablespoon melted butter
3 cups grated raw potato

Separate the eggs. To the well-beaten yolks, add the salt, sugar and milk. Gradually add the flour and melted butter, beating well. Stir in the grated potatoes. Fold in the egg whites which have been stiffly beaten. Bake at once on a hot greased griddle or heavy pan, allowing 3 minutes on each side. Serve hot and well buttered. I like my cakes with sour cream and applesauce

## MONICA'S POTATO PANCAKES

I like to make these with leftover mashed potatoes.

**Mix together**
2 cups mashed potatoes
1 egg beaten
1 cup flour
Enough milk to make thick dough

Roll ½ cup size ball in flour. Flatten and fry in lightly greased skillet.
These are the potato pancakes I make for my family.

# BASIC GRIDDLE CAKE RECIPE

1½ cups flour

1 teaspoon baking powder

½ teaspoon salt

2 tablespoons confectioners sugar

2 eggs

1½ cups milk

2 oz butter or margarine

Sift together the flour, baking powder, salt and castor sugar. Combine the well-beaten eggs with the milk. Add to the flour mixture and beat until smooth. Add the melted butter. Bake following the directions for Potato Pancakes above and serve either with golden syrup or spread with butter and sprinkled with brown sugar.

# POTATO GRIDDLE CAKES

Add 1 cup of grated raw potato to the basic recipe, omitting the sugar. When cooked, spread with butter creamed with 1 tablespoon of tomato ketchup.

Starting on Ash Wednesday, we walked to school in the morning and then all together we children marched back the mile or so to Castletara chapel to Mass and the giving out of ashes. We did all that before breakfast because at that time Catholics had to fast from midnight the night before to go to Communion in the morning. By the time Communion time rolled around there were more students passed out on the grass outside the church than there were students at the altar rail! It seemed once one went down soon others followed. Of course having passed out you were then allowed to go home; after all you couldn't go to school sick! But before you left for home you had to get ashes.

There was the story my father told. He swore it to be true, about one Ash Wednesday years before. Fr. Lynch was about to give out the ashes when a sick call came. As he rushed out the door, he asked the sacristan to have the people wait until he returned from administering the last rights. The man not being too bright said, "Tell me the words and shur I'll do it meself." The priest called back as he went out the door, "An egit y'are and an egit you'll always be." Well the poor man thinking those were the words decided to proceed with the ceremony. Soon Fr. Lynch returned and as he approached the church he heard laughter and commotion coming from inside. He ran in only to find the sacristan spitting on his thumb, dipping it in the ashes and as he made the sign of the cross on each forehead andrepeating Fr. Lynch's words, "An ejit y'are and an ejit you'll always be." Somehow I can't get through Ash Wednesday without remembering that story and usually just as I get my ashes. So much for reverence!

Of course you couldn't eat much meat during Lent like you could the rest of the year. But then we didn't have that much meat to begin with. Other than bacon and sausages we seldom ate meat, and then for the most part we had only the occasional chicken. But I do remember that during Lent we had fish. Occasionally on Fridays during Lent my father went into town and bought two fresh herring, a real treat! My father scraped the scales from the fresh fish, carefully slitting the belly to remove the roe and clean the inside. My mother placed them into the sizzling butter in the big cast iron skillet. Soon the aroma of the fish filled the air. Oh how I loved the smell as my mother fried them up. Soon the skin became crispy, covering the juicy, flaky meat beneath. Served with boiled potatoes and bread, the feast was ready. The fish were very bony, so my mother seldom let me eat much of the fish itself, but I always got the tender juicy roe. One type was granular and felt like miniature little balls in my mouth. The other was smooth, milky and tender and so delicious. What a treat! My father, who ate the fish bones and all, stuffed bread in his mouth with each bite of fish, saying that it prevented the bones in the fish from becoming stuck in his throat and choking him, while my mother carefully picked out the bones.

## FRIED HERRINGS

2 herrings
2 tablespoons Irish oatmeal or flour
butter for frying
salt

Roll the fresh herring in the oatmeal. Fry in a thick pan that has been greased with butter. Drain on absorbent paper and season with salt.

# HERRING ROES

1 pound herring roe
A pinch salt
½ cup flour
butter for frying
lemon juice
black pepper

Toss the roe in the salted flour. Fry gently in butter in a heavy pan.

Lent brought with it an increased awareness of Christ and his goodness and just how terribly unworthy people we were. It was a time when I saw God as a strong punishing God, but it seemed there always might be a chance for repentance and redemption. First everyone gave up something for Lent. It was unheard of not to. Usually it was candy or sugar. I gave up sugar one year and till this day never used sugar again on my tea. My father always gave up smoking on Ash Wednesday and Good Friday. For him, that was the supreme sacrifice, as it was for my mother, too because by noon without the smokes he was as he would say if he were honest about it, "A walkin Divil." My poor mother! It was more a penance for those who crossed his path than for him.

Of course Lent was also a time of added prayer. After school we children rushed to Castletara chapel to do the Stations of the Cross, praying and genuflecting at each one, all the while seeing who could be finished and out the door first! We went to confession every week so we could go to Communion on Sunday. I remember sitting in the last pew scared to death of going to confession and trying to remember exactly how many times at the tender age of 8 and 9, I coveted my neighbor's goods and committed adultery (whatever that was); I had no idea but it sounded good. I was really afraid that I'd forget something and have a black soul when I went to Communion. That would be an even bigger sin! I'm sure Fr. Hunt had many a good laugh at our confessions. How could he possibly have kept a straight face with the stuff we told him?

I recall the missions we used to have every year during Lent at Castletara. For weeks before there was an air of excitement as we prepared the church and our sinful souls for the time ahead.

Usually the missionary was introduced to us at Sunday Mass and then it began, every morning Mass and every night the mission. There were enough sermons to convert the worst of sinners, but all I remember from them was that they all were hell, fire and brimstone. I remember how they screamed at us the need to save our sinful souls and change our dreadful ways. They always got so worked up, that now their faces blend into one red, angry, insistent blur, pounding on the lectern, telling us how evil we were. According to them we were all headed for hell in a hand basket if we didn't repent. No loving God for them, just a vengeful God, ready to pounce on us like a cat on a mouse and send us all to hell. At least we would all be there together!

At the mission they always sold religious articles, prayer books, holy pictures, scapulars, rosary beads and medals, so many medals; St. Christopher, St. Martin, The Miraculous medal, The Sacred Heart, all of the litany. They were inexpensive, probably a penny each, and we children bought lots of them. Most of us wore them on a great big safety pin attached to our undershirt. I recall it being a kind of status symbol. How many medals you had on the pin was an indication of your devotion. I have the safety pin with my mother's medals and still treasure the silver miraculous medal my father gave to me as a teenager.

Lent was always a special time for another reason. For a couple of months groups of people in various parishes had been practicing their acting and rehearsing their lines to present a play. It was the custom for many parishes to have their own troupe. They presented their plays in their own parishes and in each others parishes. All this was in preparation for a festival of plays presented in the town over a period of one or two weeks. It was an honor for a troupe to even make the finals, and in the 1950s the group from Castletara really made a name for themselves coming in first in the competition several times. It was amazing how good these people were at acting. I remember one play, when my Uncle James had a main role playing a man with Parkinson's disease and he was able to keep tremors through the entire play. Those years had the Boylans, my uncles, John and James, Evelyn Hannigan, Joe Flatley, Paddy Cahill, Francie Kelly, Phyllis Brady, Fr. Eddie Brady, Mickey Morrow and many others in the group. From what I remember they rehearsed in their homes. Their work was wonderful entertainment for the countryside.

*1953 The Passing Day*
*Back Row: Packie Cahill, Evelyn Hannigan, James McAvinue, Phyllis Brady, Brian Boylan, Mary Boylan, James Clarke. Front Row: Sean Boylan, Joe Flatley, Eddie Brady, Francie Kelly, John Clarke.*

**The following article appeared in the Anglo Celt about a later group of Moonlight Players**

*A big attendance at Cavan Drama festival last night gave an enthusiastic reception to the Moonlight Players, Castletara who staged for the first time a three act comedy, "Venus in the Snow" by local playwright J. G. O'Reilly. The author took a curtain call at the conclusion. The adjudicator Mr. Dan Treston, said it was Marvelous that such a community spirit should exist in a parish like Castletara which had not only a drama group but could boast of having someone in the group to write their play. He particularly liked James Clarke in the role of Podge. He had natural talent and his performance was one of the nicest things he had seen for a long time. He knew how to time his lines, and when he was not on the stage the play was not so good. Mary Rooney as the mother, was quite convincing but she could afford to put a little more variety into her voice, Brien Boylan in the role of Pocher Mulberry-had given a good performance and his acting was of the same standard as Podge. Hughie Newman as the detective was very good at the end.*

On Palm Sunday we brought palm sprigs to church to be blessed. Only we didn't have real palm trees so we used small pine or cedar branches. These were blessed and brought home, put in a safe place, usually sticking out from behind a mirror in our house. There it stayed until we had the occasional thunderstorm, then my mother would break off a sprig, light it and burn it in the doorway of the house to protect our home. Storing by a mirror was the perfect spot because when it started to thunder my mother would cover all the mirrors in the house, believing they would draw lightning into the house.

# Chapter 17

# Easter

Then finally Easter and now we could eat what we wanted and could again have whatever goodies we had given up. Easter Sunday brought Kludogs - Easter eggs. These were brought by the Brown Hen along with sweets and other treats. In the area, in older days according to my mother, the children would take their kludogs up on the mountain and cook and eat them there. We cooked and ate them at home. We used both duck and hen eggs. I was never too fond of the duck eggs but my mother loved them. Easter Sunday we dressed in our best Sunday clothes for church and afterward there were usually sweets to eat and all the foods we had given up for Lent. It was a really joyous day.

Easter usually found the whole family at my grandfather's in Corratubber. Since lamb was the traditional meat for Easter, Aunt Kathleen prepared roasted leg of lamb with mint jelly on the side and all the trimmings, usually mashed potatoes, parsnips, and turnips.

*Easter Sunday - John, Mary and Monica Argue outside Castletara Chapel 1957*

Usually before Easter and Christmas the young girls, older school children, and a few women of the parish came together under the direction of Mrs. Meligan to clean the church. We scrubbed every little corner, then put out flowers from our gardens on the altar, and it was all so beautiful and grand. In between these cleanings usually a couple of the ladies and girls dusted each Saturday and put fresh flowers. It was a real honor to have your flowers on the altar, and because most families had flower gardens we really did have a beautifully decorated church. There were lots of roses, gladiolus, carnations, sweet peas, dahlias and even wild flowers too.

# ROAST LEG OF LAMB

1 clove garlic

1 tablespoon butter

1 leg of lamb, 4 to 5 pounds

10 to 12 parsley stalks

1 carrot sliced

1 onion sliced

1 tablespoon water

Crush the garlic and mix with the butter, Paint the leg with the garlic butter and set it in the roasting pan, resting on the parsley stalks, with the carrot; the onion, and the water. Roast at 350°, reducing the heat toward the end of the cooking time. Allow 20 minutes to the pound and 20 minutes over. Baste several times while roasting.

Cover and allow to rest, while making gravy. Serve with gravy and mint jelly.

## GRAVY

The sediment from the roasting pan

1 tablespoon flour

carrot and onion from the roast·

1 ¼ cups beef stock

salt and pepper

Gently pour the fat off the roasting pan without disturbing the sediment. Sprinkle in the flour. Mix well with the sediment and allow to brown. Mash the carrot and onion. Add the mashed, cooked carrot and onion. Gradually add stock Cook for 5 minutes, season and strain before serving.

All this was followed by a delicious bread and butter pudding.

# BREAD AND BUTTER PUDDING

## Ingredients
butter or margarine
8-10 slices of bread
1½ cups sugar mixed with 2 teaspoon cinnamon mixed in
1 cup golden raisins
4 cups milk heated to lukewarm
4 eggs beaten
2 teaspoons vanilla

Butter the bread and cut into smaller pieces. Grease an 8 cup ovenproof dish and put in layers of bread, sugar and raisins. Mix milk with the beaten eggs. Pour mixture over bread and fruit. Bake for 40-45 minutes at 350° F.

I sometimes make my pudding using leftover cake. Just omit butter, break the cake into chunks and continue as above.For another variety add chopped apples. And serve with Bird's custard.

As I talk about church and its celebrations there is one that I do not want to ignore, although I'm not sure that it was thought of as a celebration. Pregnancy in Ireland at that time was only whispered about as though there was something wrong about a couple having a baby. But a new baby always brought great excitement and joy. However the church at that time had a rule that a new mother was not allowed to attend Mass after the birth of a baby until she was churched (purified). For this she came to church after Mass on a Sunday, quietly made her way to the altar rail and received the blessing, or was churched as they called it. That ceremony allowed her to return to participate at Mass and the sacraments. This usually took place when the baby was just a couple of weeks old. The custom then was not to take the baby anywhere before it was baptized. This was usually after the mother was churched and within a month of the birth.

# Chapter 18

# Castletara School

Going back to Castletara School filled me with so very many feelings from all the memories. Both my parents attended that school as children in the early 1900s.

*Castletara National School*

I remember how we gathered outside the wall before school started. How many days we hoped the master or mistress would not show up, but they always did.

Mrs. Fay, our mistress, was a very nice lady, very kind and generous. She had short curly hair and was tall, I thought. She was a wonderful person. She had two sons in school with us, P.N. and Danny, and a daughter Ann. She lived the other side of Cavan town and drove her car to school every day. When I was little not many people had cars. Quite often if it was raining and she came along as we walked those several miles to school she would stop and give us a ride. I don't know how many of us she often stuffed into her little car but we really appreciated the ride.

*Mrs. Fay, Paul (P.N.), Tom and me shortly before I left Ireland, taken on our street*

Mrs. Fay had the younger children in one room of the school, babyclass, 1st and 2nd class. From her we learned our ABCs and 123s. We also learned to sew, knit and sing.

She would teach us Do, Re, Me and how to put these notes together to learn songs.

## THE MINSTREL BOY
*Thomas Moore 1779 - 1852*

Minstrel boy to the war has gone;
In the ranks of death you'll find him;
His father's sword he has girded on,
And his wild harp slung behind him
"Lord of song!" said the warrior-bard,
"Though all the world betrays thee,
One sword at least, thy rights shall guard.
One faithful harp shall praise thee!"

The minstrel fell but the foeman's chain
Could not bring his proud soul under;
The harp he lov'd ne'er spoke again,
For he tore its cords asunder;
And said. "No chains shall sully thee,
Thou soul of love and bravery!
Thy songs were made for the pure and free,
They shall never sound in slavery!"

## THE RISING OF THE MOON
*John Keegan Casey 1846 – 1870*

Oh, then, tell me Sean O'Farrell,
Tell me why you hurry so,
Husha,bhuach-aill, hush and listen";
And his cheeks were all aglow,
I bear orders from the Captain:
Get you ready quick and soon,
For the pikes must be together
At the rising of the moon.

241

**Chorus**

At the rising of the moon,
At the rising of the moon,
For the pikes must be together
At the rising of the moon.
"Oh, then tell me; Sean O'Farrell,
When the gath'ring is to be?
"In the old spot by the river
Right well known to you and me;
One word more, for signal token,
Whistle up the marching tune,
With your pike upon your shoulder,
At the rising of the moon,

**Chorus**

Out from many a mud-wall cabin
Eyes were watching through that night;
Many a manly breast was throbbing
For the blessed waning light.
Murmurs passed along the valleys,
Like the Banshee's lonely croon,
And a thousand blades were flashing
At the rising of the moon.

**Chorus**

There, besides the singing river,
That dark mass of men was seen,
Far above their shining weapons
Hung their own beloved green.
"Death to every foe and traitor;
Forward, strike the marching tune,
And hurrah my boys for freedom
Tis the rising of the moon

**Chorus**

Well, they fought, for poor old Ireland
And full bitter was their fate
Oh! what glorious pride and sorrow
Fill the names of Ninety-Eighth.
Yet thank God, e'en, still beating
Hearts in manhood's burning moon,
Who would follow their footsteps
At the rising of the moon!

**Chorus**

# A NATION ONCE AGAIN
*Thomas Osborne Davis 1814 - 1845*

When boyhood's fire was in my blood
I read of ancient freemen,
For Greece and Rome who bravely stood,
Three hundred men and three men;
And then I prayed I yet might see
Our fetters rent in twain,
And Ireland, long a province, be
A Nation once again!

**Chorus**

A Nation once again,
A Nation once again,
And Ireland, long a province, be
A Nation once again!

An from that time, through wildest woe,
That hope has shone a far light,
Nor could love's brightest summer glow
Outshine that solemn starlight;
It seemed to watch above my head
In forum, field and fane
Its angel voice sang round my bed,
A Nation once again!

**Chorus**

243

It whisper'd, too, that freedom's ark
And service high and holy.
Would be profaned by feelings dark
And passions vains or lowly;
For, Freedom comes from God's right hand,
And needs a godly train;
And righteous men must make our land
A Nation once again!

**Chorus**

So, as I grew from boy to man,

I bent me to that bidding
My spirit of each selfish plan
And cruel passion ridding,
For, thus I hoped some day to aid,
Oh, can such hope be vain,
When my dear country shall be made
A Nation once again!

**Chorus**


# SPINNINGWHEEL SONG
*John F. Waller 1810 - 1894*


Mellow, the moonlight to shine is beginning,
Close by the window young Eileen is spinning,
Bent o'er the fire, her blind grandmother sitting.
Crooning and moaning and drowsily knitting.


**Chorus**
Merrily, cheerily, noiselessly whirring,
Spins the wheel, rings the wheel, while the foot's stirring.
Lightly and brightly and airily ringing,
Sounds the sweet voice of the young maiden singing.

What's the noise that I hear at the window I wonder,
'Tis the little birds chirping the holly-bush under
What makes you be shoving and moving your stool on,
An' singing, all wrong, that old song of "The Coolun?"

There's a form at the casement - the form of her true love,
and he whispers, with face bent: "I'm waiting for you love,
Get up from the stool, through the lattice step lightly,
We'll rove in the grove while the moon's shining brightly."

**Chorus**
Merrily, cheerily, noiselessly whirring.
Spins the wheel, rings the wheel, while the foot's stirring.
Sprightly and lightly and airily ringing,
Trills the sweet voice of the young maiden singing.

The maid shakes her head on her lip lays her fingers.
Steals up from the stool - longs to go and yet lingers.
A frightened glance turns to her drowsy grandmother,
Puts one foot on the stool, spins the wheel with the other.

**Chorus**
Lazily, easily, swings now the wheel round,
Slowly and lowly is heard now the reel's sound,
Noiseless and light to the lattice above her,
The maid steps - then leaps to the arms of her lover.

**Chorus**
Slower - and slower - and slower the wheel swings
Lower - and lower - and lower the reel rings:
Ere the reel and the wheel stop their ringing and moving,
Through the grove the young lovers by moonlight are roving.

# THE MEETING OF THE WATERS

*Thomas Moore 1779 - 1852*
*Written about the Vale of Avoca in Co. Wicklow.*

There is not in the wide world
A valley so sweet
As that vale in whose bosom
The bright waters meet.
Oh, the last rays of feeling
And life must depart
Ere the bloom of that valley
Shall fade from my heart.

Yet it was not that Nature
Had shed o'er the scene
Her purest of crystal
And brightest of green.
'Twas not her soft magic
Of streamlet or hill.
Oh, no, - it was something
More exquisite still.

'Twas that friends,
The beloved of my bosom, were near,
Who made every dear scene
Of enchantment more dear
And who felt how the best charms
Of nature improve
When we see them reflected
From looks that we love.

Sweet vale of Avoca,
How calm could I rest.
In thy bosom of shade
With the friends I love best,
Where the storms that we feel
In this cold world should cease
And our hearts like thy waters,
Be mingled in Peace.

# THE HARP THAT ONCE THROUGH TARA'S HALLS

*Thomas Moore 1779 - 1852*

The harp that once through Tara's halls
The soul of music shed,
Now hangs as mute on Tara's walls,
As if that soul were fled. –
So sleeps the pride of former days,
So glory's thrill is o'er,
And hearts, that once beat high for praise,
Now feel that pulse no more.
No more to chiefs and ladies bright
The harp of Tara swells;
The chord alone, that breaks at night,
Its tale of ruin tells.
Thus Freedom now so seldom wakes,
The only throb she gives,
Is when some heart indignant breaks,
To show that still she lives.


# O'DONNELL ABU!

*Michael Joseph McCann 1824 - 1883*

Proudly the notes of the trumpet are sounding,
Loudly the war-cries arise an the gale;
Fleetly the steed by Loch Suiligh is bounding,
To join the thick squadrons in Saimear's green vale,
On every mountaineer
Strangers to fight and fear,
Rush to the standard of dauntless Red Hugh!
Bonnought and gallowglass
Throng from each mountain pass,
On for old Erin-Q'Donnell Abu!

Princely O'Neill to our aid is advancing
With many a chieftan and warrior clan;
A thousand proud steeds in his vanguard are prancing
'Neath the borderers brave from the banks of the Bann
Many a heart shall quail
Under its coat of mail
Deeply the merciless foeman shall rue,
When on his ear shall ring,
Borne on the breeze's wing,
Tir-Chonaill's dread war-cry-O'Donnell Abu!

Wildly o'er Desmond the war-wolf is howling,
Fearless the eagle sweeps over the plain;
The fox in the streets of the city is prowling,
And all who would scare them are banished or slain,
Grasp every stalwart hand,
Hackbut and battie-brand,
Pay them all back the deep debt so long due;
Noris and Clifford well
Can of Tir-Chonaill tell-
Onward to glory-O'Donnell abu!
and all his brave men.
Sacred the cause that Clann-Chonaill's defending,
The altars we kneel at, the homes of our sires!
Ruthless the ruin the foe is extending,
Midnight is red with the plunderers' fires.
On with O'Donnell then,
Fight the old fight then,
Sons of Tir-Chonaill, all valiant and true;
Make the false Saxon feel
Erin's avenging steel,
Strike for your country-O'Donnell abu!

She also prepared us for first Holy Communion. We had to learn our catechism and the Ten Commandments, though for a very long time I did not have a clue what some of them meant. With words like adultery and covet and bear false witness against my neighbor, what was that all about? We had to learn our prayers in both English and Irish. Although my Irish is in no way what it once was I still love to hear the prayers in Irish.

## BLESS YOURSELF

I n-ainm an athar, agus an mhic, agus an sprid naoimh, áiméin.

## OUR FATHER

Ár nAthair, atá ar neamh, go naomhaítear t'ainm, go dtaga do ríocht, go ndeintear do thoil ar an dtalamh mar a deintear ar neamh. Ár n-arán laethúil tabhair dhúinn inniu, agus maith dhúinn ár gcionta mar a mhaithimíd do chách, agus ná lig sinn i gcathú, ach saor sinn ó olc. áiméin.

# HAIL MARY

Sé do bheatha, a Mhuire, atá lán de ghrásta, tá an Tiarna leat. Is beannaithe thú idir na mná agus is beannaithc toradh do bhroinne, Íosa. A Naomh-Mhuire, a Mháthair Dé, guigh orainn na peacaigh,anois agus ar uair ár mbáis. áiméin.

# GLORY BE TO THE FATHER

Glóire don Athair is don Mhac is don Spriod Naomh, mar a bhí ar dtúis, mar atá fós, is mar a bheidh trí shaol na saol. áiméin.

Oddly enough I remember nothing about First Communion day, but I do remember that sometime during the week after someone took pictures of us at the school. We had to bring our communion clothes to school and change into them for the pictures. When my mother saw the pictures she was really annoyed because whoever had put my veil and headpiece on did it wrong, and she thought it looked terrible. Today I am just glad to have the pictures.

*My First Communion group outside Castletara School*

*Monica on the hill on First Communion day April 1952*

After 2nd grade (class) we still came in weekly to Mrs. Fay's classroom to further our education in sewing, singing and knitting. I remember learning to darn, making little knitted squares, putting a hole in them, then darning it. We learned to hand sew button holes, make pleats, gather, etc. I still have my practice pieces. In knitting we made sweaters and learned to turn the heel on socks. Mrs. Fay, God bless her, every winter had each of us knit wool sweaters for "the poor black babies in Africa." Often she would have one person knit the front of a sweater and another knit the back. It gave us practice knitting, but most of all, although we had very little, it taught us to share with those even less fortunate.

Then there was the time when she took a whole car load of us girls to Killashandra to visit the nuns there and to meet the "black nun from Africa." This was the first black person any of us had ever met. We wanted to touch her hands and see if they felt like ours. Her habit was snow white and that only emphasized how dark her skin was. We were fascinated. Her teeth were so white and the whites of her eyes were pools surrounding deep chocolate candy eyeballs. All these years later I still remember that day. The nuns put out a beautiful tea for us and it was a wonderful day for all of us who were there. Mrs. Fay was a nice lady and formed our concern for others very well.

About twice a year Mrs. Fay gave out prick cards that had a picture of a rosary on them. They were a means of fund raising for the missions. On the day when we got them I would rush home and then run around the area, over hedges and ditches to the neighbors to have them pay a penny per bead. As each was sold a hole was pricked in that bead, hence the name prick cards. At a penny a bead they brought in about five shillings each. As I think about this now I'm reminded of the widow who gave her last few coins in the bible story. I'm sure there were many times when people bought five or ten beads and really couldn't afford it, possibly giving their last few pennies.

The Master was something else. I do believe he was a good teacher and I appreciate how difficult it must have been for him having 3rd, 4th, 5th, 6th and when there was one, 7th grade all in his room. While he worked with 3rd and 4th graders along the wall reading Irish or English, spelling or hearing our math, the others worked at long bench desks with large inkwells doing writing and math problems. These bench desks seated about seven or eight students each. They had lots of writing scratched into them, and each space had an inkwell into which the boys liked to try to dip the girl's plaits (pigtails). We switched from the desks to the wall and back a couple of times each day.

Beside the basic Irish, English and math we learned poetry. In school we didn't just study poetry, we had to memorize it, from the simplest poems in the early grades, such as:

# THE CROW
*Cecil Frances Humphreys 1818 - 1895*

OLD crow, upon the tall tree top
I see you sitting at your ease,
You hang upon the highest bough,
And balance in the breeze.
How many miles you've been to-day,
Upon your wing so strong and black,
And steered across the dark grey sky
Without or guide or track;
Above the city wrapped in smoke,
Green fields, and rivers flowing clear;
Now tell me as you passed them o'er,
What did you see and hear?
The old crow shakes his sooty wing
And answers hoarsely, "Caw, Caw, Caw,"
And that is all the crow can tell,
Of what he heard and saw.

How is it, crow, that you can fly,
And careless see so many things,
While I have sense to think and speak,
But not your pair of wings?
Because all things in earth and air,
That live about this world of ours,
Have their appointed places set,
Their proper parts and powers.
A different nature GOD has given,
To each a different law assigned;
'Tis yours to build your nest on high,
And fly before the wind.
'Tis mine to walk the earth below,
To sail the sea, or ride the land,
With thought to ponder what I see,

And sense to understand.
We'll not despise each other's state,
But follow each our nature's law,
So sit upon your bough, old bird,
And croak your "Caw, Caw, Caw."

# THE MOON
*Robert Louis Stevenson*

The moon has a face like the clock in the hall;
She shines on thieves on the garden wall,
On streets and fields and harbor quays,
And birdies asleep in the forks of the trees.

The squalling cat and the squeaking mouse,
The howling dog by the door of the house,
The bat that lies in bed at noon,
All love to be out by the light of the moon.

But all of the things that belong to the day
Cuddle to sleep to be out of her way;
And flowers and children close their eyes
Till up in the morning the sun shall rise

One of my favorite poems was "My Shadow"

# MY SHADOW
*Robert Louis Stevenson*

I have a little shadow that goes in and out with me,
And what can be the use of him is more than I can see.
He is very, very like me from the heels up to the head;
And I see him jump before me, when I jump into my bed.

The funniest thing about him is the way he likes to grow--

not at all like proper children, which is always very slow;
For he sometimes shoots up taller like an indian-rubber ball,
And he sometimes gets so little
that there's none of him at all.

He hasn't got a notion of how children ought to play,
And can only make a fool of me in every sort of way.
He stays so close beside me; he's a coward you can see;
I'd think shame to stick to nursie as that shadow sticks to me!

One morning, very early, before the sun was up,
I rose and found the shining dew on every buttercup;
But my lazy little shadow, like an arrant sleepyhead,
Had stayed at home behind me, and was fast asleep in bed.


I might not remember what I had for breakfast but 'till this day I can rattle off those poems from so long ago. I remember the big blackboard where the master wrote our assignments and the window with the library books and the big desk, which was really a large table where the master sat. Every morning he went into Mrs. Fay's room to take attendance and always left work for all of us to do with one of the older children in charge. If he came back and found us working and quiet all was fine, but if he came back and found us talking and giggling all hell broke loose and so did he. He would yell and scream and run his fingers through his hair in fury. If he could pick out the culprit who started the ruckus that child received a real beating; otherwise, we all got it.

He had such a fury and if we didn't know lessons or failed to do our work he lashed out at us in a rage. I remember how he would rush out the front door of the school and across the road; break off a branch from the bushes and return to give us all a slap or two each with the springy stick. We had to put our hands out and if we pulled them away he really got angry and would give us that many more. Sometimes if only one person made him angry he sent the offending student across the road to bring in the stick to slap him. We thought if we put a horse hair across our hands it would absorb the blow from the rod.

There were some students he liked to pick on more than others, particularly this one boy, and the master really picked on him frequently. Then one day he beat the boy badly, slapping him so hard and often until the boy fell down. We were all terrified. Sadly the boy never came back to school again after that.

The Master also had his favorites. These he seemed to hardly ever punish. One thing to add here, if we were to get beaten in school and our parents found out we received an additional spanking at home. No questions asked, no explanations accepted.

Away from school the master was a totally different person. I was friends with his daughter and my parents were friends with him and his wife. She was a lovely lady and I always had fun at their house. He allowed us to play in his car and all over the house. I remember a drink his wife made with hops and water. She had it in a big glass container and it was fascinating to watch as the hops rose from the bottom then slowly sank back down again. It was a delicious tangy drink that I loved. I truly believe that the master was a good man, but he had a terrible temper and just used the only method of controlling us that he knew. I really don't believe he ever realized how wrong and emotionally damaging his way was. I believe that that was the acceptable way to correct children back then and probably what he had grown up with because my father often related the way discipline was doled out in that same school by the master in his time there.

As I stood there in the room that held so many memories, they came flooding back, things like reading "Sleeping Beauty" in Irish. How I loved that story. I love the sounds of Irish words.   Until this day I remember the poem "The Village Blacksmith," which I learned in that very room.

# THE VILLAGE BLACKSMITH
*Henry Wadsworth Longfellow 1807 - 1882*

Under a spreading chestnut tree
The village smithy stands;
The smith, a mighty man is he,
With large and sinewy hands;
And the muscles of his brawny arms
Are strong as iron bands.

His hair is crisp, and black, and long,
His face is like the tan:
His brow is wet with honest sweat,
He earns what e'er he can,
And looks the whole world in the face,
For he owes not any man.

Week in, week out, from morn till night,
You can hear his bellows blow;
You can hear him swing his heavy sledge,
With measured beat and slow,
Like a sexton ringing the village bell,
When the evening sun is low.
And children coming home from school
Look in at the open door;
They love to see the flaming forge,
And hear the bellows roar,
And catch the burning sparks that fly
Like chaff from a threshing floor.

He goes on Sunday to the church,
And sits among his boys;
He hear the parson pray and preach,
He hears his daughter's voice,
Singing in the village choir,
And it makes his heart rejoice.

It sounds to him like her mother's voice,
Singing in Paradise!

At one time we had mice in the master's room. We carried our lunches, usually butter bread, egg sandwiches, or soda bread and bottles of milk in our school bags. The mice soon discovered that there was food there and found ways to get at it. Many of us found that holes had been bitten in our school bags and bites taken from our lunches while we were doing our reading and sums. Often we could hear them rustle the wrappings on our food as we sat there but we dare not react to it for fear the master would become angry with our inattentiveness.

Every so often as we sat in class, a little mouse, fat from our lunches, would scurry across the floor, sending all of us into fits of giggles and that made the master angry.

As I walked back into the hall separating the two classrooms, my heart was filled with memories of time spent in there. Usually our coats were hung on pegs that lined either side and air flowed freely through it. But on rainy days the air was heavy as all of us children crowded into the small, narrow space to eat lunch and play. The boys sat at one end by the master's door and the girls at the other. It was crowded! And usually the older boys became rowdy and pushed and shoved and we girls were apt to really get crushed into the walls.

On a nice day in spring and summer we played outside. The boys climbed the walls surrounding our playground into the field next to the mistress end of the school. They played Gaelic football. It was rough and tumble and they played like it was the all Ireland finals. The Clancy boys, Hughie Newman, the Fays when not in school played football. Football was their lives. Hughie Newman's dad took him to lots of football games. Meanwhile the younger children played in the school yard. The girls played jump rope or catch in the school yard, but we also crossed the wall on occasion and played in the whin-covered rocks that went from the back of the school almost to the cross. It was a huge area to play hide and seek and occasionally someone hid too well and too far from the school. When all the others had gone in, that person was still hiding, proud that no one had found her. Eventually the realization came that it was very quiet when the noise of the others had quieted, and sheepishly she had to return alone to school and the giggles of the other children.

Outside the back of the school we had two toilets that were cold and drafty in winter. I remember being afraid I might fall into the stinking bottom when I lifted the lid. One winter my Aunt Helen sent me a very warm pants outfit for school. Girls didn't wear pants in Ireland back then, but that did not matter to my mother and on really cold days she made me wear it. Anyway to go to the bathroom I had to take off the jacket to take the pants down, and I'll never forget how cold and drafty that was in the dead of winter. Every so often the man came in a big smelly truck to clean out the toilets. I couldn't imagine a worse job.

In back of the school were two more small buildings on the mistress end of the school, one, the coal shed and another small shack we played in occasionally. I don't remember what it was used for but I do remember the year, about 4th or 5th grade. We were about to take our end of the year exams to pass on to the next class. Someone, Mary Ellen Brady I believe found the exam. We took it out into that little shack and were almost finished working the problems out together when we were discovered. Boy, the master was mad! He couldn't keep us all back, though that was what we feared. Instead he made up a new test and made it really difficult. Working out those problems was the only time in my life I ever cheated on a test. I guess I really learned my lesson.

Everyday someone had to go down to the well in the rocks to fetch water for the master and mistress tea for lunch. Usually it was a job done by a favored older boy. I am not quite sure but I think they boiled the water for their tea on a primus stove, a stove that burned paraffin oil and was also used as a heater. It was a metal cylinder that stood about two and a half feet high on four short legs and gave off quite a bit of heat. That was the only heat we had in the school on the cold damp days of winter.

### Students of Castletara National School 1951

*Front Row (left to right): Charlie Coyle, Tommy Lyons, John-Joe Lyons, Paddy Kelly, Hughie Newman, Paddy Ronaghan, Ben Coyle. 2nd Row: Pat Coyle, Danny Fay, Tom Boylan, Charlie Boylan, Eamonn McCormack, Seamus Hennessey, Frank Cusack, Sean Ruddan. Michael Flately. 3rd Row: Michael Brady, Annie Flately. Mary Ellen Brady, Nan Brady, Monica Argue, Betsy McCaffery, ........., Madeline Flately, Susan Maguire, Rose Newman, Anna McCormack, Peggy Coyle, Mary Byrd, Mary Coyle, Vera Chartors. 4th Row: John Pat Cahill, Francie Cahill, Pat Clancy, Brian Clancy, Kathleen Flately, Kathleen Kelly, Bridie Melican, Lylia Cahill, Anne Coyle. 5th Row: Josie Melican, Anne Fay, Maureen Smith. Maura Cahill. Rose Smith, Betty Coyle, Addie Melican.*

Occasionally a photographer came to the school and took pictures. He had a big camera mounted on a tripod with a large black cloth draped over it. He arranged all of us where he wanted us as above, and when he was satisfied with the pose he pulled the cloth over his head so that his head and the camera were completely covered. It is fun now over 50 years later to look at this old picture and see how many people I can still name. He also took individual pictures of each student. I have no idea where these photographers came from.

*My individual picture in that warm pants outfit on another visit by a photographer*

Another infrequent and much disliked visitor to the school was the dentist. I was very lucky to never have any cavities but others were not so lucky. He came early in the morning and set up in the mistress's room while all of us were in the master's. One by one he brought us in and checked our teeth. He filled cavities and when he deemed necessary pulled out teeth. With our hearts pounding we could hear screams from some of the children while in the other room. After a while his poor victims returned to the masters room crying and sometimes with a bit of blood on their lips or clothing. It all seemed so barbaric and was a really scary, traumatic day for all of us. I think that is the reason I still dislike going to the dentist.

Occasionally on the way home from school we would stop at Etna Callahan's shop. It was a small store that had bread, tea, essentials, and cookies and sweets. Etna had more foodstuffs to purchase than Miney's so occasionally I had to make a trip there to pick up some things my parents needed. Most of her supplies were in bulk and the amount needed had to be weighed out on big brass scales. Depending on the amount required she changed the round weights that went on the saucer-like part of the scale. Sometimes my mother gave me a few shillings before school to pick up things such as Bovril or Rinso or Bird's Custard on the way home. She always told me to spend a few pennies of the change on myself. There were so many good things there.

Because our families were poor, most of the time we children only had a penny or tuppensence to spend, if we were lucky. Some children bought gubstoppers for a penny apiece. Those were enormous hard round speckled balls that filled the mouth totally and lasted for hours. My mother didn't allow me to have them. She was afraid they would choke me or break my teeth. But really what I wanted were some Jacob's biscuits (cookies). My favorite was a plain biscuit covered with a hard, royal-type icing on one side. They came in chocolate or pink icing. I also loved a plain cookie covered with marshmallow and sprinkled with coconut. I remember standing with mouth watering while Etna weighed out thruppence worth of my favorite sweets (candy), licorice (all sorts) or my favorite biscuit.

After telling Etna how many pence worth I wanted she weighed them out carefully on the scales as I stood there salivating from the anticipation. Just tasting one brings me back to my childhood. My other favorite sweet from Etna's were the Cadbury chocolates, Carmelo, a delicious caramel filled chocolate or hazelnut, crunchy hazelnuts in dark luscious chocolate.

After Mass on Sundays my father stopped at Etna's to buy a copy of the *Sunday Independent* which he read from end to end. It had world and national news, but the most popular weekly newspaper in Cavan was by far the *Angelo Celt*. It gave all the county news and stories of local interest.

Entertainment, sales, deaths, etc. were listed. At a time when there were no telephones and cars were few and far between, the *Celt* was an important link to the outside, to the often isolated farms.

When it came to the house it was read from beginning to end, and when neighbors met articles and news were discussed. There were jokes and helpful hints in there, too, and recipes. Many a Christmas cake was made from a recipe from the *Celt*. Mr. MacEntee was editor of the *Celt*. He was married to our cousin Judy Cusack, and their daughter Eillish went to the convent school with me.

Along with his newspaper, my father usually picked up a pack of Woodbine cigarettes, which he smoked at that time.

The shop also stocked mineral waters (sodas) or minerals as we called them. Usually at home I drank either milk or tea, so minerals were a treat I seldom had. I could rarely afford such a luxury. These were only bought when someone had a spree or a wedding or some very special occasion. They were made in town by Cavan Mineral Works and my favorite then was orange. How I envied my cousin Tom who worked there. I envisioned him having all the minerals he wanted to drink.

In winter we children wore our Wellingtons or wellies as we called them to school and on really cold days their feet were lined with hay and we wore warm woolen socks often knitted at home. As winter cold waned and days began to grow a bit longer my mother took me in the horse and cart to town to buy a new pair of black patent leather shoes with a silvery buckle for good wear for church and special occasions. For school she purchased a pair of white canvas shoes that we called runners, not unlike today's keds. I sometimes even got a pair of sandals though that was not every year. I was a bit luckier than most children because most did not own two pairs of shoes.

With the first day of spring or warmer weather my friends and classmates shed their wellies and walked the several miles to school barefoot. My snow white runners stood out like two sore thumbs among all those bare feet. I even took some teasing from the other children for wearing them. Every year I pleaded with my mother to let me go barefoot but to no avail.

Then one year, well into summer, in a weak moment or perhaps to just shut me up she gave in. I could walk barefoot the three miles or so to school but I could NOT take my runners with me just in case I changed my mind. Change my mind of course I would not change my mind. I now had the chance to be like all the other children. I would fit in! I could not wait to get out the door that morning.

It was a beautiful sunny morning and I was delighted. Delighted that was, until I stepped on my first sharp stone. Ouch, but I was still determined to carry on and carry on I did. It was a long three miles of sharp rocks and gravel and muddy paths across fields and through weeds. Areas of soft grass occasionally brought some relief.

By the time I reached school both feet were cut, bleeding, bruised and very sore. I now had a whole day of school ahead. Even the smooth cement floors did not make them feel better. I had never taken into account the fact that the other children all went barefoot at every opportunity all year long.

Lunch time recess was torture. I passed up playing jump rope, my favorite playground activity, thinking that playing hide and seek in the rocks would be easier on my sore feet. Not so, the big rocks that always seemed so smooth had some rather sharp edges when tread upon by a bare foot, and even worse the prickly whin bushes that provided a fine cover for hiding shed their sharp thorns on the ground. Now I had thorns in my already sore feet. That was the one day that I could not wait to get back into school at the end of recess.

At the end of the day I still had to make the return walk home. I picked my way through the fields, back over gravel and stone, the only relief a brief stop in a small stream to soak my bloodied feet. I would like to say I was greeted by a sympathetic mother. No not her! She took one look at me and told me to go wash my feet. I would like to think she was fighting back tears but I am pretty sure it was a smile on the corners of her mouth. My feet were sore for days and wearing shoes hurt, however, I never asked to go without shoes again.

# Chapter 19

# Playtime

Looking back on my childhood I realize how very much fun I had at Castletara School and how blessed I really was growing up on our farm. I had freedom to wander through the fields, play with the animals, climb trees, so many things to do. I only wish my daughters and grandchildren could have the same freedom.

Because houses were too far from each other it was difficult for a young child to go unaccompanied to play with a friend. I learned to play alone and amuse myself. My dogs Tiny and, later, Cora were my constant companions and playmates.

I loved to play in the fields and even though I was often playing alone I enjoyed it. I had Tiny, a tan and white wire haired terrier. Later Cora, a beautiful Kerry blue collie, joined in our adventures. She was given to me by my cousin Tom when he and Aunt Mollie decided to return to America. I really loved her. She was so beautiful. Tiny was a cute little terrier and not only was she my companion, but she worked so hard as a farm dog, chasing rats, digging after them in their holes, sometimes coming out bloodied but always victorious. When we played together we had fun!

When the weather was nice I often took some of my dolls down the lane and across the road to the meadow and played with them in the little stream that bordered the meadow. There they swam and traveled over great seas in that stream. My imagination was very vivid; they traveled to places I heard of or read about that sounded very exotic. We had a book of food stamps left over from when food was rationed during the war and I used them as tickets to go on large boats or trains to faraway places. My boats and trains were simple pieces of wood or small logs.

The meadow always had a somewhat mystical feel for me. The only crop I recall ever growing there was hay, and it was sweet and fragrant as my father cut it with the scythe. The far end of the meadow close to the well dipped down sharply, and it was in the grass and moss on that slope that my father often encountered nests of bees. Though I don't know quite what his technique was, I remember how he rolled his sleeves down and in one careful, swift move retrieved the honeycomb brimming with sweet honey from its resting place. Distancing ourselves from where the hive had been, he gave the sweet offering to my mother and me. I salivate remembering its sweetness. Perhaps it was the sound of the corncrake in the nearby marshy boggy area, the smell of the new mown hay and the taste of the honey, or the call of a far off cuckoo, it always seemed a very peaceful place to sit and contemplate.

# CUCKOO SONG
*Katherine Tynan Hinkson 1861 - 1931*

Cuckoo, cuckoo!
In April
The cuckoo shows his bill,
With windflowers on vale and hill
O. Love!
Sweet was April, sweet was April!

Cuckoo, cuckoo!
In May his song was true,
And the world was new
For me and you.
In May
He sings all day,
All the long night that's sweet with hay.
O, Love!
Blithe was the May, blithe was the May!

Cuckoo, cuckoo!
Last June the roses grew
In many a place we knew,
I and you.
In June
He changes his tune.
A young man's fancy changes soon.
O, Love!
Fleet was June, fleet was June!

Cuckoo, cuckoo!
His notes are faint and few,
The lily is dying too,
For the rose there is rue.

In July
Away will he fly,
His notes blown back from an empty sky.
O, Love!
Sad was July, sad was July!

Cuckoo, cuckoo!
No more we listen to
The merry song we knew,
I and you.
In August
Go he must,
Love and lovers will turn to dust.
O, Love I
Cold is August, cold is August!

Cuckoo, Cuckoo

# THE CORNCRAKE

*James H. Cousins 1873 – 1956*
*Copyrighted 1932*

I heard him faintly, far away,
(Break! Break! Break! Break!)
Calling to the dawn of day,
"Break! Break!"

I heard him in the yellow morn
(Shake! Shake! Shake! Shake!)
Shouting thro' the rustling corn,
"Shake! Shake!"

I heard him near where one lay dead
(Ache! Ache!)
Crying among poppies red,
"Ache! Ache! Ache! Ache!"

And where a solemn yew-tree waves
(Wake! Wake!)
All night he shouts among the graves,
"Wake! Wake! Wake! Wake!"

On rainy days I played in the house with my dolls. Again playing school or doctor, sometimes I was the mommy taking care of my babies dressing them up, putting them to bed, sometimes the teacher teaching them their lessons.

I think this was when I began my love of sewing. I made clothes for my dolls from scrap pieces of material that my mother had around the house or that Aunt Mollie had given me, sewing them by hand since we didn't have a machine. As I got older I enjoyed sewing for myself. I don't recall where some of my dolls came from exactly. I think most of them I got for Christmas and some were sent to me by my Aunt Helen from New York. I'll never forget the Christmas I got a doll carriage from Santa. It was beautiful and shiny and new. Each Christmas I usually got a doll and games; Checkers, Snakes & Ladders and such. Usually I didn't get any new toys in between. We were too poor to afford such extravagances.

There was one exception that I'll always remember. We were in town shopping and went into Bannon's shop to buy rosary beads to send back to America with someone who was home on holiday and I saw a doll that I fell in love with.

I asked for her and of course was told no, but I insisted, cried, threw a real temper tantrum. Finally when it became evident that I didn't intend to leave without "my" doll, the only choices my poor mother and father had was to take me from the store screaming and kicking or do exactly as my daddy did and buy it for me. I guess he knew how much I really wanted it, or he just wanted me to have it. He always spoiled me! I was thrilled, she was beautiful!

My mother liked to play tricks on me and one that didn't turn out well was the day I was playing in the potato field with "the doll." When my back was turned, my mother took her and hid her in the pile of potato stalks. Unfortunately, by the time I eventually found her, the juice from the freshly cut stalks had damaged the paint on her beautiful porcelain-type face. She was flawed. I was devastated and very angry with my mother. Her beautiful face was never the same, but I still loved her.

Children always play out the things they and their family live. So did I. A favorite rainy day activity was playing milkman; empty wooden spools were my milk cans and an old box my cart. I'd map out the route to the creamery through the countryside using various dishes to represent the farm houses, a cup for Ruddens, a saucer for Hannigans and so on. All spread out on a kitchen table, my "cart" traveled from one to the next picking up the "milk cans," taking them to the creamery, and returning "home" with the cans now full of skim milk to be used for the animals. We never thought of drinking skim milk back then; it was considered to be part of the swill for the pigs.

As I said, there wasn't enough money to buy many toys, but one thing there was always money for in our house was books. My daddy was an avid reader and he fostered that love of books in me. Every week when he went into town he always came home with a new book for me. "Braer Rabbit," "Braer Fox," so many I've forgotten. But the one I remember most was "20,000 Leagues Under the Sea." I lived every moment of the adventure in my imagination. There it was, much more exciting than any movie of it ever could be, and I was right in the middle of it all.

To me books are more than pages bound together. They are living stories. I'm sorry for all the children who have movies and TV and won't ever really experience the wonder of a story unfolding slowly and vividly in their minds in a book.

I've mentioned radio and it too was a wonderful means of amusement for me. I'd listen to the news, but most of all I listened to children's shows. I loved listening to the songs.

I guess, though, my favorite song was really a lullaby my mother and father sang to me. Later I sang it to my children and grandchildren.

# Heshie Hoshey
*Unknown*

Heshie Hoshey hush a bye baby
Hush a by baby don't you cry
Heshie Hoshey hush a bye
Baby Mamma'll be home by and by
But to my surprise,
Before my two eyes
She was courting a soldier, six feet
There they were kissing
And hugging like fun
While I rocked the baby to sleep –
Singing Heshie Hoshey, etc.


The only toy I still have from my childhood is a little rubber lamb. I think at one time it may have been white or cream colored. It was just a little rubber lamb that squeaked but it was special to me. I believe it was given to me by the Breslins.

When my Aunt Mollie and Tom returned to the United States they gave me their Victrola, an old wind up record player, and some records. My dad was very proud of it. He played it often. It was fascinating how that record went around with the needle touching it and the sound came out, a bit fuzzy, but amazing! When someone came to visit he would wind up the Victrola, put on a record, and before you knew it he was dancing. Now there was just one thing about the old Victrola when he wound it the spring had a problem and he had to be very cautious as he placed the handle back in its slot or it would totally unwind and if his finger was in the way that handle would really strike a nasty blow. I was warned to never touch it on my own.

# Chapter 20

# Dancing

The great love of my life has always been dancing. I guess I inherited that from my father too. At sprees he was the first on the floor for The Stack of Barley, The Fling, The Versuvienna or Shoe the Donkey. And as often as not I was his partner. We were really good too. He could dance all night. Even after we came to America, and as he grew older, dances and weddings were all an opportunity for him to show off his form.

When I was old enough to take the bus into Cavan town, I joined a group of friends, the Flatleys, Anne and Merlyn, Vera Charters, and others on a weekly Saturday morning trip into town. On arriving at the bus station on Farnham Street, we crossed the bridge over the river to Railway Road Street to Miss Powers. We paid five pence each for our dance lesson. We were divided into small groups, each learning a different step dance depending on our level of ability. We started with the very simple single jig, performed to the tune of "Pop Goes the Weasel."

A penny for a cotton ball
One and two and three and four.
A hapney for a needle
One and two and three and four.
That's the way the money goes
One and two and three and four
And Pop goes the weasel
And down two three four five six seven.


And so on and so on. We learned our steps, one each week to be practiced and perfected by the next lesson. I never had to be forced to do that and I perfected my technique by practicing in front of the wardrobe mirror in my parent's room, the parlor. I remember when the weather was clear and warm enough we had our lessons in the back yard of the Power's home. In winter, when it rained, we were indoors in the back room and kitchen. Each dancing school, was recognized by the steps it did to each dance and Miss Powers School was widely known and respected. When I visited Miss Powers, she gave both my daughter and me a lesson and I was transported back so many years. She now, in her seventies, is as light on her feet and as graceful as she was back when I was a child, a truly talented, graceful Lady.

*Miss Powers and me during our visit to Cavan*

# Chapter 21

# Irish Weather

Growing up it seemed that we had really pretty good weather. Yes it rained frequently, but that was just a part of life. Winters were cold, but not terribly so, and our houses were very cozy. I don't remember the cold so much as I grew up. We didn't have a lot of snow and when we did everything seemed to close down. We jumped out of the path of the very few cars that ventured out. The countryside became a pristine picture. Grass crunched underfoot. The whole world sparkled like a million diamonds. Although I don't remember any really bad snow storms, my parents often talked about the blizzard when I was a baby, with snow so very deep that people didn't leave their homes for weeks.

Thunderstorms were only an occasional occurrence and severe ones were even less common. Usually a thunderstorm came at the end of a hot summer day when the air became heavy. My dad would herd us into the house and the cattle into their barns. He'd check the lightning and if it was just lightning up in the sky, high overhead he'd say, "Don't worry, it's just sheet lightning!" It wasn't the dangerous kind. But fork lightning alarmed him. This was great streaks of light that came from the sky to the earth below, violently streaking through the sky, and loud rattles of thunder crashed over the mountain and the fields. Such was the storm one night when I was at my grandfather's. It started late in the evening after all the young people had gone to the carnivals. The sky darkened. My Uncles James, John and Eugene were out for the evening, as were the Boylan boys. All of them at that time used bikes for transportation. Grandfather, Aunt Kathleen and I ran next door to the Boylan's. The storm raged for hours. It seemed to hang in the one place forever. We prayed the rosary over and over again as the impossible occurred, the storm got worse. The sky was like daylight, the thunder was like a continuous freight train racing through the Boylans house. We spent most of the night on our knees. Mrs. Boylan shook holy water throughout the house, burned palms at the door, covered mirrors, everything she could, but the storm raged on. One by one the boys came home, soaking wet from the pouring rain, each with their own stories of terror. Matt and I covered our eyes for most of the night so we couldn't see the lightning. I have never experienced a worse storm since then. What I remember most was the next day, a beautiful crystal clear day, betraying the terror and fury of the previous night.

# Chapter 22

# Remedies

In Ireland in the 1950s we seldom went to the doctor. If the doctor was summoned it usually meant that the person was very sick and the priest would probably also be summoned. For most ailments there were local tried and true remedies.

Whiskey, or the Irish word Uisgebeatha, water of life, blessed water, was thought to slow the aging process, help with digestion, was considered a tonic to strengthen the weak, and was frequently used to soothe a baby's teething pain. It helped encourage sleep. My mother said, "A wee bit of the grog was helpful for many ailments," Irish whiskey punch was used as a nightcap and was used to treat a bad cold or the flu.

## IRISH WHISKEY PUNCH

1½ teaspoons brown sugar
or white sugar if no brown available
boiling water
1 shot Irish whiskey
slice lemon
cloves (optional)

Dissolve sugar in a little boiling water in a heated mug. Add lemon and whiskey and then fill with more boiling water. A couple of cloves may be added if desired.

This was my mother's favorite cure for the flu. She claimed it would make you sweat the flu out of your system. Bundled up in warm flannel pajamas under heavy wool blankets you certainly would sweat!

Stout, most often called Guinness, was thought to strengthen a person recovering from illness. It was also recommended for new nursing mothers because it enriched the mother's milk. I am also sure it made for very peaceful babies.

Egg Flip was often used to add extra nourishment for the underweight or the frail or to strengthen children. Because I was a skinny little girl my mother very often gave me an egg flip. My father was troubled with really bad stomach ulcers my mother insisted that he have an egg flip every day. She felt that it was very soothing and healing for his stomach.

# EGG FLIP

¾ cup milk (scalded)
We had fresh cow's milk of course
1 egg yolk
1 teaspoon. sugar
1 shot whiskey
grated nutmeg

Whip egg yolk and sugar together, add whiskey and gently whisk milk into this mixture. Add grated nutmeg and serve in heated mug. To heat mug, let hot water sit in the mug while you prepare the flip.

My mother made this same concoction without the whiskey, of course, for me as a child as a tonic, though I really don't know why because she never hesitated to give me whiskey punch.

For a sore throat, black currant syrup was soothing but not always available.

# BLACK CURRANT SYRUP

1 pound black currants
½ cup water
1 egg white beaten
sugar to liking
Irish whiskey

Crush black currants. Add water; simmer until juice is released from the fruit. Measure the juice and discard fruit. Whisking frequently, add a beaten egg white to the juice in the pan, bring to boil. Remove the scum. Add about 1/4 cup sugar for each ½ cup of juice. When sugar is dissolved, add a teaspoon of whiskey for each ½ cup of juice.

This we seldom had because we only had currants in the summer.

Honey mixed with a little whiskey was also supposed to be good for a sore throat. That was my mother's favorite and was available year round.

Buttermilk was another cure to help relieve a hangover. Thankfully a good big glass of buttermilk was always readily available.

I remember at some point my mother boiled onions in milk and then drank the onion milk to help her sleep. This always sounded awful to me but she drank it religiously.

## BOILED ONIONS

6 medium onions – skinned and cut up
scalded milk to cover
salt to taste

Put onions in saucepan. Add milk to cover and add salt. Simmer gently until tender, about 45 minutes to 1 hour. Serve with a pat of butter and pepper.

Goose drippings were used frequently for sprains. The drippings were stored in a jar and the reserved goose drippings were rubbed into the affected area.

Nettle Soup was considered to be very healthy for the complexion. It was awful stuff, but the price of beauty was worth it. Collecting the nettles and preparing them was the most hazardous part of making this soup. Wash nettles thoroughly several times wearing gloves to avoid nettles stings.

# NETTLE SOUP

Put nettles in a sauce pan, cover with boiling water, and add a little salt. Simmer gently about 1/2 hour. Drain reserving the liquid. If you have turkeys, serve cooked nettles to the them, it was considered nutritious for them.

Flaxseed boiled with water was used for croup or any cough. What an awful taste. I got better just to avoid having any more of it.

## SENA TEA
*widely used as a laxative.*

sena tea
sena pods
water to cover

On Thursday night or Friday morning my mother would soak sena pods in lots of water, and then Friday night before bed I was given a shot glass of the horrid liquid followed by a teaspoon or two of sugar. I'm reminded of the song, "A Spoonful of Sugar Makes the Medicine Go Down." Not in that case! By Saturday morning it had worked and I got my weekly cleaning out. What a laxative!

# COD LIVER OIL

Cod liver oil was considered healthy to take as extra nourishment. As I said, as a child I was very slender and my mother thought I looked under nourished, so there was always a bottle of cod liver oil around. I got so much of it I grew to like it, so when my mother looked for the bottle to give to the chickens, it was always empty. It was good for chickens too! I often sneaked into the closet and stole it and drank it all. Just thinking about it now makes me gag.

I recall my father slapping wet mud on me when I got bee or wasp stings. Mustard poultice was also used to treat coughs and for pneumonia and bronchitis.

## MUSTARD POULTICE

Mix up a good big batch of Coleman's mustard, slather it onto brown paper and place the paper mustard side against the chest. Tape in place and put a warm sweater over that to keep the heat in. That burned!!! One thing, it was necessary to check frequently to be sure that the skin was not blistering. Combine that with the previously mentioned whiskey punch and the cough was history!

## EPSON SALTS

Epson salts melted in warm water were used to soak sprains and arthritic joints.

At one time my father developed a whittelo on his thumb. He got a cut on his thumb when he went to help kill a pig at a neighbor's farm. He claimed he got some blood from the pig into the cut and that the mixture of the pig's blood with his started the whittelo, a sore that grew and grew and filled with pus. It was extremely painful. It had to be lanced by the doctor and yet wouldn't heal. Finally Dr. Lorrigan had done all he could and nothing worked. My father went to a lady who had the cure of the whittelo. I believe her name was Reilly from Ballyhaise. She cooked up a secret mixture of herbs and plants and applied it to the infected thumb while she prayed over it. I believe he returned for several more treatments. For the first time in months he was able to sleep after the first treatment. The pain had been so bad. He was left with a nubby thumb, but that lady sure did cure it.

Cures like that were common in Ireland. I know there was a cure for rheumatism and other severe ailments. All involved plants and prayers or invocations to go with them. Whatever was in the poultices, as they called them, they worked! Cures were secret and were handed down from one person to another. How valuable it could be if we could find what it was in those plants that cured these illnesses. I wonder if they still have anyone who performs these cures today.

Uncle Ned Clarke had the cure for sprains, but unfortunately he neglected to give it to anyone when he died and so took it to the grave with him.

What was considered to be the true cure for shingles was performed by someone in Belturbet and reportedly it worked very well.

People claimed that ferret's milk was given for whooping cough, supposedly. I never saw a ferret when I was growing up and when I got the whooping cough there was no ferret's milk for me. I'm not too sure how plentiful ferrets were or how easy it would be to extract their milk. I know I would not want to be the one milking that little critter.

I remember a time when for whatever reason my dad went on a kick where he was looking for wells. I don't think it was because he wanted to dig another well, but rather he wanted to see if he had the "gift" of finding water underground. Sean Boylan had the "gift" so my father, not to be outdone by anyone, had to try his hand at it. I recall my father taking a sally limb shaped like a "Y," holding the top ends in each hand with the bottom straight out, walking along slowly, when all at once, as if pulled down with an invisible force the end would bend toward the ground, indicating the spot where an underground well existed. While he was on this kick Kathleen Reilly happened to come by and she decided to try it. Frustrated, she eventually gave up. My mother tried it. I tried it. My Father claimed that he had never seen any woman ever having the "gift". Since I never saw anyone actually dig a well where they claimed the stick indicated I'm not so sure that it really worked.

There were holy wells scattered throughout the area that were named for saints, and the people believed that the water from these wells had curative powers for various diseases. Depending on what the disease was the person would collect water from the well of a particular saint. I believe you had to rub the water on the affected area and pray to that saint.

# Chapter 23

# Deaths

When someone died certain neighbors were called on to help lay out the corpse. Mrs. Mooney and my Aunt Mollie and others did this. They washed the body, closed the eyes and dressed it in the dark brown robe that was the customary apparel for the deceased. They placed the body in their bed, hands clasped in prayer and intertwined with the person's rosary beads. Once this was done the family and neighbors took turns sitting up with the corpse. In the evenings everyone from miles around came to share in the wake. Through the night they talked, shared food and drink and took turns sitting with the corpse, praying. I remember Hugh Reilly's wake; my mother made me touch his hands and say a prayer for his soul. I will never forget how cold and hard his hands were, not at all the warm gentle hands they had been in life. Hugh was Ted's father and I liked him almost as much as I did Ted. He had always seemed older and one time when I was quite little I told my mother that "he was the best old woman in the country."

The morning after a wake the body was placed in a plain wood coffin which was hoisted onto the shoulders of six strong men and carried to the church, sometimes miles away. I don't know who the corpse was but I remember a funeral proceeding around the mountain road. The men carrying the coffin were followed by the black-clad, tearful family and friends. After a death the spouse wore black for a year. Other members of the family wore black arm bands or a black cloth diamond on their coat for a year after the death to let the world know they were in mourning. For a period of time after the death mourners did not participate in any fun activities out of respect for the dead. Included in this was refraining from sending Christmas cards for the Christmas following the death. A letter to loved ones far away would not be considered disrespectful.

After the corpse was removed from the home, the room where the body had been laid out had to be cleaned thoroughly from top to bottom. Bed linens were washed, curtains were changed, and windows were opened to air out the room.

At that time the Catholic Church did not allow anyone who committed suicide to be buried in consecrated ground. There was a man, though I do not remember who he was, who committed suicide. I just remember the neighbors talking about it. He lived near Etna's shop and not only could he not be buried in the consecrated part of the cemetery but his remains could not be carried past the chapel to the graveyard about a quarter mile away. Instead he had to be brought many miles to the Cootehill Road, to the Corratubber pass, and on to the old road around the mountain to be buried in the unconsecrated section of the graveyard without a burial Mass. What a journey and how very sad!!

As I sit here telling about funerals I'm reminded of the story about the old man lying in bed dying. He smelled beef and cabbage cooking in the kitchen. "Mary," he said in a feeble voice, "could I please have a bit of that beef and cabbage your cooking in the kitchen?" "Ah shur, John, I'm sorry but I can't give ya any of that. I'm savin it for the wake" she said firmly.


Then there was the story my father told of the funeral procession for a man who had died from poisoning. He was normal when put in the casket, but as the men carried his casket to the church his body had become so swollen from the accumulating gases that it exploded, bursting the simple wooden box apart, spewing body parts all over the men and everything and everybody around. The pall bearers and all the mourners ran for their lives in terror. No one ever knew what became of the corpse.

# Chapter 24

# Special Occasions

There were many special times to remember as I was growing up. Although we had very little, my mother always made my birthday very special. One of my most memorable birthdays was the year my mother made little luscious meringues for me and had them all ready when I came home from school. They were crisp and sweet and lighter than air. I know now how much work it took for her to beat the egg whites by hand until they were stiff and then to bake those finicky little morsels on the open fire. Needless to say with all else she had to do and the work involve in making them they were a seldom made and much loved treat.

## MERINGUES

The basic rules for meringue making
Use fine castor sugar.
Use 1 part regular sugar to 3 parts superfine sugar.
Grease will spoil meringues,
make sure all utensils including bowl are free of grease.
Separate the whites from the yolks the night before, and
leave the whites, uncovered, in a bowl.
This makes for easier beating.

## MERINGUE RECIPE:

3 oz superfine sugar

1 oz regular sugar

2 egg whites

whipped cream

Mix the sugars. Beat the two egg whites to stiff dry peaks. Add half the sugar gradually, beating well after each addition. Fold in the remainder of the sugar all at once, very gently.

Drop by heaping tablespoon on to a cookie sheet covered with wax paper, or on to a very slightly greased baking sheet. Bake for 1 hour at 250°. Turn oven off. Leave in oven to dry out completely.

Another of my favorite birthday treats was Swiss Roll. Butter sponge is needed to make Swiss Roll.

## BUTTER SPONGE

4 oz butter or margarine

1/3 cup sugar

1 teaspoon grated lemon rind

2 eggs

I tablespoon milk

2/3 cup flour

1 teaspoon baking powder

Beat the butter until light. Add the sugar gradually and beat until fluffy. Add the lemon rind, well-beaten eggs and milk, the flour sifted with the baking powder. Turn into a well greased tin and bake for 45 minutes at 350°.

## SWISS ROLL

Follow sponge recipe. When mixed turn onto well greased baking sheet. Bake at 450 for 15 minutes.

While baking dredge a cotton cloth with powdered sugar. When baked turn cake onto prepared cloth. Snip off crisp edges, quickly spread with strawberry or raspberry jam and roll up quickly. Cool and dredge with additional powdered sugar.

This sponge can also be filled with other fillings. I like Lemon.

# LEMON FILLING

2 eggs

8 oz confectioners' sugar

juice of 2 lemons

2 oz butter

Beat the eggs; add sugar, lemon juice and butter. Place the bowl in a saucepan of hot water and stir over low heat until mixture is smooth and thick. Allow to cool before used to fill sponge.

Note: This filling can be used to fill your favorite layer cake.

In summer my mother liked to fill this sponge roll with fresh whipped cream and sliced strawberries. That was a really special treat.

# ST PATRICK'S DAY

Saint Patrick's Day was and still is a holy day in Ireland, and as I walked the fields my feet pass over a carpet of shamrocks, tiny three-leaf shamrocks. I grew up knowing that here in Ireland they were the most special of all plants. As a child, a few weeks before St. Patrick's Day my mother would take me out to the fields and look for the most perfect sprigs of shamrock to send to our family in the States. We went into town, purchased St. Patrick day badges, gold harps with white, yellow and green ribbons to include in the envelope with the shamrocks, all to be worn proudly by our families on St. Patrick's Day. As I look at all these shamrocks I'm reminded of the songs we learned from Mrs. Fay in school.

## THE DEAR LITTLE SHAMROCK
*Traditional Irish*

There's a dear little plant that grows in our isle
'Twas St. Patrick himself sure that set it;
And the sun on his labour with pleasure did smile,
And with dew from his eyes often wet it.
It shines through the bog, thro' the brake,thro' the mireland,

And he called it the dear little Shamrock of Ireland.
The dear little Shamrock, the dear little Shamrock,
The dear, little, sweet, little Shamrock of Ireland.
That dear little plant still grows in our land,
Fresh and fair as the daughters of Erin,

Whose smiles can bewitch and whose eyes can command,
In each climate they ever appear in,
For they shine thro' the bog, thro' the brake and the mireland,

Just like their own dear little shamrock of Ireland.
The dear little Shamrock, the dear little shamrock,
The dear little, sweet, little Shamrock of Ireland.

That dear little plant that springs from our soil, When its little three leaves are extended, Denotes from the stalk we together should toil, And ourselves by ourselves be befriended,
And still thro' the bog, thro' the brake and the mireland,

From one root should branch, like the Shamrock of Ireland,
The dear little Shamrock, the dear little Shamrock,
The dear, little, sweet, little Shamrock of Ireland.
Probably the most venerated plant in the whole world it is a symbol of Christianity to an entire nation.


Parades and celebrations were not a part of my early St. Patrick's Days. It was a holy day, the most holy of holy days in Ireland.


# HAIL, GLORIOUS SAINT PATRICK
*Sister Agnes, of the Convent of Charleville, Co. Cork*
*~1853*

Hail, glorious Saint Patrick, dear saint of our isle,
On us thy poor children bestow a sweet smile;
And now thou art high in the mansions above, On Erin's green valleys look down in thy love. On Erin's green valleys,
On Erin's green valleys,
On Erin's green valleys,

Look down in thy love.
Hail, glorious Saint Patrick, thy words were once strong,
Against Satan's wiles and an infidel throng;
Not less is thy might where in heaved thou art--
Oh, come to our aid, in our battles take part.
Oh, come to our aid,
Oh, come to our aid,
Oh, come to our aid,
In our battles take part.
Ever bless and defend the dear land of our birth
where shamrock still blooms as when thou wert on earth;
Our hearts shall still burn where so ever we roam
For God and Saint Patrick, And our native home,
For God and Saint Patrick,
For God and Saint Patrick,
For God and Saint Patrick,
And our native home.

There is a poem that tells the story of Patrick as he began his conversion of Ireland, at Easter lighting the Paschal fire before the king lit his fire in pagan ritual on the hill of Tara. Since the high king should be the first to light a fire on that night this was considered to be a very defiant act.

## THE PASCHAL FIRE OF PATRICK
*Denis Florence McCarthy 1817 - 1882*

On Tara's Hill the daylight dies,
On Tara's plain, 'tis dead,
'till Baal's unkindled fires shall rise,
No fire must flame instead.
'Tis thus the King commanding speaks,
Commands and speaks in vain,
For lo a fire defiant breaks, From out the woods of Slane.
For there in prayer is Patrick bent,

With Christ his soul is knit;
And there before his simple tent,
The Paschal Fire is lit.
"What means this flame that through the night,
Illumines all the vale?
What rebel hand a fire dare light,
Before the fires of Baal?"
O King! when Baal's dark reign is o'er,
When thou thyself are gone,
This fire will light the Irish shore,
And lead its people on.
Will lead them on full march
Through which they're doomed to go,
Like that which led the Israelite,
From bondage and from woe.
This fire, this sacred fire of God,
Young hearts shall bear a far,
to lands no human foot hath trod,
Beneath the Western Star.
To lands where Faith's bright flag unfurl'd,
By those who here have knelt,
Shall give unto a newer world,
The sceptre of the Celt.


Early on St. Patrick's morning as the grass crunched beneath our feet, we ventured out to the fields to pick a nice little bunch of shamrocks for ourselves to wear to Mass and throughout the day. They were pinned to our coats along with one of those harp badges. We wore them very proudly! After dinner we went visiting family and friends. It was just like a Sunday.

Not long before we left Ireland, Cavan had its first St. Patrick's Day parade with several local merchants participating, many depicting the themes of various Irish songs. My father dressed up in his working clothes and boots, harnessed the horse and cart, put turf in the cart along with his turf-making tools. Off he went to town. He entered the parade as "The Turfman from Ardee."

# TURFMAN FROM ARDEE
*Patrick Akins - Traditional*

For sake of health I took a walk last week at early dawn
I met a jolly turfman as I slowly walked along
The greatest conversation passed between himself and me
And soon I got acquainted with the turfman from Ardee.

II
We chatted very freely as we jogged along the road
He said my ass is tired and I'd like to sell his load
For I got no refreshments since I left home you see
And I am wearied out with traveling
said the turfman from Ardee.

III
Your cart is wracked and worn friend your ass is very old
It must be twenty summers since that animal was foaled
Yoked to a cart where I was born, September 'forty three
And carried for the midwife says the turfman from Ardee.
I often do abuse my ass with this old hazel rod
But never yet did I permit poor Jack to go unshod
The harness now upon his back was made by John McGee
And he's dead this four and forty years says,
the turfman from Ardee.

IV
I own my cart now, has been made out of the best of wood
I do believe it was in use the time of Noah's flood

lts axel never wanted grease say one year out of three
It's a real old Carrick axel, said the turfman from Ardee.
We talked about our country and how we were oppressed
The men we sent to parliament has got our wrongs addressed
I have no faith in members now or nothing else you see
But led by blumin' hum-bugs,
said the turfman from Ardee.

V

Just then a female voice called out, which I knew very well
Politely asking this old man the load of turf to sell
I shook that stately hand of his and bowed respectfully
In hope to meet some future day
the turfman from Ardee.

# WEDDINGS

Around Fairtown weddings didn't happen very often, but when they did they were a lot of fun and caused a great deal of excitement. For some reason they seemed to always take place on a Tuesday morning. The bride and groom went to church along with the groomsman and bridesmaid and some close family and friends. While a number of friends and neighbors might go to the church, usually most neighbors did not because they were busy with their farm chores. Usually a small breakfast or luncheon followed for the wedding party in the Farmhand Hotel or some other restaurant or pub in town.

A honeymoon was not a part of life back then for poor country folk; instead the wedding night the bride and groom hosted a spree-type party in their home. As with sprees all the neighbors came, some carrying musical instruments, accordions, flutes and violins, to help them celebrate their union. Soon the party was in full swing. The lively Irish dance music poured from the thatched cabin while the assembled revelers danced and sang the happiest of their Irish songs.

## FATHER O'FLYNN

*Alfred Perceval Graves 1846 - 1931*

Of Priests we can offer a charmin' variety,
Far renowned for larnin' and piety;
Still, I'd advance ye widout impropriety,
Father O'Flynn as the flower of them *all*.

### Chorus
Here's a health to you, Father O'Flynn,
*Slainte,* and *slainte,* and *slainte* agin;
Powerfullest preacher, and
Tinderest teacher, and
Kindliest creature in auld Donegal.

Don't talk of your Provost and Fellows of Trinity,
Famous for ever at Greek and Latinity,
Dad and the divels and all at Divinity,
Father O'Flynn 'd make hares of them all.
Come, I vinture to give you my word,
N ever the likes of his logic was heard,
Down from Mythology
Into Thayology,
Troth! and Conchology
if he'd the call

### Chorus

Och! Father O'Flynn you've
the wonderful way wid you,
All auld sinners are wishful to pray wid you,
All the young childer are wild for to play wid you,
You've such a way wid you, Father avick!
Still for all you've so gentle a *soul,*
Gad, you've your flock in the grandest control;
Checking the crazy ones,
Coaxin' onaisy ones,
Liftin' the lazy ones on wid the stick.

**Chorus**

# THE HACKLER FROM GROUSE HALL
*Traditional Irish*

I am a rovin' hackler lad that loves the shamrock shore,
My name is Pat Mc Donnell and my age is eighty four
Belov'd and well respected
by my neighbours·one and all,
On SaintPatrick's Day I loved to stray
round Lavey and Grouse Hall

When I was young I danced and sung
and drank good whiskey too,
Each shebeen shop that sold a drop
of the real old mountain dew
With the poteen still on every hill the peelers had no call
Round sweet Stradone I am well known
round Lavey and Grouse Hall.

I rambled round from town to town
for hackling was my trade
None can deny I think that I an honest living made
Where'ere I'd stay by night or day
the youth would always call
To have some crack with Paddy Jack
the Hackler from Grouse Hall.
I think it strange how times have changed

so very much of late
Coercion now is all the row and Peelers on their bate
To take a glass is now alas the greatest crime of all
Since Balfour placed that hungry beast
the Sergeant of Grouse Hall.

The busy tool of Castle rule he travels night and day
He'll seize a goat just by the throat for want of better prey
The nasty skunk he'll swear you're drunk
tho' you took none at all
There is no peace about the place
since he came to Grouse Hall.
'Twas on pretence of this offence

he dragged me off to jail
Alone to dwell in a cold cell
my fine for to bewail;
My hoary head on a plank bed
such wrongs for vengeance call
He'll rue the day he dragged away
the Hackler from Grouse Hall.

He haunts the League, just like a plague,
and shame for to relate
The Priest can't be on Sunday
free the Mass to celebrate;
It's there he'll kneel encased in steel
prepared on duty's call
For to assail and drag to jail
our clergy from Grouse Hall.

Down into hell he'd run pelmell
to hunt for poteen there
And won't be loth to swear an
oath 'twas found in Killinkere.

# COME BACK PADDY REILLY

*Percy French 1854 - 1920*

The Garden of Eden has vanished they say,
But I know the lie of it still;
Just turn to the left at the bridge of Finea,
And stop when half way to Cootehill,
'Tis there I will find it I know sure enough,
When fortune has come to my call.
Oh, the grass it is green around Ballyjamesduff,
And the blue sky it over it all!
And  tones that are tender, and tones that are gruff
Are whispering over the sea.
"Come back, Paddy Reilly, to Ballyjamesduff,
Come home, Paddy Reilly to me."

My mother once told me that when I was born
The day that I first saw the light,
I looked down the street on that very first morn,
And gave a great crow of delight.
Now most new born babies appear in a huff,
And start with a sorrowful squall;
But I know I was born in Ballyjamesduff,
And that's why I smiled on them all.
The baby's a man now, he's toilworn and tough,
Still, whispers come over' the sea,
"Come back, Paddy Reilly, to me."

The night that we danced by the light of the moon
Wid Phil to the fore wid his flute,
When Phil threw his lips over "Come again soon,"
He'd dance the foot out o' her boot!
The day that I took long Magee. By the scruff,
For slanderin' Rosie Kilrain;
Then marchin' him straight out of Ballyjamesduff,
Assisted him into a drain.
Oh, sweet are me dreams, as the dudeen I puff,
Of whisperings over the sea,

313

"Come back, Paddy Reilly, to Ballyjamesduff,
Come home Paddy Reilly, to me."

# OLD SKIBBEREEN

*Patrick Carpenter - Traditional Irish Song*

*This ballad was written after the Irish Famine, when many
people were forced by starvation to emigrate to the
U.S.A due to blight in the potato crop.*

Oh father dear I often hear you speak of Erin's Isle.
Her lofty scenes, her valleys green,
her mountains rude and wild.
They say it is a lovely land
where in a prince might dwell.
Oh why did you abandon it the reason to me tell.

Oh, son I loved my native land with energy and pride
Till a blight came o'er my crops, my sheep, my cattle died
My rent and taxes were to pay, I could not them redeem
And that's the cruel reason why I left old Skibbereen.

Oh, well do I remember the bleak December day
The landlord and the sheriff came to drive us all away
They set my roof on fire with cursed English spleen
And that's the another reason why I left old Skibbereen.

It's well I do remember the year of forty-eight
When we arose with Erin's boys to fight against our fate
I was hunted through the mountains
as a traitor to the Queen
And that's another reason that I left Old Skibbereen

Your mother, too, God rest her soul,
fell on the snowy ground
She fainted in her anguish, seeing the desolation round
She never rose, but went away
from life to death's long dream

And found a quiet grave, my boy, in lovely Skibbereen.

And you were only two years old
and feeble was your frame
I could not leave you with my friends,
you bore your father's name
I wrapt you in my cotamore
at the dead of night unseen
I heaved a sigh and bade good-bye,
to dear old Skibbereen.

Oh, father dear, the day may come
when in answer to the call
Each Irishman, with feeling stern,
will rally one and all
I'll be the man to lead the van
beneath the flag of green
When loud and high we'll raise
the cry "Remember Skibbereen".

## DOWN BY THE GLENSIDE
*Peadar Kearney,18 1942*
*Author of the National Anthem*

'Twas down by the Glenside
I met an old woman
A plucking young netties
Nor saw I was coming,
I listened awhile to
The song she was humming.
Glory-O, Glory-O,
To the bold Fenian Men.

'Tis sixteen long years
Since I saw the moon beaming
On brave manly forms
And their eyes with heart gleaming
I see them all now

Sure in all my day-dreaming
Glory-O, Glory-O,
To the bold Fenian Men.

Some died on the hill-side
Some died with a stranger
And wise men have judged
That their cause was a failure
They fought for old Ireland
And they never feared danger
Glory-O, Glory-O,
To the bold Fenian Men

I passed on my way
Thanks to God that I met her
Be life long or short
Sure I'll never forget her
There may have been brave men
But they'll never be better
Glory-O, Glory-O,
To the bold Fenian Men.


# PHIL THE FLUTER'S BALL
*Percy French 1854 - 1920*


Have you heard of Phil the Fluter
Who would never pay the rent?
Whenever he was down and out
Without a single cent.
He would circulate a notice
To his neighbours one and all.
As to how he'd like their company
That evening at the ball.
And when writin' out he was careful
To suggest to them
That if they found a hat of his
Convenient to the door.
The more they put in.

Whenever he requested them,
The better would the music be
For battering the floor.

**Chorus**
With the toot of the flute
And the twiddle of the fiddle. oh !
Hopping in the middle
Like a herrin' on the griddle. oh !
Up. down. hands aroun'
Crossin' to the wall.
So come and join the gaiety
At Phil the Fluter's Ball.

There was Misther Denis Dogherty.
Who kep' 'The Runnin' Dog":
There was little crooked Paddy.
From the Tiraloughett bog:
There was boys from every barony.
And girls from ev'ry 'art'
And the beautiful Miss Bradys.
In a private ass an' cart.
And along with them came
Bouncing Mrs. Cafferty.
Little Mickey Mulligan
Was also to the fore.
Rose. Suzanne and
Margaret O'Rafferty.
The flower of Ardmagullion
And the pride of Pethravore.

**Chorus**

First little Mickey Mulligan
Got up to show them how.
And then the widow Cafferty
Steps out and makes her bow.
"I could dance you off your legs," sez she.

"As sure as you were born.
If you'll only make the piper play
The hare is in the corn."
So Phil plays up to
The best of his ability.
The lady and the gentleman,
Begin to do their share:
While young Mick was
A'prancing with agility.
Decrepit Mrs Cafferty was
Leppin' like a hare.

**Chorus**

Then Phil the Fluter tipped a wink
To little crooked Pat.
"I think it s nearly time," sez he,
"For passin' round the hat."
So Paddy did the necessary
Looking mighty cute,
Sez "Ye've got to pay the piper
When he toothers on the flute."
Then all joined in
With the greatest joviality
Covering the Buckle and
The Shuffle and the Trent.
Jigs were danced
Of the very finest quality,
The widow found a husband
And the Fluter found the rent.

**Chorus**

# MY CAVAN GIRL
*Written by Thom Moore*

As I walk the road from Killeshandra,
weary I sit down:
For it's twelve long miles around the lake
to get to Cavan Town.
Though Oughter and the road I go
once seemed beyond compare,
now I curse the time it takes to reach
my Cavan girl so fair.

Now autumn shades are on the leaves,
the trees will soon be bare:
Each red-gold leaf around me seems
the colour of her hair.
My gaze retreats, to find my feet,
and once again I sigh,
for the broken pools of sky remind
the colour of her eyes.

At the Cavan cross each Sunday morning,
there she can be found;
and she seems to have the eye
of every boy in Cavan Town.
If my luck will hold, I'll have the golden
summer of her smile,
and, to break the hearts of Cavan men,
she'll talk to me awhile.

So Sunday evening finds me, homeward,
Killeshandra bound,
to work the week till I return and
court in Cavan Town:
When asked if she would be my wife,
At least she'd not say no;
So next Sunday morning, rouse myself,
and back to her I'll go

As I walk the road from Killeshandra,
weary I sit down:
For it's twelve long miles around the lake
to get to Cavan Town.
Though Oughter and the road I go
once seemed beyond compare,
now I curse the time it takes to reach
my Cavan girl so fair.

# VAN DIEME'S LAND

*Adam Clayton – Laurence Mullen*

Come all you gallant poachers that ramble void of care
That walk out on a moon-light night
with your dog and gun and snare.
The hare and lofty pheasant you have at your command.
Not thinking of your last career
up-on Van Diemen's Land.

Poor Thomas Brown from Nenagh town,
Jack Murphy and poor Joe
Were three determined poachers
as the county well does know
By the keepers of the land, my boys,
one night they were trepanned
And for fourteen years transported
unto Van Diemen's Land.

The first day that we landed upon that fatal shore
The planters came around us there might be twenty score.
They ranked us off like horses and they sold us out of hand
And they yoked us to the plough, brave boys,
to plough Van Diemen's Land.

The cottages we live in are built with sods of clay
We have rotten straw for bedding but we dare not say nay.
Our cots we fence with firing and slumber when we can
To keep the wolves and tigers from us
in Van Diemen's Land.

320

Oft times when I do slumber I have a pleasant dream
With my sweet girl sitting near me
close by a purling stream
I am roaming through old Ireland
with my true love by the hand
But awaken broken-hearted
upon Van Diemen's Land.

God bless our wives and families,
likewise that happy shore
That isle of sweet contentment which
we shall ne'er see more
As for the wretched families see them we seldom can
There are twenty men for one woman
in Van Diemen's Land.

There was a girl from Nenagh town,
Peg Brophy was her name,
For fourteen years transported was,
we all well knew the same
But our planter bought her freedom
and married her out of hand
And she gives to us good usage
upon Van Diemen's Land.

But fourteen years is a long time, that is our fatal doom
For nothing else but poaching for that is all we done
You would leave off both
dog and gun and poaching every man
If you but knew the hardship that's
in Van Diemen's Land.

Oh, if I had a thousand pounds all laid out in my hand
I'd give it all for liberty if that I could command,
Again to Ireland I'd return and be a happy man
And bid adieu to poaching
and to Van Diemen's Land.

For nothing else but poaching for that is all we done
You would leave off both dog

and gun and poaching every man
If you but knew the hardship that's
in Van Diemen's Land.

Oh, if I had a thousand pounds all laid out in my hand
I'd give it all for liberty if that I could command,
Again to Ireland I'd return and be a happy man
And bid adieu to poaching
and to Van Diemen's Land.

The stout for the men and port wine for the ladies flowed freely. Lots of food including tomatoes, sliced ham, pan loaves of bread and all kinds of salads was laden on the kitchen table. The biggest attraction was the beautiful wedding cake, usually baked months earlier by the bride and her mother. This cake was the traditional Irish fruitcake, the same recipe as a Christmas cake with a layer of marzipan under the crunchy snow white royal icing. The cake was decorated with flowers made from the icing; tiny, shiny, silver balls were arranged like necklaces around the cake. Traditional symbols of good luck, tiny silver high heel shoes, silver horseshoes and silver leaves embellished the top.

The young ladies in attendance took a small piece of the wedding cake to place under their pillow that night, hopefully to dream of the man that they themselves would marry some day. After all had enjoyed a piece of the delicious cake, it was carefully put aside to have small pieces cut from it the next day to be mailed to members of the couple's families in America and other countries. Not doing so would be a very big disappointment for those awaiting the piece of cake which would allow them to participate in just a small way in the festivities. Usually, at some point during the night, some of the young men from the area who were not at the party arrived dressed up in crazy clothes, stuffed with straw; hence they were called straw boys. Dressed in this manner they knocked on the door, interrupting the party. Of course, since this was expected, the groom was prepared to pay them off with enough money to buy them stout so they could celebrate the marriage too, upon which time the party resumed. The straw boys proceeded to town to toast the happy couple with a few pints.

The wedding that I remember most was Nell and Ted Reilly. I really enjoyed it! I still have a little silver shoe from their cake. Ted and Nell were two of my favorite people, sweet and gentle. Ted was always especially kind to me. One time when it looked like I was going to get a really good spanking he happened to come by and talked to my dad, calming him down and saving me. He and Nell had two daughters, and when I came to America I gave them my dolls to play with.

*Ted Reilly on their street*

*Nell with her daughters*

*Castletara Chapel*

*Ted and Nell Reilly's wedding*
*Best man Sean Boylan and bridesmaid Nell's sister Kathleen*

# MIDNIGHT MASS

For me Midnight Mass at Christmas was always very special. Having spent the day in Cavan town we arrived home, Santa came, and my mother put a beef roast, a rare treat, bought earlier it the butchers, in the pot to cook for hours. She then made for me, by hand, an outfit to wear to midnight Mass. I remember one year in particular when she made a plaid pleated skirt to wear with the new red sweater we had bought earlier in Providers. Just buying something new to wear was a very rare extravagance that we could hardly afford.

Late in the evening we began to prepare to go to Castletara. My parents dressed in their Sunday best and I in my new skirt and sweater. Pile some more turf on the fire; check on the roast as it hung low from the crook, oh the aroma! One last look around and we were out the door into the crisp, frosty night. We brought our collars and scarves closer around us. Daddy would walk with us, no bike.

We met up with the Ruddens at the foot of our lane. The evening was cold but there was no need for a flashlight, the full moon so bright that we could see everything around us bathed in silver. The frost on the grass mirrored the stars twinkling in the winter sky. It was magic! As we walked along we greeted and were greeted by the cheery voices of our neighbors, "Happy Christmas," as they joined us, shadows walking in the moonlight. We children excitedly talked about Santa as we skipped and played along ahead of the adults. Eventually we reaching the Chapel, so welcoming in the moonlight, lanterns lit, and candles, too, with light streaming from its windows. Now silent we all went in to pray. While most took their accustomed seats some of us went upstairs to the gallery to sing all those beautiful Christmas songs we had been practicing so hard with Mrs. Melligan. Christmas Eve Mass was always so special and I will never forget singing Silent Night in that little lantern lit church. The unheated church sent shivers up our spines but at the same time felt cozy and peaceful.

One year Father Hunt, not liking having to be out at midnight started his sermon by announcing "This is a cod (joke). 'Tis at home in our beds we all should be." Mass finally ended, we all started for home wishing "Happy Christmas and goodnight" to each other as we parted at each family's lane.

By the time we returned home to a house that smelled so good from the roasting beef it was almost 2 a.m. Being hungry from fasting so long before Communion, it was not long before my mother had a meal of the roast beef with potatoes roasted in the pan with the meat on the table. The following is my mother's recipe for roast beef and potatoes.

# ROAST BEEF

4-pounds sirloin or rib roast
1 carrot
1 onion
dry mustard
3 tablespoons bacon fat

Preheat the oven to 400° Coat the meat lightly with mustard. Put it into the roasting pan with the quartered onion, the carrot cut into one inch chunks, and the fat. Baste with the hot fat every 20 minutes. Reduce the heat to 350° after a half hour. It is cooked after 45 to 50 minutes. Allow the meat to rest in the pan for 10 minutes before carving to keep the juices from escaping. The mustard helps to seal in the juices.

## GRAVY

Gently pour the fat off the pan without disturbing the residue. Sprinkle a little flour on the pan and mix it well in with the residue. Allow this to brown and gradually add stock, or the water in which potatoes or vegetables were cooked if available. Cook gently for 5 minutes, season, and strain.

# ROAST POTATOES

6 medium potatoes
1 tablespoon flour
salt and pepper

Peel the potatoes and leave to steep in cold water for one hour. Dry well. Add salt and pepper to flour. Toss potatoes in the seasoned flour and put in the pan beside the meat when you are cooking a roast beef. Baste whenever you baste the roast. When cooked, they should be crisp and brown outside, while the inside is light and floury.

Because back then Christmas Eve was a day of

abstinence and we couldn't eat meat now it was 2 a.m. Christmas Day and we thoroughly enjoyed roast beef! We might not have that for another year but tonight it was good, the start of a really good Christmas. Christmas Day was spent in Corratubber with the family. Aunt Kathleen roasted a big goose that had been foraging around in the fields for months and now was very fat. We had it with all the trimmings, all topped off with Christmas cake and plum pudding with Bird's custard. I usually spent the day playing with my new dolls and usually at some point we went next door to visit the Boylans. Matt and I were the same age so we spent some time playing together. Late in the day, full of such a good meal and the love of family, we returned back to Fairtown.

## CHRISTMAS GOOSE

1 fat goose 13 to 14 pounds
2 bitter apples cut in chunks

Put the apples inside the cavity. They help to counteract the fat. Lay the goose on a grid standing over the roasting pan. Put into a hot oven (400°) for a half-hour. This will help to crisp the skin. Reduce the heat to 350° and prick the skin lightly with a fork from time to time to allow the fat to escape. Do not damage the flesh. Bake for 2 ½ to 3 hours.

Aunt Kathleen always made the goose with mashed potatoes and toasted parsnips. My mother usually made parsnips by boiling them as in the following recipe but roasting them for Christmas was special.

# TOASTED PARSNIPS

2 or 3 parsnips, 1 pound each
½ tablespoon butter
½ teaspoon sugar
salt and pepper

Peel the parsnips. Cut them in 2-inch lengths across the grain. Cut the lengths down into quarters or eighths. Boil them in salted water until tender, 20 to 25 minutes. Drain them thoroughly and put a folded cloth on top of the saucepan to enable the parsnips to dry off. Melt the butter in the frying pan. Toss in the cooked parsnips, sprinkled with the sugar. Pepper well and brown on all sides. I like to put the buttered parsnips under the broiler and toast. Of course back then we did not have a broiler.

# MINCE PIES
## MINCEMEAT

1 large apple
2 cups raisins
2 cups currants
1 cup sultana raisins
½ cup candied fruit peel
½ cup almonds
1 orange

330

1 lemon

1 cup sugar

¼ teaspoon salt

¼ teaspoon cinnamon

¼ teaspoon allspice

¼ teaspoon powdered cloves

½ cup melted butter

¼ cup Irish whiskey

Core the apple but do not peel. Coarsely chop apple, raisins, currants, sultanas, peel and almonds. Grate the rind off the orange and lemon and squeeze out the juice. Mix the grated rinds with the sugar, salt and spices. Add the melted butter and spiced sugar to the chopped fruit, together with the juice of the lemon and orange and the whiskey. Mix, thoroughly by hand. This mixture can be made ahead of time and stored in airtight jars.

## *PIECRUST*

2 cups butter (cold)

4 cups flour

A pinch of salt

Ice water

Rub the butter into the salted flour. Bind to a stiff dough with a little ice water. Divide into two balls making one slightly larger than the other. Chill for one hour. Roll out the pastry very thinly. Ease the larger circle into greased pie plates. Put enough mincemeat in shell to fill fully. Cover with smaller circle. Pinch the edges together. Stick the point of the knife several times into the top of the pie to allow the steam to escape. Bake at $400^0$ until the pastry is golden. The pie is traditionally eaten hot, with a light dusting of confectioners' sugar but may also be enjoyed cold later. This recipe will also make 12 small single serving pies. Just divide dough into 24 small circles and proceed as above using small pie cups.

The day after Christmas is St. Stephen's day. St. Stephen was a martyr for his faith. The story goes that he was running from the soldiers who were chasing him. Upon finding a large bush Stephen hid behind it. The soldiers were almost past when a small wren rustled the leaves of the bush attracting their attention. They found Stephen and he was put to death. To commemorate this event in Ireland each December twenty sixth young men and boys collect feathers and present them as an effigy of a wren. As they went from house to house they knocked on doors and sang the wren song, begging for money to bury the wren.

## THE WREN
*Traditional*

The wren, the wren, the king of all birds,
St. Stephen's Day, was caught in the furze.
Although he was little, his honour was great.
Jump up, me lads, and give him a treat.

### Refrain
Up with the kettle
And down with the pan,
And give us a penny
To bury the wren

We followed the wren three miles or more,
Three miles or more, three miles or more,
Followed the wren three miles or more,
At six o'clock in the morning.

### Refrain

We have a little box under my hand,
Under my hand, under my hand.
We have a little box under my hand.
A penny or tuppence will do no harm.

### Refrain

Missus Carthy's a very good woman,
A very good woman, a very good woman,
Missus Carthy's a very good woman.
She gave us a penny to bury the wren.

### Refrain

# CONFIRMATION DAY

Confirmation was another of those special occasions that come to mind. Mine was April 9, 1956. I know that because I still have the "The Child's Picture Prayer Book" that Rose Reilly gave me with the date and her best wishes inside the cover. It's now yellowed, pearly cover with a picture of St. Joseph holding the child Jesus is somewhat beaten up from years of use but is still a treasure.

For months before the big day we were preparing, memorizing the Catechism. We were warned that demonstrating the importance of the occasion, the Bishop of

Kilmore would be the officiating clergy. He would ask us questions about our faith and we had better know them or he would refuse to confirm us. We were scared to death of him. He was also going to give us a slap on the cheek to show that now we were soldiers of God. We wondered how hard that slap would be. Also we would be signed with the oil of chrism, which would show our maturity and wisdom in the Church as we received the seven gifts of the Holy Ghost. We were also required to "take the pledge," a solemn promise or pledge to not have an alcoholic drink before the age of twenty one. While that sounded like a wonderful, easy thing to do, we were only eleven years old and making such a promise.

When the day finally arrived it was a complete blur because I was so nervous and excited. We were to be dressed in white dresses and veils like First Communion. The boys in their Sunday best all looked very smart. I wore a beautiful long dress and embroidered scalloped veil and the sheerest white gloves I have ever seen, all borrowed from a cousin. I carried my new prayer book and rosary beads. To emphasize the importance of the occasion my parents rented a car for the trip to Ballyhaise, which was the main church for our parish. We from Castletara were combined with the children from Ballyhaise. Our teachers acted as our sponsors with Mrs. Fay standing up for the girls and the master standing up for the boys.

As I said, the ceremony was a blur; but afterwards there was lots of discussion about it when we gathered with our families in Young's in Ballyhaise for a meal and drink. We, the newly confirmed, were toasted several times and minerals were provided for us since we had just taken the pledge! I have often wondered how many young people kept the pledge until their 21st birthday. Now having said that, many older people took the pledge also and joined the pioneers, wearing the pioneer pin on their lapel to show that they had promised not to drink alcoholic beverages.

*With my parents on Confirmation day*

*My Confirmation April 9, 1956*

# THE CIRCUS

Thanks to the advertising in the *Celt* it was with great anticipation that we waited the arrival of the circus in Cavan town. My parents and I would get all dressed up and off we would go. I was bursting with excitement. This was a really big deal to get to go. I remember being mesmerized by the trapeze artists as they swung high in the air and the tight rope walker as he moved slowly along the rope. The elephants were so huge and could do so many tricks and their riders were so beautiful. The dogs did tricks I could not believe, and the tigers looked so ferocious and scary, but my favorite were the clowns. Their funny antics and painted faces made me giggle with glee. What a treat to go to the circus!

# Chapter 25

# Visitors

Visitors coming to stay with us was always an exciting time for us. For weeks before the arrival my mom would scrub everything in the house until it was shining. Curtains were washed and starched and bed linens washed and hung out to dry so they smelled fresh and clean. A fresh coat of whitewash was applied outdoors to both the house and the outer buildings and new thatch was applied to any spot on the roof that looked even a bit shabby. If at all possible a whole new coat of thatch might be applied in special cases.

Then just before the arrival extra food was made ready and bought. My mother would bake not only her soda bread but a fancy cake and make what she called a fussie. A fussie could be as simple as an apple pie with Bird's custard or one of her famous trifles. A fussie was pretty much any fancy desert that we would not have that frequently.

# MOMS TRIFLE

package lady fingers or sponge cake sliced

package Jello

package Bird's custard

can fruit cocktail drained

raspberry jam

brandy

fresh whipped cream

Make Jello according to package directions, when soft set add fruit. Refrigerate until almost completely set. Meanwhile spread lady fingers with jam and sprinkle well with brandy. Make custard according to package directions. Line bottom and sides of trifle bowl with lady fingers. Layer the Jello, custard and remaining lady fingers, finishing with custard. Whip cream and spread over custard.


I have included a second trifle recipe that Aunt Kathleen made. She often made her own fresh custard.

# AUNT KATHLEEN'S TRIFLE

1 stale sponge cake

4 tablespoons raspberry jam

1/3 cup Irish whiskey

2/3 cup sherry

1 cup heavy cream

½ tablespoon sugar

½ cup almonds, blanched and split

2 cups egg custard (given below)

Split the sponge cake into 4 layers. Spread the layers generously with the jam and restack. Put them in a straight sided glass dish or trifle bowl. Mix the whiskey and sherry and pour over the layered cake. Cover with a plate and leave to soak for an hour.

## FOR THE CUSTARD

1 egg

2 egg yolks

1 tablespoon sugar

2 cups milk

Beat the egg and egg yolks together with the sugar. Scald the milk and pour over the eggs while beating. Cook the custard over a pan of hot water until it thickens to a cream. Pour it over the cake while hot. Leave to get cold.

Whip the heavy cream with a half tablespoon of sugar, and pile over the trifle. Decorate with the blanched and split almonds, which are spiked into the cream.

## GINGER BREAD LOAF

1 1/8 cups flour

4 tablespoons butter/margarine

3 tablespoons sour milk

1 egg

½ teaspoon baking soda

½ teaspoon ground ginger

¼ cup ground almonds

½ cup raisins

¼ cup candied fruit

¼ cup Treacle

Mix dry ingredients, rub in butter. Add almonds and fruit. Mix treacle with the milk and beaten egg then stir into dry ingredients. Put into a greased baking pan and Bake 375° for 1 ¼ hours.

While we occasionally had a roasted or boiled chicken for Sunday dinner which was usually stretched to last several days for company my mother often made a large stuffed roasted chicken. My father usually killed the bird and my mother plucked the feathers off, then burning off the last of the very fine pin feathers which were impossible to pluck with a match. I still remember the stench of those little feathers. She removed the innards and cleaned it out, saving the liver and gizzards for gravy.

My father told the story about the first time he, as a young man, killed a chicken. He had an idea how to do it so he took the poor old hen, holding her head in one hand and securely holding her body in the other. Being sure to completely do the job, with all his strength he pulled and twisted her neck, wanting to break her neck and so kill her. However he was just a touch to strong and he looked down to find her head in one hand and disconnected from it her struggling body in the other. In his shock at what he had done he dropped the body, which continued fluttering across the yard.

# STUFFED ROAST CHICKEN

1 chicken, 4 to 4 ½ pounds, with its giblets

2 slices fat bacon

½ cup water

salt

pepper

## STUFFING

1 onion

4 tablespoons melted butter

3 cups white breadcrumbs

4 tablespoons chopped parsley

1 teaspoon chopped thyme

2 cloves of garlic, crushed

1 egg beaten

salt and pepper

water or chicken broth

Chop the onion and fry lightly in the butter. Add this to the bread crumbs, parsley, thyme, garlic, and seasonings, which have been well mixed in a bowl. Add the egg. Mix it by hand, and if it is too dry, moisten with a little water or chicken broth if available. Place the under the flap of skin at the neck. Secure the skin over the stuffing, Cover the breast of the chicken with the fat bacon and secure with string. Paint the legs and other exposed flesh with soft butter. Dust the bird with salt and pepper. Place the bird in the roasting pan, breast up, together with the neck and gizzard. Add a half cup of water to the pan. Cover loosely with aluminum foil and bake at $350^0$ for 1 ½ to 2 hours. In the last half-hour remove the foil and the bacon to let the bird brown.

Occasionally my mother's Aunt Mary and her daughters, the Smiths, came from Scotland and we really enjoyed their company. Aunt Mary was a very large woman and seemed to have trouble getting around. I really enjoyed my time with her daughters Cathy who was older and Margaret who was close to my age.

*Cathy Smith, Mary Argue, Me, Aunt Mary Smith, John Argue, Margaret Smith*

The most excitement I remember over people coming was when the Yankees, that would be Aunt Helen and Uncle Mike and their son Tommie, came in 1949. Every nook and cranny was scrubbed, painted and made to shine like the sun. The parlor was made ready to be their bedroom while they were there. It never looked so beautiful. It had been years since Helen, or Ellie as my dad called her, had come home to Ireland, and Uncle Mike, who was from Kilkenny, had never been to Cavan.

Helen was my dad's twin sister and had always been so special to him. They spent many hours reminiscing about their childhood and all the fun they had growing up. Tommie was eight or nine and had never been on a farm before, so everything fascinated him and amused him. We had a lot of fun together. We dug two large holes in the garden because Tommy wanted to get to China that way. I had no idea what he was talking about, but he convinced me that if we dug deep enough we would get there because it was on the other side of the world.

Of course in spite of the fact that we had visitors my father still had to do his work on the farm. When my father worked in the fields with the horse, my dog Tiny and I were right there at his heels up and down the rows plowing, harrowing and digging. I would "harness" the dog using pieces of rope and string. Aunt Helen tells the story of when she, on awakening one morning heard, as she explains it, me a 4 year old, a dainty, innocent, blonde curly headed little girl and Tommy a city boy, let loose in the country outside her window. That morning my father was harnessing the horse, so I proceeded to harness the dog under the patient eye of Tommie Who wanted to "work" with the dog. Every few minutes he asked, "now can I have him?" Each time, "Not yet, Tommie." Finally the dog was all harnessed. Tommie became impatient and asked one more time. I told him "in a minute," picked up a big stick, smacked the dog on the butt, and yelled "get on outta there ya auld bitch ya." Just like my dad would have done with the horse. Till this day Aunt Helen still laughs at this sweet little girl with the not so nice mouth. When we moved to the US we left Tiny with my grandfather, but she died within months. A vet told my grandfather he couldn't cure a broken heart.

*John and Mary Argue, Bunnie Smith, Uncle Mike Maher, me, Hugh Reilly (seated) and Tommy Maher on our street when Aunt Helen, Uncle Mike and Tommy were home from America*

# Chapter 26

# Work, Sundays and Relaxation

This farm as I understand it had been in my father's family for generations. And although it supported generations of Argues, my Dad found it difficult to make ends meet from the farm alone so when the Land Reclamation Project came to the area, he got a job with them. He was paid about five pound a week for the back-breaking job of digging drainage ditches in fields, placing red terra cotta pipes in the ditches, then covering them over with dirt. The idea was to remove excess water from wet fields. This program gave employment to a lot of the area men. Whether it really made a difference in the amount of moisture in the soil I do not know.

After he came home from his job and on Saturdays he worked on our farm, tending to the potatoes, oats, hay, and taking care of the animals. My mother helped him a great deal with all of it, but there was a lot he had to do himself, such as taking the horse to the forge to have new shoes. The blacksmith would remove the old ones, pare down the horse's feet, and fit new shoes to them, securing the new shoes with special nails. In Ireland it was a custom to keep an old horseshoe over the door for good luck. I still have one of Fannie's shoes over our door.

Sundays were his day to rest and I really never remember him working on a Sunday other than the necessary work of milking cows and feeding all the animals. We always took seriously the commandment to keep holy the day of the Lord. On Saturday night we bathed thoroughly. People in Ireland back then didn't have the facilities to bathe daily and bathing was a task. Extra water had to be brought from the well; the water was boiled on the fire and put in the big wash tub. The houses were cold and damp even in summer, so getting into a tub if we had one would not be too enticing. But we needed to get ready for Sunday, so Saturday night we bathed with a wash cloth as my mother would say, "Wash up as far as possible and down as far as possible and possible if you can." We washed our hair after which my mother would roll my already curly hair around rags and secure them tightly so that on Sunday morning my uncontrollable curls would fall down my shoulders in neat ringlets usually held off my face with a big bow to match my dress. On Sunday morning, we put on our best clothes. Dad put on his suit, my mother and I walked to Castletara Chapel to Mass while Daddy rode his bike. As we walked we met up with other women and children, Mary and Jemmie Mack, the McCaffreys and eventually the Flatleys and Coyles. We children skipped and played ahead as our mothers followed behind, catching up on the gossip.

On reaching the church the men were already there, all having ridden their bikes, all standing around chatting and smoking by the old vault. It was like the ladies and children were on review as we passed by on our way into Mass, a rather uncomfortable feeling as I grew older. As we went into the church we paid our penny seat offering at the door, so it was called the penny offering. Two men from the parish sat at the table keeping a record of it.

Upon entering the church we sat in our socially accepted places. The women sat on the left, young girls of school age in the front of them in the first few rows. The men sat on the right, boys in the front of them. Those of us lucky enough to be in the choir sat up in the gallery and made beautiful music under the direction of Mrs. Melligan, "Faith of our Fathers Holy faith, we will be true to thee 'till Death." I remember so many beautiful hymns, the mystical "Silent Night" at midnight Mass in the dimly light church, "Tantum ergo" at Benediction. The heady smell of the incense filled the air as it wafted through the air above the pews to the gallery in that little church when we had benediction.

Mass back then was in Latin and we all had our prayer books to follow along in English. Many of the women prayed the rosary during Mass. Because we didn't understand what was being said boredom usually set in at some point. Combine that with the fact that the priest's back was to us, we children found lots of opportunities to become distracted and have some fun that usually led to some giggles. But the most fun was the occasional fly that made its way into church and seemed to know just when to land on someone's back and crawl around and set a bunch of little girls giggling.

At the point for the collection everybody put in what they could afford, usually no more than one or two shillings. For poor farmers even a shilling was a lot of money.

Back in those days we had to be fasting to go to Communion. By the time we got up, dressed and walked the several miles to church it was not surprising that frequently children passed out in church. Maybe the fact that first we went to school and then to Mass made this happen more frequently on school days during Lent. Of course fainting was contagious, and I remember one morning when five or six children were laid out on the grass outside, still coming to after fainting inside.

Mass finished with the Deprefundus to guard and protect against the action of the devil through black magic. After Mass people stood around and talked for a while then headed home to Sunday dinner and later visits with friends and neighbors. Some folks drifted off into the graveyard to say a prayer for their deceased loved ones.

In Castletara the graves were usually kept very well, especially in summer, with beautiful flowers; roses, gladiolus, geraniums, etc. But no time were they more beautiful than for the blessing of the graves. That was always a special Sunday. The people of the parish spent the week before preparing for it; they cleaned off their family plot of any grass or weeds and planted new flowers and then added a wreath of fresh flowers to the grave. Most of these wreaths were homemade because there really wasn't the extra money to buy them, but they were still beautiful. Even as a young girl I loved to make wreaths of mosses and fragrant flowers to be placed on the graves before Mass. Cannon Maguire came up from Ballyhaise and concelebrated Mass with Father Hunt. Then after Mass everyone processed to and through the graveyard with the priests stopping and blessing the graves with holy water along the way. There is also an ancient graveyard behind the church. It was very overgrown then and we never went in there. The priests just stopped at the gate and shook the holy water toward the graves. It was a special festive day in Castletara. The old graveyard has now been cleaned up and it is so wonderful to be able to walk through it and pray there for my long dead ancestors. Although many graves are unmarked and some headstones are not legible this is where they would have been buried.

*The old graveyard by Castletara Chapel*

Although we school children were more than a bit scared of the graveyard, occasionally we would go in there to play among the headstones on our way home from school. Usually it ended with us running for our lives if we heard a strange sound. And even though I would never ever go in there alone I can remember when one time a pack of gypsies came down the road and I practically flew over the graveyard ditch to hide. I was more scared of the gypsies than the "ghosts." I remember once staying overnight with Jean McCormack. We had a lot of fun and stayed up most of the night, but I was really scared to go to sleep because their house was across the road from the church and graveyard.

On Sunday afternoons after dinner was our time to relax. One of my father's favorite Sunday pastimes was following the hunt. All the farmers gathered together with their hunting dogs and once a fox was routed, the dogs took chase over hedges and ditches with the farmers in hot pursuit on foot, no horses. They were running but of course they couldn't always keep up with the dogs, so frequently they went from one high hill to the next to follow their progress. When the hounds lost the scent of the fox the dogs and men regrouped, found another fox, and they were off again. In this manner they often traveled miles over many town lands. As dusk set in they returned to their homes excitedly discussing the days hunt. After milking the cows and doing evening chores they very hungrily ate their supper, which was made for them by their waiting wives.

My dad's other passion on Sunday afternoons was football. If there was a game on in Breffni Park, he was there cheering on his favorite team. He was more intense about it than the players! A couple of times a year he went to Dublin to the all Ireland semi-final and final, especially if Cavan was playing. There was real rivalry between the counties in football. Cavan was competitive, but Kerry, Mayo and Galway always seemed to be on top.

Gaelic football is a very rough, dangerous sport, especially when the players don't care what or where they kick the opponent. Many a good man has suffered permanent injury from a "friendly" game of football. Unlike American football where players are paid a lot of money to play, Irish football players were paid nothing and came from all walks of life. It was a totally amateur game, but the rivalry was strong and competition was tough. After a game my father would come home and recount all the events of the game to my mother who was always anxious to know how the game went, especially if her cousin Johnny Cusack was playing for Cavan. She always worried that he might be injured.

While my dad did his own thing on Sunday my mother and I did ours too. Sunday was our day to do some serious visiting. After dinner we got the horse hitched up to the trap, if we were going a distance, and off we went, often to Aunt Maggie Ruddy's or Aunt Mary Cusack's. In later years occasionally we hired a car to drive us. Occasionally we walked but it was quite a walk to either one. Although we did visit Uncle John Clarke of Alackin, I don't remember being there to much, but I do remember Teasie and Joan.

I really enjoyed going to Ruddy's and Cusack's. Aunt Maggie's house was wonderful, a pretty house, tidy and clean. She had really beautiful things. She served tea in delicate china cups. She had an elegant touch. Her tea tasted better than any other. It must have been the cups. During our visits her husband Paddy Ruddy would take us on a tour of his barnyard and garden where everything was clean and orderly. He seemed so proud of it all. Aunt Maggie, my mother's aunt, and Uncle Paddy had no children of their own, but they had a "daughter" Annie Foster. She was actually a niece whose mother had died at her birth. She was raised by the Ruddys and still lives on that farm today, while her husband of many years Francie Cahill is now deceased. I remember when Annie and Francie were courting, my mother would ask Francie to take us up to Lavey to visit Aunt Maggie on Sundays and Francie was always very happy to oblige. It gave him the opportunity to spend the day with Annie because it seems dating was all done in secret at that time until a wedding date was announced.

*Paddy Ruddy his wife, Maggie Clarke Ruddy,*
*And her brother my grandfather James Clarke*

*Grandfather James Clarke, Uncle Paddy Ruddy*
*Merlyn Flatley, Francie Cahill, my mother,*
*Aunt Maggie Ruddy, and me*

Aunt Mary's, also my mother's aunt, was a fun place to go. She always wore black, long black skirts, long-sleeved black tops. She was a robust woman with beautiful long, snow white hair that she had pulled up into a bun on top of her head. I remember her sitting by the fire. Her farm was fun and I enjoyed playing in the out houses and sheds.

There was a mill there also and lots of interesting things to see and do. Often her grandchildren Maisie, Seannie and Ita Cusack were over when I was there, and I really enjoyed their companionship playing in the yard. But the best fun of all was when her sons, Gene and Johnny, the football player, were there. They both spoiled me.

*Eileen and me during our 1986 visit to Ireland*

Aunt Mary's daughter Maud lived in Dublin. She helped her Uncle Hubert raise his family. His wife Lena had died soon after the birth of their youngest child, Bernadette, who incidentally was born the same day I was. Hubert had an off the premises liquor store and Maude helped him with that too. She was like a mother to his children. Some of them spent summers with us, particularly Eileen. We had a wonderful time together. I loved to see her come and hated to see her go back to Dublin. Cora and Bernadette also came, but it was Eileen that was my friend. She loved the farm and I enjoyed sharing it with her.

Other Sundays we walked to neighbors and friends houses like Fitche's or McCullum's up on the old road near Philip Brady's. I love to go there and play in the rocks and then come in for tea. They always had delicious goodies for tea time. Sometimes we walked down to Bennie McCaffreys. Betsy and I were close in age and we would play together while our mothers talked in the parlor. They had a big house and instead of sitting in the kitchen as you would in the thatched houses, tea was served in the parlor. It was a lovely two story home with a beautiful flower garden out front.

One of the terrific things about Ireland has always been its gardens and every house we went to had beautiful gardens, each one prettier than the one before. Roses, geraniums and fuchsia that grew into bushes, Sweet Williams and sweet peas grew to unbelievable size. Beautiful scents, a palate of colors; red, yellow, purple, pinks, each brighter than the other. It seems flowers grow wild in Ireland with the moisture and mild weather. I remember the daffodils on a large mound in the field behind Mick Brady's house. Every year they appeared with their beautiful yellow trumpets in a cloud of golden color.

# DAFFODILS
*William Wadsworth ~1815*
*Out of Copyright per Wordsworth Trust*

I wandered lonely as a cloud
That floats on high o'er vales and hills
When all at once I saw a crowd,
A host, of golden daffodils;
Beside the lake, beneath the trees,
Fluttering and dancing in the breeze.

Continuous as the stars that shine
And twinkle on the milky way,
They stretched in never-ending line
Along the margin of a bay:
Ten thousand saw I at a glance,
Tossing their heads in sprightly dance.

The waves beside them danced; but they
Out-did the sparkling waves in glee:
A poet could not but be gay,
In such a jocund company:
I gazed--and gazed--but little thought
What wealth the show to me had brought:
For oft, when on my couch I lie
In vacant or in pensive mood,
They flash upon that inward eye
Which is the bliss of solitude;
And then my heart with pleasure fills,
And dances with the daffodils.

The Cahill's home was also a favorite place to visit. They had a big new house on the Old Road and Lila always kept me well amused. I recall when they built that house. As was the custom in Ireland at that time when a new house was built, before the family moved in the priest came to say Mass in it and bless the house. All the neighbors were invited. After Mass a big breakfast was set out and a great celebration ensued. That evening when everyone was gone home the family settled in and spent their first night in their new home. No one would dare risk living in a house that had not been blessed.

*My parents, John and Mary Argue, Aunt Kathleen Clarke, Francie Cahill and me outside Cahill's new house on the day it was blessed*

*Jack Cahill*
*me and Leila*

That was a time when a lot of families started to replace their thatched cabins with new homes and we frequently were going to house blessings. Others that I can remember were The Hannigans, Boylans, my grandfather's and many more. A lot of the new homes were lovely modest three-bedroom bungalows with a large kitchen, scullery and dining room/parlor. Most of them did not have bathrooms. However the new large two-story homes had a bathroom built in, whicht was surely something new for a country house. But not everyone who had a full bath really felt compelled to use the tub, and one family made the comment that the tub was a great place to store the coal for the cooker or the turf for the fire, much better than going outside to bring it in on a cold winter night.

In Cavan town my dad had a cousin Katie McManus and for whatever reason I always called her Aunt Katie. When we went into town we frequently stopped in to see her. She was a lovely lady and I always enjoyed visiting her. Sometimes she came out to our house on a Sunday to visit, and when she did it was always a special day for me. She always brought goodies from the bakery in town, a treat we seldom could afford. Katie had a sister, Ellie Agnew, who also lived in town. For some reason we visited her less often, but she or a member of her family often came out to visit our house with Katie. Later the Agnew's son Desie taught a group of us how to play the accordion. He played beautifully! We had our classes in what had to be Aunt Mollie's house and occasionally we had a party there with dancing and singing. It was an opportunity for us children to show off how much we had learned. This was a time when there was a revival of all things Irish. The thirty-two counties were enjoying their freedom from English rule and the opportunity to be completely Irish and practice their centuries old heritage and culture.

*Mary Agnew Phelan, Jim Phelan, Aunt Helen Argue Maher*
*and Katie Mc Manus holding my dog Tiny.*
*My father, John Argue, and Me.*
*This picture was taken during Aunt Helen's visit in 1949*

*My Mother and Me, Uncle James in background, Jimmy
Mack, Cousin Mary Argue in Foreground*

# Chapter 27

## Corratubber

I think though that my mother's favorite place to be was Corratubber, and I believe that she always thought of it as home. Fairtown was home and she took good care of the house and farm so very well, but Corratubber was where her heart was. She loved to go there on Sunday, as did I. It was an opportunity for her to spend time with Aunt Kathleen and for my mother an opportunity to also spend some time with Maggie Boylan. The three of them would talk over the gate between their streets for hours. The two families were like one, each one caring so much about the other, like brothers and sisters. Matt, the youngest Boylan, is my age. The twins, Tom and Charlie, are a bit older, Brian somewhat older than them. Sean, Geramie and Mary were all out of Castletara School before I entered there. Mary was someone I truly adored. First of all, I always thought she was the most beautiful girl I knew. She had luxurious shiny black hair. I remember how she loved to brush and braid my long blond curly hair. She was always kind and sweet to me. After she had been in the America for a few years she and her friend Margaret Lyons came home to visit. I was so excited seeing

Mary. She was beautiful and now her beautiful black hair had grown long to her waist and seemed shinier than ever, like black satin. I was in awe of her. She was so glamorous! I thought she looked like a film star.

*Charlie Boylan, Uncle John, Tom and Brian Boylan and Tom Breslin*

*Sean Boylan with the horse and cart*

Visiting the Boylans again made me see how things have changed. John and Mrs. Boylan have passed on. Matt and his wife Rose now have the farm. Actually Matt no longer has all the variety of farming that his father had. He has a mushroom farm selling to buyers in Europe. The mushrooms are grown in three large black buildings. These commercially grown mushrooms are as delicious as the ones I used to pick in Fairtown years ago. But some things haven't changed. Matt's little boys are back and forth between their house and Kathleen's and Rose and Kathleen still stop for a chat across the gate.

I have already talked about some of my time in Corratubber with Kathleen. Visiting Aunt Kathleen was always quite an experience. She was a rather accomplished cook. I was not the only one who thought so. Fr. Comey knew how well she cooked and had her cook for him often. Every year she was invited to go into the bishop's house for a special two weeks of meetings with dignitaries. She would pack and go move into the bishop's palace and oversee the existing kitchen staff and cook very special meals. I have included here some of her old recipes.

It seemed she could make a full meal from nothing. Mashed potatoes became special by her hand. I remember so many good meals that Aunt Kathleen cooked; roast goose at Christmas, roast chicken, beef roast, all mouth watering. But what I remember most of all were the Christmas cakes, cherry cakes and plum puddings. I loved to spend time with her. At least a month before Christmas my mother and I would go to Auntie Kathleen's to spend the day making these rich luscious cakes and of course plum puddings. We would start first thing in the morning and keep at it all day long. There was so much to do. All the fruit came whole or in big chunks and had to be chopped into small pieces, the candied citron, orange peel, cherries, ginger, etc. had to be all chopped, unlike today when you can buy them that way. For the plum pudding big chunks of beef suet were grated till they were like fine meal. Kathleen directed while my mother and I chopped and grated for what seemed like hours. All three of us would take turns beating the egg whites in a great big bowl with a large wooden spoon, until stiff peaks formed. No electric beaters at that time! Finally when everything was ready Aunt Kathleen mixed her cakes and put them into big round pans and onto the fire to bake for several hours. Of course once she got her stove this was made much easier than when she did them on the open hearth, which was for many a year! Cakes baking, we proceeded to put the plum pudding together; stout, brandy, bread crumbs, fruit, suet and all! We poured it into several cloth lined bowls, tied it, and then placed these bowls in pots of hot water to steam for hours and hours. Oh the aromas of those puddings and cakes baking. Not only will I never forget them but now I repeat them each year in my own home. At the end of the day, usually well into the evening my mother and I returned home with our share of the goodies to be wrapped in white cloths soaked in rum or medira and stored in cake tins until Christmas. Every few weeks they were removed, the cloth re-soaked and re- wrapped and stored

# OLD FASHIONED CHRISTMAS CAKE

*5 pound cake*

1 pkg 15 oz dark raisins

½ teaspoon cinnamon

1 pkg 15 oz white raisins

½ teaspoon cloves

½ pound currants

½ teaspoon mace

½ cup dark rum

½ teaspoon allspice

½ cup madeira

¼ pound slivered almonds

½ pound candied cherries

¼ pound Whole pecans

½ pound candied pineapple

2 cups butter

1 ½ Tablespoons black treacle (molasses)

½ pound candied citron

1 cup dark brown sugar

2 oz candied orange peel

5 eggs separated

2 oz candied lemon peel

1 teaspoon almond extract

2 cups sifted flour

marzipan

1 teaspoon taking soda

royal icing (see separate recipe)

In a large bowl, combine raisins, currants, rum and madeira; let stand, covered, overnight. Add candied fruit and mix well. Sift flour before measuring and again combined with the spices, soda and 1½ cups of the flour. Add to fruit mixture and toss lightly. In a small bowl, combine the remaining ½ cup flour with nuts, coating the nuts with the flour. Add to the fruits and mix lightly. In another large bowl, cream together butter and sugars until light-colored. Beat in treacle. Lightly beat egg yolks and almond extract; combine with butter-sugar mixture and beat well. Add fruit and nut mixture to this batter and blend well. Beat egg white until stiff and fold into batter. Turn into a well greased 10-inch tube or spring form pan; two 9" x 5" x 3" pans can also be used. On the bottom rack of the oven, place two shallow pans filled with one inch of hot water. Bake the large cake for 3 ½ to 4 hours in a preheated 275° oven; the small cakes take half that time. Either size is finished when a cake tester or broom straw inserted in the center comes out dry.

Remove the pans of water during the last 15 minutes of baking. Cool cake in pan for 30 minutes, then loosen and remove to a wire rack. When cake is cold, wrap it in a cloth that has been saturated with rum or madeira. Seal cake and cloth in airtight foil, place in a tightly covered tin, and store in a cool place. Allow at least six weeks of storage in this liquid, adding more every two to four weeks before serving. Days before serving, roll out marzipan/almond paste to cover the cake. Ice the cake with royal icing. Royal icing should look smooth, light and shiny, almost like meringue. Add icing sugar carefully, as directed, or the icing will become stiff and heavy.

Christmas cake covered with royal icing should always have a protective coat of almond paste to prevent crumbs, grease and moisture coming through to the icing. Before applying the rolled out paste, brush the cake with hot, sieved apricot jam. Let the almond paste rest at least two days to dry on the cake.

Make sure that the icing sugar is dry and free from lumps. Eggs will whisk more easily if older.

Before covering a rich fruit cake with almond paste, brandy may be added to the cake.

Save ¼ of the royal icing to decorate. This should be stiffer than that for coating the cake, but it should be soft enough to pipe easily.

Ice the cake completely coating it with icing. Decorate to your liking.

## ALMOND PASTE

This quantity is enough to cover the top of one 8-inch round cake or one 7-inch square cake. Make double quantities if the sides of the cake are to be covered or the cake is larger. I would double for a 10 inch cake, which I usually make.

9 ozs. ground almonds (9 heaped tablespoons)
4 ½ ozs. icing sugar (powder sugar) (4 well-heaped tablespoons and one lightly rounded tablespoon) sieved
4 ½ ozs. superfine sugar (4 rounded tablespoons and one level tablespoon)
1 teaspoon lemon juice
2 drops almond essence
approximately one small beaten egg

Put the ground almonds, icing-sugar and superfine sugar into a mixing bowl and mix together. Add the lemon juice, almond essence and enough beaten egg to mix into a fairly dry paste. Gather together with the fingers. Turn out on a board dusted with sieved icing sugar, and knead until smooth. Now prepared almond paste is available commercially.

# ROYAL ICING

This quantity is sufficient to coat all over one 8-inch round cake or one 7-inch square cake, *excluding* piping decoration. Again I use twice this amount for my 10 inch cake.

Approximately 1 ½ pounds. powder sugar
3 to 4 egg whites
2 drops fresh lemon juice
1 ½ teaspoons glycerin (optional)
a few drops coloring (yellow, red, etc.)
for color icing for decorating

Sieve the powder sugar. Put the egg whites and lemon juice into a mixing bowl and beat with a fork or whisk until frothy. Add the icing sugar **a tablespoon at a time**, beating each addition in very thoroughly until it is completely smooth and white. When about half the icing sugar has been beaten in, use a wooden spoon to beat in the remainder until the icing stands up in straight points when the spoon is lifted up quickly.

When this stage is reached, stop adding sugar. Beat in the glycerin (if used).

Divide and add the coloring to part saved to decorate. I cover the entire cake with plain icing and then divide remaining portion to color for decorations. Cover the bowl with a cloth wrung out in cold water to prevent a skin forming. Keep covered all the time, only removing the cloth to lift out some of the icing, but covering again immediately.

# PLUM PUDDING

1 pound finely chopped beef kidney suet

(almost as fine as flour)

1 pound sultana raisins

1 pound muscatel raisins

¼ pound cleaned currants

1 pound finely crumbled stale bread

1 pound brown sugar

3 (2 teaspoon) nutmegs grated

½ oz ground ginger

½ pound candied lemon

½ pound candied citron

½ pound candied orange

(the last three ingredients to be cut into small pieces)

½ oz cinnamon

pinch salt

All ingredients to be thoroughly mixed together, dry in a large crock or basin

2 small bottles Guinness's stout

Pour all round edges of material and mix together so that nothing dry shall remain, with a large wooden spoon or silver tablespoon. Cover down tightly with a plate and weight on it

THIS SHOULD BE DONE 1 to 3 days
BEFORE REQUIRED !

8 - 10 eggs - well beaten

8 oz glass brandy

mix eggs with mixture in bowl

add the glass of brandy

This will make a very large pudding or two or three small puddings which should boiled in a buttered and floured cloth or in a queen's pudding bowl. Two can be made if the pudding bowl is used and no cloth is then needed

**_Boil for 6 hours_**

Filling the pot from time to time with boiling water. If boiled in a cloth, tie tightly, giving an inch of space between the tying and pudding to allow for swelling. Put a plug of flour at the opening at top to prevent water from getting into the pudding. When boiled in a cloth, a plate should be put under it in a saucepan.

If given a first boiling the day before using, 4 hours will do for the first day and 3 hours the day of use.

At table pour ¼ cup brandy over pudding on rimmed serving dish or pie plate.

Light brandy and serve with custard either homemade or Bird's custard when flame is out.

# GUINNESS CAKE

1 pound flour

¼ teaspoon salt

1 teaspoon baking powder

1 cup sugar

½ teaspoon nutmeg

½ teaspoon mixed spice

8 oz butter or margarine

1 pound sultanas

¼ cup chopped peel

1 cup porter / stout

2 eggs

Sieve the flour, salt and baking powder, and add the sugar, nutmeg and spice. Rub in the butter finely. Add the fruit, then the porter which has been mixed with the beaten eggs. Bake in a well-greased tin for 2½ hours at 350°.

# IRISH STEW

## Ingredients

2 pounds boned lamb

2 pounds potatoes

2 large onions

Salt and pepper

1 tablespoon fresh, chopped thyme and parsley or

1 teaspoon dried thyme

1½ cups water

chopped parsley for garnish

Trim the meat, leaving a little of the fat on and cut into chunks. Peel and slice the potatoes and onions. Season the meat and vegetables with salt, pepper and herbs. Then, starting and finishing with a layer of potatoes, layer the potatoes, meat and onions in a large saucepan. Add the water and cover tightly. Simmer on a very low heat on the top of the stove for 2 - 2½ hours. The pot stirred occasionally to prevent the potatoes from sticking and add additional liquid if it has dried out. The finished stew should not be too liquidly, the potatoes should thicken it enough. If not, I use a little potato flakes or flour to do so. ½ cup Guinness can be substituted for ½ cup water for more robust stew.

# SCONES
### *(Kathleen's)*

1 cup self rising flour

1 teaspoon baking powder

4 Tablespoon margarine

1/3 cup super fine sugar

1 egg

4 Tablespoon milk

Mix all ingredients together. Roll out to about ½ inch and cut with a glass or cookie cutter. Bake 325° 12 to 15 minutes.

# SCONES
### *(Mary Boylans)*

4 cups self rising flour

¼ pound butter / margarine

1 cup sugar

½ cup raisins

1 egg

1 ½ cups buttermilk

1 teaspoon salt

4 teaspoon baking powder

Mix together and then roll out about ½ inch thick
Cut circles with cutter or use a glass
Brush tops with milk and Sugar
Bake 350° 25 minutes

# SODA BREAD
### *(Kathleen's)*

1 pint buttermilk

2 2/3 cups flour (soda bread flour)

4 Tablespoon margarine

½ teaspoon salt

1 teaspoon baking soda

¼ cup fine sugar

1½ - 1¾ cups sultanas

Mix flour, sugar salt and baking soda together. Rub margarine into flour mixture. Mix well together with fingers. Add the buttermilk and sultanas, stir into soft dough with a wooden spoon. Flour fingers and form into a ball. Turn onto flowered baking sheet or put in round baking pan and flatten to about 1 1/2 inches thick. Make a cross across top. Bake in 425° oven for 35 minutes.

# BROWN BREAD
*(Kathleen's)*

4 cups whole wheat flour

2 cups white flour

1½ teaspoon salt

1½ teaspoon baking soda

2 cups buttermilk

1 tablespoon butter

Mix flours, salt and baking soda together. Rub butter into flour mixture. Mix in buttermilk with wooden spoon to form soft dough. With floured fingers form into ball and turn onto floured baking sheet or round pan. Flatten to about 1½ inch thickness. Make cross in top and bake at 425° for about 35 minutes.

# TREACLE BREAD
*(Kathleen's)*

3 tablespoon treacle

½ cup milk

4 tablespoon butter/margarine

¼ cup brown sugar

1 egg

2 tablespoon powder sugar

¼ teaspoon baking powder

1 cup raisins

1 cup flour

1 Tablespoon ground ginger

Mix milk and treacle and warm. Cream the brown sugar and butter, then add to the treacle mixture. Mix flour, baking powder and ginger and add gradually to the creamed mixture, beating well. Then add the beaten egg and raisins. Pour into a greased baking pan lined with parchment paper. Bake at 375° for one hour. When cooled completely cut into squares and sift powder sugar on top.

This treacle bread was one of my favorites with lots of homemade butter. These are just a few of the things I learned to make from Aunt Kathleen.

One of my most fond memories has been the time I spent alone with Aunt Kathleen as I learned to cook. I walked or later rode my bike to Corratubber early in the morning. Then we would decide what to make that day and we were off and cooking. I'd help her beat the eggs and butter and sugar together. Help her mix all the ingredients for a cake, line the pans, pour the cake and put it in the oven. Then as the aroma of a cake baking filled the house, we had our time together. One of her favorite things was to have me practice walking with a book balanced on top of my head, so I would learn to walk tall. She told me that models walked this way and we would strut around the kitchen.

I remember how she used to say, "Aw be the gaws" or "Be Jasus!" about things. She was so funny! After some time the cake came out of the oven and many times we sampled it after it cooled a bit. Oh, the taste of it. Maybe because treats were very rare and just making ends meet was difficult, I enjoyed it even more. She always made me feel good about myself! I had a great time with her. We talked and she always listened to what I had to say.

Now there was the time Aunt Helen sent my parents a package from America and in with the clothes were included two cake mixes. My Dad, who liked to cook on occasion, took this opportunity to do some baking. Now mind you the cake mixes were meant for oven baking and we only had the open fire. Anyway my dad added what was called for as best he could, for we had no measuring cups. He lined the pan with wax paper, included in the package, beat the batter with a spoon and poured it into the pan. Then, to the best of his ability, he baked it on the open fire for the prescribed time. Out came the most beautiful angel food cake I've ever seen.

The next day being Sunday my dad took it to Kathleen's for critique. She cut a piece, looked it over and tasted it, "Wow!" she kept saying, "Be Jasus, the texture of it, the texture of it!" "I used 13 egg whites, Kathleen," He told her because that's what the package said it contained. "Aw Jasus its beautiful John." "Be Jasus, it's a great cake." She could hardly believe her taste buds! Till the day she died I don't think she ever knew it was a box mix. Aunt Kathleen came by her interest in cooking honestly, my grandfather fancied himself as a good cook. Down the lane from Aunt Kathleen was Miney's shop. It was just one room in their home. They kept staple-type foods, creamery butter, bread, sugar and, of course, big jars of candy. When I visited Aunt Kathleen, she often sent me on an errand there, and it was a special treat for me to buy three pence worth of candy. I wonder if she didn't find an excuse to send me just so I could get the treat.

Going to Corratubber was also a chance to spend time with my uncles John, Eugene and James and most of all to spend time with my grandfather. My uncles were young men when I was a child and John and Eugene were often off to the dances or carnivals and having a good time as young men should. James was more a stay at home man but so very quiet that I never really knew him well until my first visit back to Ireland; he took me around and he really was a lot of fun. Once when I was about eleven Eugene took me to Stradone carnival. It was the first time I had been to it and I had a great time. He also took me on the bar of his bike into Cavan town to see my first movie, Bing Crosby in *Little Boy Lost*. I was amazed by that!

*Uncle James Clarke*

*Uncle Eugene Clarke drawing water from the well during a visit to Corratubber*

*May 1959, Uncle John and me lapping hay the Sunday before we left Ireland*

Now, about my grandfather, suffice to say I adored him. He was tall and handsome, with red hair turning gray. He was a proud man with shoulders held back and head held high, a moustache framing his upper lip. He always dressed in a jacket, shirt and tie. He had an air of authority about him that commanded respect. He was proud of his home, family and heritage; after all, he was a Clarke from Alacken, as my mother would say. He worked very hard on his little farm and with Kathleen and my uncles made it a really lovely place to live. I remember when they built the new house, all working together. It was beautiful! They were all so proud of it but none more than my grandfather.

*My Grandfather James Clarke*

As I said, he liked to think of himself as a bit of a cook, too, and my father tells the story of one of his cooking lessons from his father-in-law. It was early in my parents' marriage when my father was visiting Corratubber and Grandfather was making pancakes. He was anxious to impress his son-in-law with his cooking prowess. Seeing that my father was interested in his technique, he decided to give his new son-in-law a lesson. "Do you know how to toss a pancake, John?" he asked. My father responded that he did not know how it was done. My grandfather said, "Well, watch me now I'll show you." He carefully moved the pancake around in the big black iron pan and with a strong twist of the wrist up in the air and over it flipped. Beautiful! Perfect! Only he failed to get the pan back under the pancake soon enough and his masterpiece landed in the open fire. He muttered and cursed at the now blazing pancake. My father could hardly contain his amusement but knew better than to laugh. So ended his cooking lessons from his father-in-law! It was never mentioned in my grandfather's presence.

Unfortunately I never knew my grandmother Clarke. She passes away at quite a young age before I was born. John was probably only sixteen years old when she died. I wish I had the chance to know her.

Maybe because my Grandfather Clarke was the only grandparent I ever knew he was that much more special to me.

*grandmother and grandfather Clarke*
*This is the only picture I have of my grandmother Clarke*

The field behind the house was where my grandfather had his vegetable garden. That field is where my Uncle John now has his home and in the corner where he has his greenhouse is where the vegetable garden was. Like everything else my grandfather was proud of it. I know he had all sorts of vegetables in neat tidy rows but what I remember most were the peas. I would sneak up there and creep between the rows of peas, popping open the pods and eating the sweet peas from inside, leaving the empty pod hanging on the vine. I do not know if he ever knew I did it, or being a loving, kind grandfather he choose never to say a word about it. I know I ate my fill before I headed back to the house.

*A picture of the back of my grandfather's new house, with the old house on the left and the byre on the right as it was in earlier days.*

*This picture was taken later. My Mother with Tom Breslin in the field behind grandfather's where he had his vegetable garden and where Uncle John's house now stands. Miney's shop in the background on the left.*

*Uncle John on the tractor is gathering hay into rows.*

*Uncle John and Aunt Kathleen making hay*

Corratubber has always been special for me. It was the place where all the family gathered, especially in the summer. Frequently Aunt Annie and her family came from Belfast for a weekend. Uncle Paddy Breslin's family lived nearby so they could visit both families easily. We would all gather at Corratubber. Aunt Kathleen would cook one of her big delicious meals. We children had lots of fun playing together on the farm, and that was a treat for the Breslins who lived in Belfast. These frequent visits kept the family close and gave us cousins the opportunity to get to know each other. Aunt Brigid and Uncle Patrick Mulheron sometimes came from Donegal with their two daughters, Bridie and Maureen. Their third daughter Anne was born later. Though they were not able to come as often as the Breslins I loved when they came. They were from the country and younger than I but I really enjoyed playing with them. Those family gatherings were wonderful, with everyone there enjoying good times together before we all went separate ways. John went to England, we to the States and Eugene eventually to the States, too, and James died of brain cancer at an early age. But each time when we go back the family still meets in Corratubber. As in the past when we all get together we inevitably end up on the front steps taking pictures. Through some are missing, there are new cousins and new stories, new memories to make and lots of fun.

*Uncle Eugene and his sons Steven and James getting the milk cans ready for the creamery on one of their trips to Corratubber*

*My favorite picture of Uncle John*

Unfortunately my grandfather died in 1965, so I never got to see him again after I left Ireland in 1959. A year later it was with great sadness that I visited his grave in Castletara Cemetery. I was twenty one years old and when I visited Corratubber there was an empty spot that could never be filled.

Grandfather had a big beautiful horse and a dog named Piro, both of whom he was very proud. He thought Piro was the smartest dog in all of Ireland, and he was proud to display the two of them.

*Grandfather with his horse and Piro the dog outside their new house*

*Uncle James Clarke, John Argue and Granfather Clarke,*

*Granfather giving Piro advice*

*Grandfather with Uncle John, Aunt Annie and her family*

*Aunt Kathleen, Grandfather, Uncle James*
*Uncle John on the steps of the new house*

*Grandfather Clarke and Ivan Black*
*In front of our house*
*Note the wellies left to dry on the bushes*

*Great Grandmother Clarke and her daughter,*
*Aunt Maggie Clarke Ruddy*

*The cousins and Aunt Brigid the Sunday before we left*
*Ireland, May 1959*

*Family and neighbors came by to say goodbye before we left for the United States*

*In later years Aunt Annie, Uncle Eugene, Aunt Brigid and Uncle John*

*Philip Brady, Eddie Fitzsimmons, Fr. Johnnie Cusack,*
*Uncle James and Aunt Kathleen*

*Uncle Paddy, Aunt Brigid, Uncle Patrick, my mother, Aunt*
*Annie and my cousins visiting Corratubber, 1964*

*Mrs. Boylan, Tom Boylan and Philip Brady,*
*Sean Boylan, Kathleen, 1962*

# Chapter 28

# The Convent School

After Castletara National School I started the newly established Convent school in Cavan. It was run by the Poor Claire nuns and was already building a good reputation. Mary Ellen Brady and I were the only two girls from Castletara or the surrounding area going there so we rode our bikes together every day, meeting at the end of the Corratubber pass each morning and coming home late. Sometimes in winter it was almost dark before we returned to the pass again. Studies at the Convent school were tough. We had French, Latin, English, Irish, Geography, History, Algebra, Geometry, Religion, Cooking, Sewing, Dancing and Music. Add to that we had a school play. All this was accomplished Monday through Friday with a half-day on Saturday. We were required to memorize poetry back then and my favorite poem was "O Captain My Captain" about the American president Abraham Lincoln. It was intended to be an excellent example of extended metaphor, but it also awakened us to a whole chapter of American history.

# O CAPTAIN MY CAPTAIN
*Walt Whitman 1819 - 1892*

O Captain! my Captain! our fearful trip is done;
The ship has weather'd every rack,
the prize we sought is won;
The port is near, the bells I hear, the people all exulting,
While follow eyes the steady keel,
the vessel grim and daring:

But O heart! heart! heart! O the bleeding drops of red, Where
on the deck my Captain lies, Fallen cold and dead.

O Captain! my Captain! rise up and hear the bells;
Rise up—for you the flag is flung—for you the bugle trills;
For you bouquets and ribbon'd wreaths—
for you the shores a-crowding;
For you they call, the swaying mass,
their eager faces turning;
O Captain! dear father! This arm beneath your head;
It is some dream that on the deck,
You've fallen cold and dead.

My Captain does not answer, his lips are pale and still;
My father does not feel my arm, he has no pulse nor will;
The ship is anchor'd safe and sound,
its voyage closed and done;
From fearful trip, the victor ship, comes in with object won;
Exult, O shores, and ring, O bells! But I, with mournful
tread, Walk the deck my Captain lies, Fallen cold and dead.


One of my most remembered classes there was cooking. I think that was because it was held in the convent kitchen. It was the biggest, brightest, shiniest kitchen I could have ever imagined. We sat at long tables to copy down our recipes to be made at our next class. Somewhere in my belongings I still have the orange covered notebook I used. We made roly poly pudding and every manner of eggs, boiled, fried and poached. Each direction was covered in our notebooks to the minutest detail. Following are copies from my class notebook which I have kept all these years.

Object in Cooking food

1 To make it more appetizing and pleasing to the eye.
2 To make it more nurishing.
3 To lessen the danger of infection
4 To develop new flavours.
5 To mix foods so as to increase the food value.

Methods of Cooking food

1 Roasting
2 Boiling
3 Stewing
4 Steaming
5 Baking
6 Frying
7 grilling
8 Soups

# Raspberry Buns

½ lb flour      pinch salt
2 ozs Sugar      1 tea sp baking Powder
2 ozs marg.      raspberry jam
1 egg    new milk

Sieve flour.    Cut in margarine and
make crumbs add salt and sugar mix
well (till) to a loose dough with egg
and milk.    Turn on to a floured
board and knead. Form into a rool

9/

and divide into pieces with flour fingers
make a hole in each, Drop in jam
and cover well. Brush with egg and
Sprinkle with sugar.    Bake in a
hot oven 10-15 mins.      ✓

# Porrige

1 Pint Boiling water
2 ozs flaked meal
¼ Tea sp Salt.

Use a double saucepan. Boil water
and add meal and salt. Stir well
an boil till very soft. Serve with
cream and sugar in pyrex bowl.

402

# Roly Poly Pudding

| 3 or 4 table sps jam | above |
|---|---|
| serve with jam sauce. | ingredients for the suet pastry. |

method. make suet Roll into an oblong shape ¼ inch thick. Damp round the 4 edges of the pastry with cold water. spread the jam to 1 inch from edge of pastry. Roll up and seal the edges

together. Wrap up the pudding in the scalded cloth leaving room for it to swell. Tie ends with twine and leave a bit twine for a handle.
Sew the opening. Pplunge the Pudding into boiling Water and boil 1½ hours. Lift out of the water and drain well. Remove the cloth and roll on the to a hot dish. Pour a little jam sauce round the pudding and serve the remainder of the sauce.

note.
Suet Puddings are suitable for winter because of the lead and energy with they give. They require long cooking to make them light.

*Suet Pastry.*

| | |
|---|---|
| 4 ozs flour | ½ tea sp. Baking P. |
| 2 ozs suet | ¼ " " Salt |
| 2 ozs breadcrumbs. | Cold Water — |

Sive flour salt and Baking P. in bowl.

add the chopped suet and breadcrumbs. Mix to a stiff dough with cold water, using a knife for mixing. Turn out on a floured board. Knead with tips of fingers untill smooth. Roll Roll out and use for Roly Poly pudding or dumpling.

The best part was we got to eat what we made but that, too, was covered as we learned to set a table for breakfast, lunch and dinner. Everything had to be proper, befitting young ladies. On reading the notebook I am reminded how we were trained to also clean the kitchen, including the washing of kitchen cloths in hot soapy water and rubbing them on a board. We were to rinse in hot then cold water, mangle, and hang to dry.

Directions for cleaning were also included and practiced. Very detailed daily cleaning directions for both gas and coal stoves as well as necessary weekly cleaning were also included. Cleanliness was next to Godliness according to the nuns!

There was a great emphasis on our Catholic education with it being the center of our curriculum. I still have the prayer book "Our Lady's Altar" that Mother Mary Francis gave to us in December 1958. One of the prayers we were required to memorize from it was:

# THE MAGNIFICAT

My soul doth magnify the Lord.
And my spirit hath rejoiced in God my Savior.
Because he hath regarded the humility of His handmaid:
for behold from henceforth all generations
will call me blessed.
For He that is mighty hath done great things to me,
and holy is His name.
And His mercy is from generation to generation,
to them that fear Him.
He hath showed might in His arm: He hath scattered the
proud in the conceit of their heart.
He hath put down the might from their seat.
And He hath exalted the humble.
He hath filled the hungry with good things,
and the rich He sent away empty.
He hath received Israel His servant,
being mindful of His mercy.
As He spoke to our fathers,
to Abraham and to his seed for ever.
Glory be to the Father and to the Son and to the Holy Spirit.
As it was in the beginning, is now and ever shall be. Amen.

We frequently went to Mass in the beautiful convent chapel, but for special occasions we went to the Cathedral for Mass. At that time our lay teacher, Miss Joy, accompanied us because the nuns being of the Poor Clares were cloistered and couldn't leave the grounds of the convent. So they lined us all up two by two and off we marched behind Miss Joy down Asch Street to Farnham Rd. to the Cathedral. That was fun especially because we got the attention of the area shop boys on the way. I'm sure we were impressive marching along in our navy blue pleated uniform with white blouse, accented with green tie belt and tie, black flat shoes and tights. In colder weather we wore a warmer navy blue jumper (sweater). The trip to and from the Cathedral was more exciting than the reason for going.

*Miss Joy and me in convent yard*

*The Beautiful Cavan Cathedral*

*The convent yard where we played,*
*the Chapel left foreground.*
*The left rear just beyond the chapel*
*was where we had our classes.*
*This picture was taken from the garden*
*on the hill behind the buildings.*

Mary Ellen Brady and I became good friends, and when I first came to the United States I really missed her. We truly enjoyed the Convent School and all of us there worked hard and had lots of fun in our free time. Our classrooms were on the second floor along McDonald's yard and every chance we girls got, when the teacher left the room, we were hanging out the windows calling down to the shop boys in the yard. I don't ever remember getting caught but if we had we would have been in really big trouble with the nuns. Mother Mary Bonaventure was in charge of us and she was a really sweet sister, while some of the others were much sterner. I often felt that we were just a nuisance to be reckoned with.

But the convent also had sadness in its past. It had originally been and still was when I went to school there a home to many orphan children. Years earlier when my dad worked there, which he seldom liked to talk about, there was a terrible tragedy,. This is how he told the story. It seems a fire broke out in one of the buildings where the children were housed. When the fire broke out the nuns tried to put it out by themselves, but it quickly spread. The nuns moved the children into another area, still not trying to get the fire brigade. Maybe because of their cloister, when help arrived they couldn't or wouldn't open the doors. Some believed that they refused to let the firemen in because the children were in their night shirts and the nuns didn't want them to be seen undressed. For whatever reason, it really didn't matter. Finally with the fire way out of control it became too late and many innocent children were burned to death.

My dad was one of the men who helped bring out the bodies of dead children. As he recounted the horrible story of burned flesh, sadness came over him and tears filled his eyes when he'd say, "Those poor innocent children never had a chance. It should never have happened." After the fire, things were different at the convent. Although the nuns still were not allowed to leave the compound, they opened their doors to others to come in and the children were able to come out and shop in town. The story is documented in a book "The Children of the Poor Clares." During the time I went to school there two or three of the orphan girls from the convent were in class with us. I remember how beautiful the convent was with shiny marble floors and walls. I thought the orphans had to keep them that way. I know they had chores to do and were discouraged from really socializing with the rest of us, at least that was how it seemed. Although I never really got to know them, they seemed like nice young girls. I'm now reminded of a line from "ANNIE" as Mrs. Hannigan makes the children scrub, "till this place shines like the top of the Chrysler building."

*Eillish MacEntee and me on the steps at the Poor Clare Convent School, 1959*

*With friends Una, Teresa, Catherine and Mary, 1959*

*Visiting Poor Clair's School
before leaving for America*

*My Class with Miss Joy on the
Merry-go-Round at the convent school*

*May 1959, my class at the Convent School*
*just before I left Ireland*

# Chapter 29

# Cavan Town

When I was little, until I learned to ride my bike I always went into town with my mother. My father would harness up the horse to the cart or, later when we got one, the trap. My mother and I, all dressed up for the outing, would put whatever we had to take into town, radio battery to be recharged, and usually a dozen or two eggs to sell at McDonald's. I believe sometimes we also took potatoes to sell. When all was ready off we went, with advice from my father on how she should drive the horse. Fanny was a pretty placid, laid back animal so there was no need to worry really, and she followed my mother's guidance with the slightest movement of the reins. When we reached town we proceeded to McDonald's yard where we parked the horse and trap, tied up to a post while we proceeded to do our errands.

Because we did not make the trip very frequently, going into town was always exciting for me, all the stores, so many things for a country girl to see. We frequently stopped at the post office. It always seemed a very formal, serious place. I was a bit nervous about going into it but I had to so we could mail our letters to my aunts in America. Wheelan's was one of my favorite stores and it was next to the post office. They had all kinds of wonderful things, small toys, candy, statues, rosary beads and prayer books. I remember my mother frequently going in to buy rosary beads or holy water fonts for visiting Americans to take back with them to the United States. She would have these objects blessed by Fr. Hunt and then proudly give them to those leaving Ireland as a really beautiful souvenir.

It was also to this shop that we went every Christmas Eve so I could see Santa. I was always so excited and nervous while we waited. When it was finally my turn I'd sit on his lap and inform him as to what I wanted for Christmas while my parents stood close by. After he gave me a small toy I said good-bye and we went shopping for Christmas. At some point my parents went separate ways. I'm sure that was when my dad bought me my Christmas gifts. Meanwhile my mother took me to Provider's shop. We would go up stairs to the drapery department where she would purchase a couple of yards of plaid material to make a new skirt for me, then buy a new wool sweater to match it. I remember all the different materials and I often wished I could have something other than the traditional plaid. I remember the hollow sound of our boots on the wooden floors and steps as we moved around the store from floor to floor. They had a lot of lovely things. Upstairs was filled with housewares, material and clothing, while downstairs they sold groceries, meal, flour, coal, like a general store.

Our grocery shopping was always done at McDonalds. Tom Boylan worked there and usually waited on us. Our tea we bought loose by the pound. Just past the grocery area in McDonalds and past the office was the bar, where the men gathered for a pint, especially on fair day. There they gathered to recall the day's events. The ladies never sat at the bar, but gathered in the back room at tables where they were served their port wine passed through a small opening in the wall separating it from the bar.

Each week, while shopping, we also bought 2 ounces of pipe tobacco, which they cut from a large richly scented block with a very sharp knife. To use this tobacco my father would pare off strips with his penknife, then to bring out the flavor he would crush the slivers between the palms of his hands, all the time rotating his hands around and around. He then packed it into his pipe. Oh how I loved the smell of his pipe tobacco as I sat on his knee by the fire while he told his stories. It was only in later years that he smoked cigarettes.

The Bank of Ireland is still on Main Street. We didn't go there because of the money we had but rather to exchange to pounds, the dollars my aunts sent us from America. Those few extra pounds often helped us make ends meet and made life much better for us. I still remember how grateful and delighted my parents were when a letter arrived and the dollars fell out. Only those who have lived with so little can know how much a five dollar bill could mean to us. It was a chance to pay a bill or buy some necessity and was never squandered. Up town, I think it was over Smith's shop, was a little tea shop. I recall going up there with my mother and having tea and delicious pastries. That was always a real treat. Those flaky, cream-filled delicacies were one of the few splurges we ever had.

*Main St. Cavan late fifties*

Our shopping done, we headed back for home feeling satisfied with our purchases. Usually this was quite uneventful since I think Fannie knew the way just as well as we did, and you just had to point her to the Cootehill Rd. However on one occasion it did not go so well. In fact it was a near disaster. We were just a little past the Drumalee Cross outside of town when we heard an airplane approaching. Already this made Fannie a bit nervous and she pricked her ears back in fear. As I said earlier, American pilots got their kicks out scaring the people and animals by swooping low over them in the fields. So it was that this one who decided to amuse himself by swooping low over us, scaring not just my mother and me, but terrifying the poor horse. She took off at a full gallop down the road, no longer under my mother's control. All we could do was hold on for dear life and pray that the trap, now bouncing along precariously, would not turn over and that she would soon slow down. To pull on the reins to stop her would possibly make her rear up and that would be the real disaster. She galloped all the way home, arriving at our gate slathered in sweat. My father was very upset when he heard what had happened and saw the state the poor horse was in, not to mention the state of my mother. She was never very secure taking the horse and cart or trap into town without him again.

*My Mother, Anna Mae Brady and me with Fannie and the cart ready to go for a ride.*

*Note how my father had clipped the horse's hair for summer.*

# Chapter 30

# Dark Moment

There was one very dark time for me growing up in Ireland. I had never intended to write about it in this manuscript. In fact, before this moment, I have only shared the incident with my very immediate family and a few very select people. Today I attended a session at our parish on protecting our children and I was so moved by the stories of those children that I knew that I needed to tell my story for this to be complete.

For some reason I can't remember exactly how old I was at the time, but I think I was about eight, and certainly no more than nine when this occurred.

One day my parents sent me to a neighbor's house to borrow their grape. This was not unusual, for this man and my dad to occasionally borrow things back and forth, and so my dad sent me off to get it from him. I recall going into the byre with him to get the grape. I had no reason not to trust him, I had been to his house many, many times before and he had always been exceptionally nice to me, so I followed him in there. He handed me the grape and as we turned to leave the byre it was then that I felt his hands on me as he proceeded to molest me. I was terrified! My heart was pounding. I was only a child and I didn't really understand what was going on but somehow deep inside I knew it was wrong. I vividly remember thinking that I could hit him with the grape as I stared at its prongs resting on the straw on the floor, but he was bigger than me and I was sure that he would turn it on me. Somehow, I don't remember how, eventually I was able to tear myself free and I ran home as fast as I could. Even though I did not understand what had happened to me and I could not put it into words, I felt violated and dirtied and I was too scared to tell my parents anything.

Some time, maybe a couple of weeks went by and one day this neighbor came to our house. A soon as he set foot on our street I became hysterical. Needless to say my parents were dumbfounded when I kept screaming for them to make him go away. My mother took me inside the house and somehow was able to get me to tell her what was wrong. After that I'm not sure how things happened but I remember my Dad yelling at this man. I remember my dad cursing at him so much I was afraid my dad would kill him. My parents never spoke to him again and he never spoke to us either. I avoided even going past his house for the remainder of the years we lived in Ireland. I thank God that my parents did what they thought was right in the circumstances, but I wonder if he molested other children and forever changed their lives too.

I have chosen not to include the name of this individual and I will never divulge it. There would be nothing to be gained by doing that. He had a very wonderful wife and children, including girls. My parents never told his wife or children, though I'm sure his wife might have wondered why for years they never darkened their door. Sharing his name would only hurt them and I have no intention of doing that. They should not be hurt by their father's sins. I know that some people will try to guess who this person might be, butdo not waste your time for he is not worth even that. He is long since dead and has had to face the good Lord. Therein will be justice. During subsequent visits that my parents made to Ireland after his death they happily visited his wife and family, holding no ill will against them because there was no reason to. I am thankful that the friendship with the family was renewed.

This type of abuse was never mentioned in Ireland at that time, and I'm sure that there are some people who will say nothing like that ever happened around Cavan. I do not tell this story for the drama of it but rather because I really do not believe that I was the only one who suffered this type of abuse at the hands of another. I want to let other possible victims know that they are not alone. They were not the only one. It just was not something that was ever talked about and we children, unfortunately, were never prepared for it.

I choose not to dwell on this or any other difficult times in my childhood. They were what they were and we coped the best we knew through them.

# Chapter 31

# Beyond Cavan

Often through my childhood my parents spoke of places they had been in their younger years. They both had lived outside of Ireland at one point during the early years of World War II, she in London and he on a farm in Wales. He loved it there but the war had brought sad changes to the area and he returned to Ireland. My Mom also worked in Dublin and loved it there. She and Meg Cusack enjoyed the social life and she often told stories of their escapades in Bray and Phoenix Park and other places in the Dublin area. How difficult it must have been for her to return to farm life after life in the big city. She often told me stories about it and I really could not picture it. After all Cavan Town was the biggest town I knew and it fascinated me. I just could not fathom any much bigger.

*My mother Mary Clarke and Meg Cusack when they were young women in Dublin.*

I was particularly fascinated when she told me about lights in the street that when they turned red all traffic stopped and when they turned green all traffic moved again. I just could not believe that a light in the street would have that much power to do that.

So it was even with all her stories I was in no way prepared for my first visit to a big city, Belfast. My Aunt Annie and her family came down and brought me to Belfast for two weeks. I had always been fascinated by trains, that chug, chug sound they made, but until that summer I had only heard their music in the distance. Now Aunt Annie took me to Belfast on one. It was huge and seemed to fly through the countryside as it rocked to and fro on the rails. I felt like I was being rocked to slumber but I was much too excited to sleep. We changed trains in Newry and before I knew it we were pulling into the station in Belfast. Till this day my heart quickens at the sound of a train.

## FROM A RAILWAY CARRIAGE
*Robert Louis Stevenson*

Faster than fairies, faster than witches,
Bridges and houses, hedges and ditches;
And charging along like troops in a battle,
All through the meadows the horses and cattle:
All of the sights of the hill and the plain
Fly as thick as driving rain;
And ever again, in the wink of an eye,
Painted stations whistle by.
Here is a child who clambers and scrambles,
All by himself and gathering brambles;
Here is a tramp who stands and gazes;
And there is the green for stringing the daisies!
Here is a cart run away in the road
Lumping along with man and load;
And here is a mill, and there is a river:
Each a glimpse and gone forever!

Now there was the city for me to see. I was eight years old and had never seen anything like it. I never knew there were that many cars in the world, let alone in one city. There were huge buses and all the chaos of the traffic was controlled by, you guessed it, those traffic lights, and I could clearly see why they were necessary. Everything there was so different.

They lived on Clondara St. and to me it was a world away from Fairtown. They had electricity and every so often someone had to go outside to put a penny in the box to keep it on. They had running water and a real bathroom with a tub that even a grown up could fit in, and a toilet and toilet tissue, no dalkin leaves used there. There were no dalkins! Since it was a row house there was only a little backyard and no front garden, just one step down to the sidewalk. However there was a big area at the far end of the street where the residents could have a garden, and so my Uncle Paddy grew some vegetables in a little plot.

I loved my holiday in Belfast. That was at the beginning of the troubles and Belfast was still untouched by the bombs and was a beautiful city. While there Aunt Annie and Uncle Paddy took me to the zoo for the first time. The Belfast Zoo had a whole new world of animals I had only read about; monkeys, zebras, giraffes, and tigers, elephants, too, but I had seen them at the circus in Cavan when it came to town. It was amazing to me. I will never forget that day.

That trip to Belfast opened a whole new world to me. We rode buses through the city, went to stores bigger than I could ever have imagined, and saw sights I could never have dreamed of. One of the day trips Aunt Annie and Uncle Paddy took me on was a trip to the seaside. The vastness of the ocean spread out before me was overwhelming. We children jumped from rock to rock as they tumbled into the sea. I thought all oceansides were rocky. I watched with fascination as the waves thundered toward us, splashing white billows of foam over the huge boulders then quietly retreating to the sea. I tasted the salty sea for the first and only time as a child in Ireland. For the first time I heard the call of seagulls and ocean's mighty roar as the waves broke, foaming, on the shore.

## AT THE SEA-SIDE
*Robert Louis Stevenson*

When I was down beside the sea
A wooden spade they gave to me
To dig the sandy shore.

My holes were empty like a cup.
In every hole the sea came up,
Till it could come no more.

Just a short distance away from my aunt's house, at the top of the street, was a main road and on the other side of it was the Falls Road, a street that would in later years be a big player in "The Troubles." I remember to the left was the Catholic church and across that road was a park with the most beautiful green lawn I had ever seen. It was while there in Belfast I became aware of the tension between the Catholics and Protestants.

Uncle Paddy's brother Tom and his family lived in another area of the city and had a small corner store. It was early July and it was a Protestant area so we had to be cautious; but one night while we were there the Protestants started a huge bonfire near their shop, which was on the ground floor of their home. I had never seen such a fire right there in the middle of the street. They were throwing anything they could get onto it and soon the crowd was huge and getting out of control. Uncle Tom closed the shop and although they tried to hide their fear we children knew the grownups were anxious. As the night wore on we somehow escaped, slipped by the rowdy mob unnoticed and made our way to catch a bus back to Clondara Street and safety. Maybe life in the big city was not so good after all. After all these years that trip has stayed with me. On a more recent trip we visited Belfast, and I was saddened by all the damage that has been done to that beautiful city through the years of the Troubles.

When we left Belfast the Breslins also took me with them to visit my Aunt Bridie and her family in Donegal for a few days. What a beautiful area with mountains much higher than I had ever seen in Cavan. My aunt and uncle and their daughters also lived on a farm. They had a really pretty thatched cottage and I loved being there. It was a very hot July and we cousins had lots of fun playing together. Some of us girls slept in a little alcove that jutted out from the back of the kitchen. The one really sharp memory that I have was losing a tooth on the way up the lane and I was so upset that I could not find it. I wanted to bring it home with me for the tooth fairy.

*Beautiful Donegal Mountains*

*Beautiful Donegal Mountains*

I still think Donegal is one of the most beautiful places in Ireland. On one visit back to Ireland my Uncle Patrick had caught a huge salmon just that morning and had it stored in a barrel of cold spring water by the end of the house. Later that evening Aunt Bridie baked it. I love salmon and that was the most delicious I have ever tasted.

## POACHED SALMON

3 pounds fresh salmon
enough water to cover salmon
½ cup salt

Bring the water and salt to the boil. Put in the piece of salmon. Cook with the lid off at a gentle simmer for 10 minutes. Remove the saucepan from the heat. Put the lid on the saucepan and let the fish finish cooking in the warm liquid. When the water has come down to about the temperature of a hot bath lift the fish from the water. Now skin and serve with melted butter or sauce of your of your choice. Salmon should be served warm, not hot.

# BAKED SALMON

Whole Salmon gutted, cleaned and gills removed
(about 5 pounds)
butter
lemon slices if desired

Preheat oven to 350°

Coat the entire fish with butter and place on large piece of heavy duty aluminum foil. Place lemon slices on salmon. Fold foil making sealed parcel. Place the parcel in a large roasting pan. Bake for 10 minutes per pound. Allow the salmon to cool slightly before removing from foil. Carefully remove the skin.

Enjoy leftovers the next day either plain or made into salad. Whichever you choose. Allow the fish to reach room temperature before eating.

The song "The Homes of Donegal" sums up the feelings I have for beautiful Donegal.

# THE HOMES OF DONEGAL
*Sean MacBride - Traditional*

I've just stepped in to see you all
I'll only stay a while
I want to see how you're getting on
I want to see you smile.
I'm happy to be back again
I greet you big and small
For there's no place else on Earth just like
The homes of Donegal.

I long to see the happy faces
Smiling at the door
The kettle swinging on the crook
As I step up the floor.
And soon the teapot's fillin' up
My cup that's far from small
For your hearts are like your mountains
In the homes of Donegal.

To see your homes at parting day
Of that I never tire
And hear the porridge bubblin'
In a big pot on the fire.
The lamp a-light, the dresser bright
The big clock on the wall
O, a sight serene celestial scene
In the homes of Donegal.

I long to sit along with you
And while away the night
With tales of yore and fairy lore
Beside your fires so bright.
And then to see prepared for me
A shake-down by the wall
There's repose for weary wanderers
In the homes of Donegal.

Outside the night winds shriek and howl
Inside there's peace and calm
A picture on the wall up there,
Our Saviour with a lamb.
The hope of wandering sheep like me
And all who rise and fall
There's a touch of heavenly love around
The homes of Donegal.

A tramp I am and a tramp I've been
I tramp I'll always be,
Me father tramped, me mother tramped
Sure trampin's bred in me.
If some there are my ways disdain
And won't have me at all,
Sure I'll always find a welcome
In the homes of Donegal.

The time has come and I must go
I bid you all adieu,
The open highway calls me forth
To do the things I do.
And when I'm travelling far away
I'll hear your voices call,
And please God I'll soon return unto
The homes of Donegal.

*Uncle Patrick, Anne and Aunt Bridie Mulheron
with Uncle Paddy and Aunt Annie Breslin, Sean Breslin,
Bridie and Maureen Mulheron and Tom Breslin.*

*Uncle Patrick, Anne, Aunt Bridie,*
*Bridie and Maureen in Donegal*

The trip home from Donegal was quite an experience. The fastest way to get to Cavan from Donegal was to cross the border into the north and continue through there. Now the only problem was that the day of our trip was the 12th of July, which is one of the biggest Protestant holidays in the North. We had no sooner crossed the border than we wound up smack dab in the middle of an "Orangeman's" parade. All the men were dressed in their parade regalia with wide orange sashes around their shoulders and down to the opposite hip. They were marching to big bands with drums deafeningly loud, banners and flags with long ribbons waving in the hot summer sun. There seemed to be thousands of them and there we were a Catholic family in a Vauxhall right in the middle of the parade. Aunt Annie was obviously distressed with the situation but Uncle Paddy, trying to stay calm just kept driving like we belonged there, warning us children in the back seat to be quiet and not say a word. He didn't have to worry about that. We were scared to death! I do not know how we got into it, but I do know that we were very relieved when we finally were able to escape it and traveled on to the safety of the South.

It was many years after that before I left Cavan again. This time we traveled to Dublin to go through the testing to come to the United States. We stayed with the Clarke family and Maude Cusack at their home, an off license liquor store where they lived and where my mother had spent so many happy times as a young woman. As I think about it, that was her first time back in Dublin since she had married my father many years before.

The days there were taken up with our testing and physical exams like I had never experienced or imagined, even chest X-rays and blood tests. We were poked and examined, questioned and talked to for two whole days. At the end we were given our passports and documents necessary to come to the States as permanent residents. Like

Belfast, Dublin was a very busy bustling city, and going to Moore Street I was reminded of the song "Cockles and Muscles."

# COCKLES AND MUSSELS
*Unknown – Traditional*

In Dublin's fair city,
Where the girls are so pretty,
I first set my eyes on sweet Mollie Malone.
She wheeled her wheel-barrow
Through streets broad and narrow,
Crying, "Cockles and mussels, alive, alive, oh!

"Alive, alive, oh!
Alive, alive, oh!"
Crying, "Cockles and mussels, alive, alive, oh!"

She was a fishmonger,
But sure 'twas no wonder,
For so were her father and mother before.
And they both wheeled their barrow
Through streets broad and narrow,
Crying, "Cockles and mussels, alive, alive, oh!

"Alive, alive, oh!
Alive, alive, oh!"
Crying, "Cockles and mussels, alive, alive, oh!"

She died of a fever,
And none could relieve her,
And that was the end of sweet Mollie Malone.
But her ghost wheels her barrow
Through streets broad and narrow,
Crying, "Cockles and mussels, alive, alive, oh!"

"Alive, alive, oh!
Alive, alive, oh!"
Crying, "Cockles and mussels, alive, alive, oh!"

*My parents and me outside Clark's in Dublin the day we took our tests to come to America*

I was fourteen years old and we were ready to leave everything I had ever known behind and start a new life. We went back to Cavan and made preparations to sell all our belongings. A package arrived from Aunt Helen with new clothes for us to wear and three one-way tickets for our trip to the US. We were to spend our last few days staying at my grandfather's in Corratubber while our cherished things were sold at auction. Since it would not be appropriate for my mother and me to be there, we were not at the auction at our house. My Dad reported on it that evening and it was much discussed by the family afterward. He paid all our bills and we were now ready for the future. It was May 1959, and so with five pounds in my father's pocket and everything we had in one cardboard suitcase we were driven to Shannon and boarded a TWA prop plane for New York and a whole new life.

## FAREWELL TO THE FARM
*Robert Louis Stevenson*

The coach is at the door at last;
The eager children, mounting fast
And kissing hands, in chorus sing:
Good-bye, good-bye, to everything!

To house and garden, field and lawn,
The meadow-gates we swang upon,
To pump and stable, tree and swing,
Good-bye, good-bye, to everything!

And fare you well for evermore,
O ladder at the hayloft door,
O hayloft where the cobwebs cling,
Good-bye, good-bye, to everything!

Life in Ireland was not easy in the late 1940s and 1950s, but I had a wonderful childhood filled with the love of family and friends. I had a freedom that today's children can only dream of. It was a simple life filled with fun and laughter and experiences that I would never trade. So today I hold onto my five stones that nest in a Bovril bottle on my kitchen sink and remember and cherish my memories of the people and all those good times so long ago. I thank God for those fourteen years for they made me who I am.

On my many trips back to Ireland since that painful one in 1986 I choose not to return to Fairtown again until 2009. I wanted to share the farm with my grandchildren. With great apprehension I climbed that lane, not knowing what lay ahead. I picked some strawberries with my granddaughter. Soon we came to a clearing and there where the house once stood was a stone-covered area so clean and tidy. The fields where now I watched my grandchildren romp, where I had played, were now beautifully cared for. Tears rolled down my cheeks again but this time tears of joy. I had come home again.

## BORN IN IRELAND
*continued*

When I die please take me back to Ireland
Where I'm free from worry and from care
And lay me down by Mom and Daddy
And let me sleep forever there
And when it's springtime in the mountains
And the purple heather glows
I'll be happy here in Ireland
As in the days of long ago

# Recipe Index

Printed in Great Britain
by Amazon